This is an urgently needed book wit... Qureshi masterfully argues for the gospel while painting a beautiful portrait of Muslim families and heritage, avoiding the fearmongering and finger-pointing that are all too pervasive in today's sensationalist world. I unreservedly recommend this book to all. It will feed your heart and mind, while keeping your fingers turning the page!

—*Josh D. McDowell, author and speaker*

Nabeel describes the yearning in the hearts of millions of Muslims around the world. This book is a must-read for all seeking to share the hope of Christ with Muslims.

—*Fouad Masri, President and CEO, Crescent Project*

Fresh, striking, highly illuminating, and sometimes heartbreaking, Qureshi's story is worth a thousand textbooks. It should be read by Muslims and all who care deeply about our Muslim friends and fellow citizens.

—*Os Guinness, author and social critic*

Nabeel Qureshi's story is among the most unique two or three testimonies that I have ever heard. His quest brought together several exceptional features: a very bright mind, extraordinary sincerity, original research, and a willingness to follow the evidence trail wherever it took him. His search led to the cross and to Jesus Christ, who was resurrected from the dead.

—*Gary R. Habermas, Distinguished Research*
Professor, Liberty University

In his personal quest to know the truth, Nabeel Qureshi paves the way for an analytical study of the faiths, dissecting the Christian and Islamic arguments, specifically citing numerous Islamic hadith and early Christian texts, so that the reader can see a logical progression to the analyses. But it is also a deeply personal heartwrenching and tear-evoking saga of the life of a young Muslim growing up in the West, a gripping biography that is impossible to put down.

—*James M. Tour, Professor of Chemistry, Computer Science,*
Mechanical Engineering, and Materials Science, Rice University

For anyone seeking understanding of their Muslim neighbors or colleagues, this is a book to read. We go on a journey from the inside out. We are introduced to the depth of spirituality, the love and honor of family, and the way a person "sees" and "feels" in a devout Muslim home. This is a profound book that skillfully shows the core differences between the gospel and Islamic claims. I highly recommend it.

—*Dr. Stuart McAllister, Regional Director The Americas,*
Ravi Zacharias International Ministries

This book offers the fascinating story of the conversion of a sincere young Ahmadiyya man who tried his best to seek Allah and eventually fell in love with Christ. I trust that this book can be a powerful encouragement for all Christians to pray for many Muslims to find Jesus Christ.

—*Mark Gabriel, author and former lecturer,*
Al-Azhar University in Cairo

Seeking Allah, Finding Jesus is a brilliant book with an authentic and challenging message. Nabeel Qureshi tells the powerful story of his journey to Jesus, a story that began with a doubtful investigation and ended with a beautiful transformation. Jesus isn't intimidated by our questions; this story celebrates that truth! You won't be able to put this book down.

—*Louie Giglio, pastor, Passion City Church;*
founder, Passion Conferences

SEEKING ALLAH,
FINDING JESUS

SEEKING ALLAH,
FINDING JESUS

A Devout Muslim Encounters Christianity

THIRD EDITION WITH BONUS CONTENT,
NEW REFLECTIONS

NABEEL QURESHI

ZONDERVAN
REFLECTIVE

ZONDERVAN REFLECTIVE

Seeking Allah, Finding Jesus
Copyright © 2014, 2016, 2018 by Kathryn Michelle Qureshi

Conversation between David Wood and Nabeel Qureshi copyright © 2018 by Zondervan

ISBN 9780310092674 (audio)

ISBN 9780310092650 (ebook)

Requests for information should be addressed to:
Zondervan, 3900 *Sparks Dr. SE, Grand Rapids, Michigan 49546*

This edition: ISBN 978-0-310-09264-3 (softcover)

The Library of Congress has cataloged the original edition as

Qureshi, Nabeel.
    Seeking Allah, finding Jesus : a devout Muslim encounters Christianity/ Nabeel Qureshi.
        pages cm
        Includes bibliographical references.
        ISBN 978-0-310-51502-9 (softcover)—ISBN 978-0-310-51503-6 (ebook)
    1. Qureshi, Nabeel. 2. Christian converts from Islam—Biography. I. Title.
BV2626.4.Q74A3 2014
248.2'46092—dc23
    [B]   2013035814

Published in association with the literary agency of Mark Sweeney & Associates, Bonita Springs, Florida 34135

Cover design: *ThinkPen Design*
Cover photography: *Howard Korn Photography*
Interior design: *Matthew Van Zomeren and Ben Fetterley*

THIS BOOK IS DEDICATED TO MY PARENTS.

Ammi and Abba, your undying love for me even when you feel I have sinned against you is second only to God's love for His children. I pray you will one day realize His love is truly unconditional, that He has offered forgiveness to us all. On that day, I pray that you would accept His redemption, so we might be a family once again. I love you with all my heart.

CONTENTS

FOREWORD

WHAT WOULD YOU DO if someone challenged the very core of your deeply held beliefs? How would you respond if your most cherished traditions were called into question?

This is the riveting story of one man's quest to set aside his preconceptions and pursue answers to the most pressing issues of life and faith, despite enormous pressure to maintain the status quo.

When his world was being rocked twenty centuries ago, Pontius Pilate simply scoffed, "What is truth?" and chose to wash his hands of the matter. But my friend Nabeel Qureshi was courageous enough to chase down the truth with intellectual integrity, no matter the personal cost.

I'm thrilled that you'll meet Nabeel in the following pages as he describes his circuitous—and, yes, even supernatural—journey to satisfy his mind and soul. You'll experience what it's like for someone immersed in Islamic culture to risk everything to determine the true identity of God. It's a personal story of family, friends, and faith, intertwined with insights into Islam that will help you understand the Muslim world in new ways.

I've seen Nabeel's formidable intellect up close. (He was a medical doctor, had two master's degrees, and was working on a PhD.) And I also came to know his empathetic and compassionate heart. He had an uncanny ability to ask probing questions that bore down to bedrock. But I never saw him use his intelligence to intimidate or bully anyone; invariably, Nabeel extended a helping hand to anyone who was intent on discovering which road of faith really leads Home.

I know what it's like to have the legs kicked out from under my foundational beliefs. As an atheist, I was challenged to use my journalism and legal training to investigate whether there's any cred-ibility to Christianity. What I found turned my life upside down.

So I can relate to Nabeel's journey as he asked uncomfortable questions and resisted easy answers. He carefully sifted through the evidence of history and adroitly navigated the mazes of philosophy and theology. He was persistent and unflinching, even in the face of discoveries that eroded the beliefs that had ruled his life from childhood.

Regardless of where you are on your pathway of faith, I predict you'll benefit deeply from reading Nabeel's account. You'll come to see Nabeel as a friend who cared deeply enough to share what he learned and to coax you forward in your spiritual journey. I'm con-vinced that Nabeel's saga needs to be read far and wide, by all people who value truth and who ache to know God personally.

So read on and see how God uses Nabeel's story to shape your own.

—Lee Strobel, author,
The Case for Christ and
The Case for Grace

ACKNOWLEDGMENTS

I AM HUMBLED by the staggering personalities whom God has brought into this project for guidance and assistance. I would like to begin by thanking my dear friends and family who read and commented on segments of this book. Their encouragement and advice was invaluable. I especially would like to thank Carson Weitnauer and my dear sister, Baji, for their extensive feedback when I needed it most.

Thanks also go to Mark Sweeney and Madison Trammel for their friendship and professional expertise as they diligently worked to make this book into a reality.

Without a doubt, one of the greatest blessings of this book is the input from many amazing minds. I am indebted to Lee Strobel, Dan Wallace, Ed Komoszewski, Rob Bowman, Keith Small, Gary Habermas, and Josh McDowell for their heartfelt and insightful contributions. I am blessed beyond belief to even know them, let alone to consider all of them dear friends.

An extra dose of gratitude is due to Abdu Murray, not only for his contribution but also for his regular fellowship and spiritual support from afar. Having fought the battle from Islam to Christianity a few years before me, his insights have been invaluable. I acknowledge him as the older brother I never had.

Similarly, Mike Licona's mentorship over the years has helped me to grow in both my thinking and my scholastic efforts. Much of my ministry would not have happened without him, let alone this book.

Another whose impact extends far beyond his contribution is David Wood. I am eternally indebted to him for his faithful fulfillment of the call to reach out to a young, zealous Muslim despite all the odds. May it be that our friendship and ministry together is only beginning.

If there is one person without whom this book would not have been written, it is Mark Mittelberg. From the very first stage of suggesting the book, to finding an agent, to choosing a publisher, to helping me write the book, to contributing to the book, to marketing the book ... I am left wondering how much of the book is actually mine! Mark, your consummate mentorship and friendship is inspiring and compels me to be the best I can be. I will never be able to thank you enough.

Finally, I would like to thank my bride, Michelle. For bearing weeks of separation so that I could write this book, for diligently reading it late into the night, for having an unfaltering love for a fallen man, and for not once complaining in the least, I will never be able to pay you back. It's a good thing we have our entire lives together for me to try!

To all my friends and family who took part in the shaping and support of this book, your help is inexpressibly appreciated. I pray the Lord will repay you all in kind.

INTRODUCTION

THE PAGES THAT FOLLOW contain my most powerful memories and personal thoughts, my very heart poured out on ink and paper. By reading this book, you will enter into the circle of my family and friends, take part in the bliss of my Islamic youth, and struggle with me through the culture clash of being an American-born Muslim. By looking over my shoulder, you will be privy to the offensiveness of Christianity to Muslim eyes, begin struggling with the historical facts of the gospel, and feel the ground that shook beneath me as I slowly learned the hidden truths about Islam. By reading my personal journal entries, you will encounter the visions and dreams that gave me the spiritual confidence I needed to approach the Bible as the Word of God.

By reading this story, you will travel with me through life and know me intimately, and I pray you will be transformed as I was by an encounter with the living God.

THE PURPOSES OF THIS BOOK

But this book is more than just my story. It is designed with three purposes in mind:

1. To tear down walls by giving non–Muslim readers an insider's perspective into a Muslim's heart and mind. The mystical beauty of Islam that enchants billions cannot be grasped by merely sharing facts. By entering into my world, I hope Christians will understand their Muslim neighbors and begin to love them as Jesus loves them. The first two parts of the book are designed for this purpose, and if they

seem pro-Islamic, they are serving their purpose of conveying a past love for my former faith.

2. To equip the reader with facts and knowledge, showing the strength of the case for the gospel contrasted with the case for Islam. History powerfully testifies to the foundational pillars of the gospel: Jesus' death on the cross, His resurrection from the dead, and His claim to be God. By doing so, history challenged my Islamic theology, which was grounded in the foundational pillars of Islam: the divine origin of the Quran and the prophethood of Muhammad. As I studied Islam carefully, what I learned shook my world: there is no good reason to believe that either Muhammad or the Quran speaks the truth about God. Since this book is far too short to share all the facts and arguments I learned over the years, I have written another book for people interested in the details, *No God but One: Allah or Jesus?* In this book, I provide only the broad contours of what I came to grasp in parts 3–8, and how this led me away from Islam toward Jesus.

3. To portray the immense inner struggle of Muslims grappling with the gospel, including sacrifices and doubts. As you will see in parts 9 and 10, it is in the midst of this struggle that God is known to reach people directly through visions and dreams.

HOW TO READ THIS BOOK

Glossary

There are many Islamic terms that you will come to know as you read the book. I have defined them for you upon their first instance in the text, and you will find all these terms defined once again in the glossary.

Expert Contributions

The expert contributions are truly the hidden treasure of this book. Ranging from prolific evangelists to a distinguished Quran scholar, learned experts who are passionate for the gospel and compassionate toward Muslims have graciously added their voices to this work, lending their academic credibility and experienced insights. Three of these experts played personal roles in my journey to Jesus. There is one contribution for each of the ten parts of the book, and I recommend that you read each immediately after its related part. You will find them in the "Expert Contributions" section in the back of the book.

A Note on Narrative Biography

Since we have entered the digital age, it is unfortunately and increasingly true that people exact inappropriate standards on narrative biographies. By its very nature, a narrative biography must take certain liberties with the story it shares. Please do not expect camera-like accuracy. That is not the intent of this book, and to meet such a standard, it would have to be a twenty-two-year-long video, most of which would bore even my mother to tears.

The words I have in quotations are rough approximations. A few of the conversations represent multiple meetings condensed into one. In some instances, stories are displaced in the timeline to fit the topical categorization. In other instances, people who were present in the conversation were left out of the narrative for the sake of clarity. All of these devices are normal for narrative biographies — normal, in fact, for human mnemonics. Please read accordingly.

FINAL INTRODUCTORY REMARKS

I am genuinely grateful that you have decided to read this book. There are many views of God, and the differences matter. There is nothing like the one true God! If I had known just how boundless is the love of God, just how transformative His grace and mercy, just how liberating His exemplary life and death, I would have run to Him years sooner with all my might. It is my prayer that this book will release readers to run with abandon toward their Father. That is why Jesus came, that we might have life and have it abundantly (John 10:10). I am honored that you would allow my story to be part of your journey.

PROLOGUE

SEEKING ALLAH

I LAY PROSTRATE in a large Muslim prayer hall, broken before God. The edifice of my worldview, all I had ever known, had slowly been dismantled over the past few years. On this day, my world came crashing down. I lay in ruin, seeking Allah.

Fading footsteps echoed through the halls of the mosque as the humid summer evening drew to a close. The other worshipers were heading back to their homes and families for the night, but my thoughts were still racing. Every fiber of my being wrestled with itself. With my forehead pressed into the ground and heart pounding in my chest, my mind scrutinized each word my lips whispered into the musty carpet.

These were not new words. I had been taught to recite this Arabic phrase 132 times, every single day, from a time before I even knew my name. It was the *sajda*, the portion of the ritual prayers in which Muslims lower themselves before Allah, glorifying His loftiness. The words had always flowed with ease, but this day was different. As my lips exercised their rote rituals, my mind questioned everything I thought I knew about God.

Subhana rabbi al-ala.
Glorified is my Lord, the Highest.

"Glorified is my Lord ... Who is my Lord? Who are You, Lord? Are You Allah, the God of my father and forefathers? Are You the God I have always worshiped? The God my family has always worshiped? Surely You are the one who sent Muhammad ﷺ[1] as the final messenger for mankind and the Quran as our guide? You are Allah, the God of Islam, aren't You? Or are You ..." I hesitated, fighting the blasphemy I was about to propose. But what if the blasphemy was the truth?

"Or are You Jesus?"

My heart froze, as if indignant at my mind for risking hell. "Allah, I would never say that a man became equal to You! Please forgive me and have mercy on me if that's what I said, because that's not what I mean. No man is equal to You. You are infinitely greater than all of creation. Everything bows down before You, Allah *subhanahu wa'tala*.[2]

"No, what I mean to say is that You, O Allah, are all powerful. Surely You can enter into creation if You choose. Did You enter into this world? Did You become a man? And was that man Jesus?

"O Allah, the Bible couldn't be right, could it?"

As if on parallel timelines, my lips continued to pray in sajda while my mind relentlessly fought with itself. The Arabic phrase was to be recited twice more before the sajda would be complete.

Subhana Rabbi al-ala.
Glorified is my Lord, the Highest.

"But how is it conceivable that Allah, the highest being of all, would enter into this world? This world is filthy and sinful, no place for the One who deserves all glory and all praise. And how could I even begin to suggest that God, the magnificent and splendid Creator, would enter into this world through the birth canal of a girl? *Audhu billah*,[3] that's disgusting! To have to eat, to grow fatigued, and to sweat and spill blood, and to be finally nailed to a cross. I cannot believe this. God deserves infinitely more. His majesty is far greater than this.

"But what if His majesty is not as important to Him as His children are?"

Subhana Rabbi al-ala.
Glorified is my Lord, the Highest.

"Of course we are important to Him, but Allah does not need to die in order to forgive us. Allah is all powerful, and He can easily forgive us if He chooses. He is *al-Ghaffar* and *ar-Rahim*![4] His forgiveness flows from His very being. What does coming into this world to die on a cross have to do with my sins? It doesn't even make sense for Allah to die on the cross. If He died, who was ruling the universe? *Subhanallah*,[5] He cannot die! That is part of His glory. There is no need for these charades. He can simply forgive from His throne.

"But how can Allah be just if He 'simply forgives' arbitrarily? God is not arbitrary. He is absolutely just. How would He be just if He forgave arbitrarily? No, He cannot 'just forgive us if He chooses.' The penalty for my sins must be paid."

Rising from the ground and sitting on my heels, I recited the *takbir*.

Allah-hu-akbar.
God is great.

"God, I know that You are great in reality, but some of what the Holy Quran teaches is far from great. I am having a very difficult time understanding it, Allah. Please, have mercy on me. I don't mean to doubt You, and I ask for Your mercy on my lack of knowledge and understanding. Please, Allah, may all this doubt not anger You. I must have misunderstood something, but there's no way You, being good and loving, would have given some of the commands found in the Quran. I have found so much violence and contempt in its pages, the pages of a book I have read and loved every day because it is Your word.

"But maybe You are showing me that the Quran is not Your word after all? So much of what I've been taught about it has turned out to be false. I was taught that it has never been changed, but *hadith* and history show that it has. I was taught that it has supernatural knowledge of science and the future, but when I asked You to help me see it with my own eyes, I could find none. So much that I thought I knew about the Quran simply is not true. Is it really Your book? O Allah, have mercy on me.

"Who are You?"

At-tahiyyatu lillahi, was-salawatu wat-tayyibatu. As salamu 'alayka ayyuha n-nabiyyu wa rahmatullahi wa barakatuh. As salamu 'alayna wa-'ala 'ibadi llahi salihin.

All compliments, prayers, and good things are due to Allah. Allah's peace be upon you, O Prophet, and His mercy and blessings. Peace be on us and on all righteous servants of Allah.

"I praise You, Allah. All homage is certainly due to You. But there is so much I do not understand. Why am I speaking to Muhammad ﷺ in my prayer? He cannot hear me. He is dead! I should not be praying to any man, even if it is the Prophet. And why am I wishing peace upon him? I am not his intercessor. I know these words were first recited when he was alive, but why does Your greatest prophet need anyone to pray peace over him? Could You not have given him assurance and peace? If he cannot have peace and assurance as the Prophet, what hope is there for me?"

Following the traditions of the Prophet and the guidance of my parents, I pointed my forefinger skyward while reciting the proclamation:

Ashhadu alla ilaha illa llahu wa ashhadu anna Muhammadan 'abduhu wa-rasuluh.

I bear witness that there is none worthy of worship except Allah, and I bear witness that Muhammad is His servant and messenger.

"O Allah, have mercy on me. How can I bear witness that Muhammad ﷺ is Your messenger? It used to be so easy! Ammi taught me to love Muhammad ﷺ because he was the greatest man who ever lived, and there was no close second. She taught me that his generosity was abundant, his mercy was incomparable, and his love for mankind was beyond measure. I was taught that he would never wage war unless he was defending the *ummah*,[6] and that he fought to elevate the status of women and the downtrodden. He was the perfect military leader, he was the ultimate statesman, and he was the exemplary follower of Allah. He was *al-Insan al-Kamil*, the perfect man. He was *Rahmatu-lil alameen*, God's mercy personified for all the world. It was easy to bear witness that such a man is *Rasul Allah*, the messenger of God.

"But now I know the truth about him, and there's too much to sweep under the rug. I know about his first revelation, his raids on caravans, his child bride, his marriage to Zainab, the black magic cast upon him, his poisoning, his assassinations, his tortures, and ..."

My thoughts slowed as they arrived at the one issue that I simply could not overlook. "And how could Muhammad ﷺ, my beloved Prophet, have allowed ... *that*?"

Awash in empathy, my mind drifted from the prayers. I was still grappling with what I had come across while investigating the Quran. How could he? I envisioned the horror from the vantage point of the victims. What if that had been my family? Where was the Prophet's famed mercy?

I imagined that I was there, under the red sky of the desert, at that very moment. Anger quickly swelled within me as I surveyed the ruins of my people. Blood and death. A few young soldiers hungrily made their way through the corpses and approached Muhammad. They made their barbarous desires known and asked Muhammad for his guidance. Muhammad's face flushed and began perspiring. He was receiving revelation from Allah.[7] When he announced it to his soldiers, an evil glee spread across their faces. They disappeared into their tents, eager to proceed. Allah had sanctioned their activities. For a moment, all lay calm.

Suddenly, an unbearable noise pierced the desert sky and my soul.

It was my mother, screaming.

My eyes shot open as I snapped back to reality. I was still in the mosque, still praying the *salaat*. My overwhelming revulsion toward Muhammad suddenly met with immediate contrition. I had been impudent before Allah. Muhammad ﷺ was still my Prophet. I still swore allegiance to him. I had gone too far.

How could I continue like this? *Astaghfirullah.*[8]

Quickly, I finished the rest of the ritual prayers, ending by turning my head to the right and the left:

Assalaamo alaikum wa rahmutallah.
The peace and mercy of Allah be upon you.

After a pause, I let my face fall into my hands. Tears blurred my sight. The ritual prayers had ended, and now it was time for my heart's prayer.

"God, I want Your peace. Please have mercy on me and give me the peace of knowing You. I don't know who You are anymore, but I know that You are all that matters. You created this world, You give it meaning, and either You define its purpose or it has none.

"Please, God Almighty, tell me who You are! I beseech You and only You. Only You can rescue me. At Your feet, I lay down everything I have learned, and I give my entire life to You. Take away what You will, be it my joy, my friends, my family, or even my life. But let me have You, O God.

"Light the path that I must walk. I don't care how many hurdles are in the way, how many pits I must jump over or climb out of, or how many thorns I must step through. Guide me on the right path. If it is Islam, show me how it is true! If it is Christianity, give me eyes to see! Just show me which path is Yours, dear God, so I can walk it."

Although I did not know it, that peace and mercy of God which I desperately asked for would soon fall upon me. He was about to give me supernatural guidance through dreams and visions, forever changing my heart and the course of my life.

Part 1

CALLED TO PRAYER

The edifice of my worldview, all I had ever known . . .

Chapter One

PRAYERS OF MY FATHERS

AT DAWN ACROSS THE ISLAMIC WORLD, sonorous voices usher the sun over the horizon. The core beliefs of Muslims are repeatedly proclaimed from rooftops and minarets, beginning with the *takbir:*

> *Allah-hu-akbar!*
> *Ashado an-la illaha il-Allah!*
> *Ashado an-na Muhammad-ur-Rasool Allah!*

> Allah is Great!
> I bear witness that there is no god but Allah!
> I bear witness that Muhammad is the messenger of Allah!

It is the start of the **adhan**, the call to prayer. The call reminds Muslims to dedicate their lives to Allah the very moment they awaken. From memorized occasional prayers to elaborate daily rituals, devout Muslims are steeped in remembrance of Allah and performance of Islamic traditions. The adhan calls the Muslims, resonates within them, rallies them, and brings them together in unified prostration before Allah.

Adhan: The Muslim call to prayer

To the alien observer, it might seem that the adhan is the very thing that rends the night sky, separating dark from day, infusing life into the Muslim lands and people.

It is no surprise, then, that Muslims use the adhan not just to awaken one another for the day but also to awaken one another into life. It is a **hadith**, a tradition of the prophet Muhammad, that every Muslim child should hear the adhan at birth. When I was born, my father softly spoke the adhan into my ear, echoing the words that his father had whispered to him twenty-eight years earlier. They were the first words ever spoken to me, in accordance with tradition.

My family has always paid particular attention to following the hadith. We are Qureshi, after all, and the Qureshi are the tribe of Muhammad. When I was old enough to realize the prestige of our name, I asked my father if we inherited it from the Prophet.

"*Abba*, are we the real Qureshi, like Muhammad ﷺ?"

He said, "*Jee mera beyta,*" **Urdu** for "Yes, my son." "Muhammad ﷺ had no sons who survived childhood, but we are descendants of Hazrat Umar." Umar was one of the four **khalifas**, the men that Sunnis consider the divinely guided successors of Muhammad. Our lineage was noble indeed; it's no wonder my family was proud of our heritage.

> **Hadith**: Muhammad's words or actions recorded in tradition
>
> **Urdu**: The language of Pakistan
>
> **Khalifa**: The position of supreme leader over Muslims; usually the title is used to refer to one of Muhammad's four successors

When my father left Pakistan in the 1970s, love for his family and heritage was his motivation. He was driven to provide a better life for his parents and siblings. When he came to the United States, he joined the navy at the instruction of his older brother. As a seaman, he sent money from every paycheck back home, even when it was all he had. It would be a few years before he briefly returned to Pakistan, once his marriage to my mother had been arranged.

Ammi, my mother, had also lived a life devoted to her family and her religion. She was the daughter of a Muslim missionary. Her father, whom I called *Nana Abu*, had moved to Indonesia with her mother, *Nani Ammi*, shortly after their marriage to invite people to Islam. It was there that my mother was born, followed by her three sisters. With Nani Ammi working to help support the family and Nana Abu often absent on mission, my mother had a large role in raising her younger siblings and teaching them the way of Islam.

At the age of ten, Ammi returned to Pakistan with her siblings and Nani Ammi. The community received her family with great respect for dutifully performing the call of missionaries. Since Nana Abu was still an active missionary in Indonesia and returned to Pakistan only on furlough, Ammi's caretaking role in the home intensified. Ultimately she had five siblings to manage and care for, so although she graduated at the top of her undergraduate class and was offered a scholarship for medical school, she declined the offer. Nani Ammi needed the help at home, since she invested much of her day volunteering as a secretary at the local *jamaat* offices.

Jamaat: The Arabic word for assembly, usually used to mean "group" or "denomination"

Nani Ammi herself had spent virtually all her life sacrificing in the way of Islam. Not only was she the wife of a missionary but, like Ammi, she had also been the child of a missionary. She was born in Uganda, where her father served as a physician while calling people to Islam. Raised as a missionary child, transitioning into the role of missionary wife, and living her last able years serving the jamaat, she had garnered great respect and prestige from the community. Through it all, Nani Ammi was perhaps Ammi's greatest role model, and Ammi wanted nothing more than to carry on the legacy through a family of her own.

And so, though I did not know it at the time, the man who whispered the adhan into my ears was a self-sacrificial, loving man who bore the noble name of Qureshi. The woman who looked on was a daughter of missionaries, an experienced caretaker with an ardent desire to serve Islam. I was their second child, their firstborn son. They were calling me to prayer.

Chapter Two

A MOTHER'S FAITH

I LIVED A VERY PROTECTED CHILDHOOD, physically, emotionally, socially, and otherwise ineffably. I was sheltered in ways I am still trying to comprehend. The few scars I have from those days are all physical, results of minor mishaps, and they come with vivid memories. The largest scar—no more than two inches, mind you—was from an open window that fell on my hand when I was three. That day is emblazoned on my mind because of what I learned about my mother's faith.

At the time, Abba was stationed in Norfolk, Virginia. He was in his eleventh year with the navy, having spent the past few working by day and studying by night for a master's degree. After officer commissioning school, he was promoted from petty officer first class to lieutenant junior grade, and he was deployed shortly afterward. Of course, I didn't know much of that at the time. All I knew was that Abba worked hard for us, and though I never felt a lack of love, I didn't get to see him as much as I wanted.

Ammi, on the other hand, was an ever-present ballast and encouraging influence in our lives. She always seemed able to do everything. From making our food to preparing our clothes to teaching us the *aqeedah*, she never seemed to fatigue or complain. She had only two hard and fast rules for her sanity: no whining after nine o'clock at night and no interrupting her while she was drinking chai, which she did quite often.

> *Aqeedah*: Deeply held Islamic beliefs

When we had visitors, she exemplified the highest caliber of hospitality, considering it an honor to receive and serve our guests. More food would be prepared than the visitors could hope to eat, the house would be cleaner than the day it was built, our clothes would be crisply pressed, and our calendar would be cleared for the day of the visit and the next, in case the guests chose to stay. It was normal for us when she deeply apologized for the lack of food and our unkempt appearances anyway. It was part of the protocol. The guests knew to assure Ammi that they had not had such wonderful food in years, that homes in heaven couldn't be much cleaner, and that her children were role models for theirs. At this, everyone would be quite content: the guests for being so honored, Ammi for being so praised, and we kids, just for being mentioned in grown-up conversation.

Sometimes the guests would stay with us for months at a time, Ammi's hospitality and diplomacy never waning. When I consider the array of people who stayed at our home, two of the most prominent are Nani Ammi and her older sister, whom we called Mama. Mama was a delightful woman, a big heart with a big laugh in a tiny body. She was always ready to play board games with me, unending in her patience for three-year-olds and always willing to look the other way when I cheated.

On the day of the mishap, Mama was at our home. She and Ammi were upstairs, and I was playing with my Hot Wheels, little toy cars that Ammi would buy me so I would stop annoying her in grocery stores. *Baji*, my older sister, and I had a mutual understanding. She would play with me and my Hot Wheels if I played with her and her My Little Pony collection. She'd choose the cars she wanted, and I'd pick the ponies I wanted. I chose my ponies brazenly, spending the rest of my time convincing Baji that I had picked the best one. She'd always pick the Lamborghini, and I'd spend the rest of my time convincing her that the Pontiac I was left with was better.

Baji had just finished playing with my Hot Wheels and had gone to get the ponies while I continued playing with my Pontiac, racing it along the floor and in between the couches. I looked up and saw the window, the kind that slides up to open. On a whim, I decided it was time for the Pontiac to crash. I raced the car along the windowsill with a gust of finality and slammed it against the pane.

To this day, I cannot recall the window actually coming down. I just remember the piercing pain, the immense amount of blood, and my scream for Ammi amid gasping sobs. And I recall what happened next.

When Ammi came downstairs and saw the accident, she almost began to cry herself, but in the very next instant she stayed her emotions. Being a navy wife, she had learned to play the roles of both mother and father, and now was not the time for tears. She chose instead to act swiftly and give her fear to Allah.

She raised the window, wrapped my hand in a towel, and deftly donned her *burqa*. Leaving Baji under Mama's care, Ammi lifted me into the car to take me to the clinic. The whole way there, Ammi recited *du'aa*. She offered du'aa from portions of the Quran, from sections of hadith she had memorized, and by impromptu prayers of her own. Her dependence on the sovereign care of Allah gave her strength, firmed her resolve, and allayed her fears.

> *Du'aa*: Muslim prayers recited at specific occasions, as opposed to the ritual prayer called salaat; these may be memorized or improvised

When we arrived at the clinic, I had a rude introduction to the concept of stitches. The doctor tried to dismiss Ammi so she would not have to watch, but I refused to be separated from her. As they stitched my hand, Ammi continued to pray audibly, indifferent to the questioning looks of the doctors and nurses. American Muslims were not common in those days, much less a naval officer's Muslim wife who was wearing a full burqa and murmuring aloud in Arabic and Urdu.

Her resolute du'aas and her steadfast reliance upon Allah, even in the face of a screaming child and judging eyes, was a testimony of her faith that I have never forgotten. Throughout the rest of my childhood, she taught me many du'aas from the Quran and hadith, and I guarded them close to my heart because I knew their power. I had seen them strengthen her in a time of fear and need, and that left a mark on me far deeper than any physical scar.

Chapter Three

A COMMUNITY OF FOUR

AS I GREW, I felt like my family and I never really fit in with the people around us. I have always felt disheartened thinking about it. Aside from the Islamic traditionalism, my life was a mix of 1980s cartoons, plastic toys, and temper tantrums. I should have fit in with the other boys just fine. Unfortunately, people are afraid of what they do not know, and my Muslim heritage was a deterrent for many would-be friends and their families. I was very lonely.

What made it even worse was that the navy moved my family fairly regularly. We never had time to develop any roots. Most of my early memories are snapshots of either moving out of a house, traveling to a new one, or settling in and learning to call a new place "home." But these memories are still dear to me, and I vividly remember, for instance, our move when it was time to leave Virginia.

> My Muslim heritage was a deterrent for many would-be friends and their families. I was very lonely.

As strangers took our furniture, I stood by the screen door on the front porch crying. I cried inconsolably, not understanding who these men were or what I had done to deserve this fate, but Ammi was there to comfort me. True, she chuckled at times, and I do remember some teasing when my favorite chair was taken away by a stranger. But I also remember her consoling caress and her comforting voice.

"*Kya baat hai?*" she asked, as she took my face into her hands and drew it close in embrace. "*Kya baat hai, mera beyta?*" "What's the matter, my son?"

"They took the chair! The one with strawberries!"

"And is the chair more important to you than your Ammi? I'm still here. And so are Abba and Baji. Allah has given you everything! What more do you need, Billoo?" Billoo was the nickname that only my parents used for me, and they used it specifically when they wanted to express their love. They rarely said "I love you" directly; that is too crass for traditional Pakistani ears. Love is implicit and understood, expressed through provision by the parents and obeisance by children.

That implicitness is one reason why a child's obedience is paramount in Muslim culture. In my teen years, Ammi would often reprimand my obstinacy by saying, "What good is it to tell me you love me when you don't do what I say?" Later still, when I was considering following Jesus, I knew I was contemplating the one choice that would be far and away the greatest disobedience. Not only would my parents feel betrayed, they would be utterly heartbroken.

But at the sheltered age of four, heartbreak and family strife were the farthest things from my mind. I just wanted my strawberry chair back.

When everything was packed and we were ready for our journey, Abba gathered the family and said, "Let's pray." I raised my cupped hands to waist level, copying Ammi and Abba. We all prayed silently, asking Allah for a safe and swift journey.

When we finally arrived at Abba's new duty station, we were in Dunoon, Scotland. Looking back, I still feel like Dunoon was my first real home. It wasn't that I built any friendships at school or that I knew many boys in the neighborhood—even the strawberry chair went missing in the move—it was that I grew closer with my family and deeper in my faith during those years. I had my Ammi, Abba, and Baji. I did not need anything besides them.

Chapter Four

THE PERFECT BOOK

BY THE TIME I ARRIVED IN SCOTLAND, I had not yet learned English well. We always spoke Urdu at home, and if we were going to learn any script, it would be Arabic. The reason for this was simple: the Quran was written in Arabic, and it was imperative that Baji and I learn to recite it.

Muslims believe that every single word of the Quran was dictated verbatim by Allah, through the Archangel Gabriel, to Muhammad. The Quran is therefore not only inspired at the level of meaning but at the deeper level of the words themselves. For this reason, Muslims do not consider the Quran translatable. If it is rendered in any language other than Arabic, it is not Quran but rather an interpretation of the Quran. A book can be a true Quran only if written in Arabic.

This is why it is such an important belief for Muslims that the Quran has always been exactly the same—word for word, dot for dot. Imams and teachers regularly declare that the Quran was perfectly preserved, unchanged from the moment Muhammad heard it from Gabriel and dictated it to his scribes. Of course, Muhammad had nothing to do with composing the Quran; he was simply the conduit of its revelation to mankind, and he dutifully preserved its exact form. Had he not, and had the words been even slightly altered, the Quran would be irretrievably lost. But such a tainting of the words was unfathomable. No one doubted the perfect transmission of the Quran. The words must be perfect.

In fact, the emphasis on the words themselves leads many Muslims to neglect the meaning of those words. Muslims who recite the Quran regularly are regarded as pious, whereas Muslims who only contemplate the meaning of the Quran are regarded as learned. Piety is the greater honor, and most Muslims I knew growing up could recite many chapters of the Quran from memory, but rarely could they explain the meaning or context of those verses.

Imams and teachers regularly declare that the Quran was perfectly preserved.

Ammi had it in mind to teach us both the recitation of the Quran and the translations, but recitation was first. Every day as far back as I can remember, Ammi would put a traditional Muslim skullcap on my head, sit me down beside her, and teach me to read Arabic. We began with a book called *al-Qaeda*, "the Guide." It taught us Arabic letters in their various forms with their respective sounds. Right after moving to Scotland, I "graduated" from the Qaeda to the Quran.

I remember that moment vividly because my momentary elation was curtailed by horror. After finishing the last page of the Qaeda, Ammi reached next to her, picked up a Quran, and presented it to me. It was my Quran, the very first book I was ever given.

Thrilled, I ran to Baji to show it to her. Baji was playing on the floor near Ammi and Abba's room, so I got down next to her and placed the Quran on the ground to show it to her.

All of a sudden, I heard Ammi emit a heart-stopping scream while running in my direction. "Nabeel!" I was too shocked to respond. I had never heard her scream like that, nor had I ever seen her run. In a flash she picked up the Quran. "*Never* put the Quran on the ground!"

"Okay."

"Always raise it high. Put it in the most honored place, wash your hands before touching it, and only touch it with your right hand. This is not just any book, it is the word of Allah. Treat it with the respect He deserves!"

"Okay."

"*Jao*, go." She was deeply disturbed, and I did not hesitate to leave.

From then on, whenever I carried the Quran, I raised it high. Baji also learned from my mistake, so the next time Ammi called us to read the Quran together, we came holding our Qurans as high above our heads as we could, arms fully outstretched. Ammi was smiling. This was not exactly what she meant, but she was pleased.

Baji was the elder, so she went first. Ammi pointed to each word Baji was to read, slowly moving her finger across the page from right to left. Baji was not so much reading the words as singing them. We were taught to read the Quran melodically, making the sound of the recitation as beautiful as possible. Some men dedicate their lives to this practice, perfecting their pitch, tempo, pronunciation, and melody.

But Baji and I were no experts. She had a few years' head start on me, and she had only just learned to recite the Quran acceptably. When she finished, it was my turn. I had never read the Quran before, and I was terribly excited.

"Billoo, what do we recite before we start anything?"

"*Bismillah-ir-Rahman ar-Raheem.*"

"And what does that mean?"

"In the name of God, the Most Gracious, Most Merciful."

"Why do we recite this prayer?"

"So that we remember everything belongs to Allah, and so that we do only good things."

"*Shabash*, good job. Do you know where this prayer comes from?"

"No."

"It is found at the beginning of every **surah** in the Quran."

"Every surah?"

> **Surah**: A chapter of the Quran

"Every surah except one."

"Why did Allah leave it out of one surah, Ammi?"

"Allah was very upset with people in that surah, beyta, so He didn't give us the blessing of the *bismillah* there. But He loves us very much, so He put an extra one into another surah. And how many surahs are there?"

"114."

"Shabash. And you will read them all soon, *inshallah*. Baji finished the Quran when she turned seven, and I want you to do it by the time you are six. Let's go."

As the days progressed, I became increasingly familiar with the Quran. I learned that there were two ways the Quran was divided: one was into 114 chapters, and the other was into thirty parts. The latter is a system that Muslims devised long after the Quran was compiled, mainly so that the entire Quran could be easily recited during the thirty days of *Ramadhan*. But the thirty parts were important to me for another reason: whenever I finished one, Ammi bought me a congratulatory gift. The Mario Bros. trash can was my favorite.

By the time I reached an acceptable pace, Ammi and I had developed a rhythm. We would sit down with my Quran, open it to the last page we had read, and Ammi would point to my ending spot for that day. For some reason I preferred to recite exactly eighteen verses. If Ammi picked more for the day, I would complain, and if she picked less, I would consider reading a few extra to make her happy.

And so the days went on. I ultimately finished the Quran just before I turned six, much to Ammi's delight. Concurrently, Ammi had helped me memorize the last seven surahs to recite during the daily prayers. My favorite was *Surat al-Ikhlas*, number 112, because it was short, melodic, and memorable. Plus it was the first surah I memorized, and I repeated it many times a day during salaat. It was one of Ammi's favorite chapters as well but for a different reason: in a hadith, Muhammad told his companions that *Surat al-Ikhlas* is so weighty and consequential that reciting it is like reciting one third of the whole Quran in one sitting.

What was the message that Muhammad considered so important? Essentially this: God is not a father, and He has no son.

For much more detail on the Muslim view of the Quran, read part 4 of No God but One, titled "The Quran or the Bible: Two Different Scriptures."

Chapter Five

STORIES OF THE PROPHET

"WE'RE LATE, LET'S GO!"

It was a Saturday morning, and Abba was standing by the door waiting for us. Every Saturday, our family would travel from Dunoon into Glasgow to the jamaat *masjid*. It was our favorite time of the week, when we would get to spend time with other Muslims, almost all of them of Pakistani heritage. They were all just as out of place as we were, so we fit together perfectly. Ammi seemed to live for that day of the week since it was the only place she really let her hair down outside of the home—figuratively, of course, but also literally. Muslim women take off their burqas in each others' company, and they are usually quite fashion conscious at such times.

Masjid: A Muslim place of worship, often called a mosque

As much as Ammi looked forward to it, she was always running late. Always. In Pakistani culture, punctuality is not nearly as important as it is to Westerners. Social considerations take priority. It's often seen as uptight to be punctual, and to show up to someone's home at the invited time is actually considered somewhat rude. What if they are making last minute preparations for your arrival? It would impugn their hospitality to arrive before they are ready. Fifteen or thirty minutes late is a safe bet.

Abba, on the other hand, had left this aspect of our culture at boot camp. He was now a military man, and our tardiness perturbed him. Try as he might, he was never able to change Ammi's ways. She always did whatever she wanted, and Abba always reminded her that he was the man of the house. She would listen for a few minutes and then slowly charm her way into his heart, bringing him back into a good mood. That lovers' tiff might as well have been on the calendar every Saturday morning.

But this particular Saturday came only once a year. It was the day our jamaat celebrated *Sirat-an-Nabi*, the life of the Prophet. It wasn't Muhammad's birthday, just a day that the community chose to gather and tell stories about Muhammad's life.

Muslims consider Muhammad's life exemplary, and devout Muslims emulate him as much as possible. To do so, Muslims learn stories about his life from books of **sirah** and hadith. They almost never read the stories themselves; rather they hear them in sermons at the mosque. It is prestigious to be well-learned in the hadith, able to quote and recite them in their appropriate contexts. Thus, going to the mosque was important for both religious and social reasons.

> **Sirah**: Biographies of Muhammad's life

But we were late.

"*Challo*! Come on!"

The mornings were virtually scripted for Ammi, Baji, and me: after waking up and reciting the morning prayers, Ammi dressed me and Baji, fed us, and then put on her makeup. She would shout, "I'm ready!" right after the foundation and right before the lipstick. This Saturday, she brought the lipstick with her into the car. Soon, we were on our way to Glasgow.

To get to Glasgow from Dunoon, we had to cross Holy Loch. The loch was a berth for American nuclear submarines during the Cold War. Abba was the safety and environmental officer for the submarine repair ship. Of course, I did not know that at the time. All I knew was there were two ferries that took us across the loch, a small red one and a big black one, and the black one had a lounge where we could get cheese sandwiches. Usually Ammi and Abba had stopped squabbling by the time we got on the ferry, and on this day, they decided to stay in the car and prepare us for Sirat-an-Nabi day.

Ammi quizzed us, and either Baji or I responded, depending on who knew the answer. "*Batao*, tell me, when was Muhammad ﷺ born, and where?"

"AD 570, in Mecca."

"Shabash, good job! *Ub batao*, now tell me, who was his father?"

"His name was Abdullah, but he died before Muhammad ﷺ was born."

"And his mother?"

"Her name was Amina, and she died when he was six."

"So who took care of Muhammad ﷺ when she died?"

"His grandfather, Abdul Muttalib, but only for two years. Then he died."

"And after that?"

"His uncle, Abu Talib. He lived until Muhammad ﷺ was much older."

These were routine questions, all part of a proper Islamic education for young Muslims. Parents often pride themselves in their children's rote knowledge of Islamic facts and recitations, and Ammi and Abba were no exception.

"Okay, this one is difficult. Tell me one thing that happened to Muhammad ﷺ before his mother died."

Baji answered. "One day, when Muhammad ﷺ was playing with some of the other kids, two angels came to him and opened up his chest. The other kids were scared and thought the angels might be *jinn*. They ran away. The angels took out Muhammad ﷺ's heart and cleaned it until it shined. Then they put it back into his chest and left."[9]

Jinn: Spiritual beings often considered analogous to demons

"Shabash, *guriya*!" That was Ammi's nickname for Baji, which means "doll."

"Since you answered that, Nabeel, batao: who was Muhammad ﷺ's first wife, and how did they get married?"

This one was easy. "Muhammad ﷺ's first wife was Khadija. She was a rich widow, and Muhammad ﷺ worked for her as a merchant. When she saw how good he was at business and how honest he was with money, she offered to marry him."

"And how old were they?"

"Muhammad ﷺ was twenty-five, and Khadija was forty."

"Good, but maybe that wasn't difficult enough. Ub batao, Billoo, how did Muhammad ﷺ find out he was a prophet?"

"He was praying in a cave one day ..."

Abba interjected, "What was the name of the cave?"

"The Cave of Hira. He was praying, and an angel came to him and asked him to recite. But Muhammad ﷺ did not know how to recite, so the angel had to ask him three times. Then the angel gave Muhammad ﷺ the first verses of the Quran."

"Shabash," Ammi continued. "And what surah was that?"

Neither Baji nor I knew the answer to this question. It was harder than it might appear, since the Quran is not in chronological order. It wasn't a separate question in the books we had read, so we hadn't paid specific attention to it.

"No problem, don't worry. In case anyone asks you today, remember that it is *Surat al-Alaq*."

"*Jaani*, no one is going to ask them what surah it was. Ask them the important questions." *Jaan* or *jaani* is an Urdu term of endearment that means "my life." It is used for loved ones, and the way Abba used it here, it roughly meant "my darling."

But Ammi wasn't having any of it. "So the name of a surah isn't important, but the name of a cave is? Okay, fine. Let the man of the house ask questions!"

"Okay, I will. Challo, batao: Who was the first person to accept Muhammad ﷺ as a prophet?"

"His wife Khadija."

"And among men?"

"His best friend, Abu Bakr."

"And what is special about Abu Bakr?"

"He became the first khalifa when Muhammad ﷺ died." This was an important issue about which **Shia** disagree, but Baji and I did not know that yet.

"Good. Who accepted Islam first among children?"

"Muhammad ﷺ's cousin Ali."

"And what is special about Ali?"

"He became the fourth khalifa."

> **Shia**: Followers of Shi'ism, one of the two major branches of Islam

"How did most of the other Meccans receive Islam?"

"They persecuted the Muslims, insulting them and attacking them for years."

"So what happened?"

"Muhammad ﷺ had to flee to Medina."

Abba grew silent. Waves lapped softly at the ferry's hull as it began to dock. Juxtaposed with the rapid-fire questions, the brief pause served to magnify the mood. What was Abba thinking about?

When he finally spoke, his voice was contemplative, almost remorseful. "Billoo, batao, what was the first battle Muhammad ﷺ had to fight? Give me details."

"It was the Battle of Badr. The Meccans came to Medina to attack the Muslims and destroy them. They brought one thousand soldiers and many horses. The Muslims had only 313 men, very little armor, and only a few horses."

"Who won?"

"We did, of course!"

"Why?"

"Because we were better."

"No, beyta. They had the upper hand in every way. We won because Allah helped us. If this battle had gone naturally, we would have lost, and Muhammad ﷺ would have been killed, audhu billah. God will always help the Muslims, because we are His people. Okay, *beytee*, now you tell me, what were the other battles that were fought at Medina?"

"The Battle of Uhud and the Battle of the Trench," Baji responded, perhaps too cheerfully for the subject matter.

"Why did the Muslims fight these battles? Were we attacking anyone?"

"No, Abba. Muslims only fight to defend themselves. The Meccans were attacking the Muslims."

"So what did the Muslims have to do to stop the Meccans?"

"They conquered Mecca."

"And where was this prophesied?"

I interjected, "In the Bible! Deuteronomy!"[10] There was a whole field of Islamic polemics called "Muhammad in the Bible," and our books of Islamic knowledge were full of references to biblical prophecies about Muhammad. I was fascinated with them. Plus, I loved saying "Deuteronomy," though I had no idea what it was.

"Okay, last question. When Muhammad ﷺ conquered Mecca, what did he do?"

"He forgave all the Meccans!"

"Yes . . ." Abba trailed off again, and this time I could tell he was preparing to make an impassioned point. Sometimes his love for Islam overwhelmed him, and he would even pontificate to the wind if no one was there to listen. It did not happen often, but when it did, I loved it. I soaked it in.

"Yes, he forgave everyone. These are the same people who killed Muhammad ﷺ's uncle, who are responsible for the death of Khadija, who persecuted Muslims for years and then launched many wars against the defenseless community. When Muhammad ﷺ finally had a chance to strike them down, no less than they deserved, he gave mercy to them all. Is it any wonder Muhammad ﷺ is called *rehmatullah*, the Mercy of Allah?"

Abba's eyes were fixed on the horizon. We hung on his every word, brimming with respect and pride for our prophet.

"Many of the Meccans saw Muhammad ﷺ's mercy that day and couldn't help but proclaim the beauty of Islam. The whole of Arabia was so in awe of Muhammad ﷺ that they all became Muslim. The Messenger and message were irresistible, and soon, the Muslim empire expanded from Spain to India. It was the greatest civilization the world had ever seen. While the West was in its Dark Ages, Islam was in its Golden Era."

"Western society owes much to Islam. Science, medicine, mathematics, philosophy . . . Muslims had a huge impact in all these fields. That's why we still find Arabic words in all of them, like 'algebra' and 'alchemy.' Unfortunately, when the Western civilizations conquered, they destroyed everything. Muslim scholars were murdered, libraries were burned, cities were razed. The Spanish Inquisition is just one example of how Christians treated Muslims."

"But why would the Christians treat Muslims that way?" I wondered aloud. "Didn't they follow *Hazrat Isa*?"

"Beyta, they weren't following Hazrat Isa. They stopped following him a long time before. They turned Jesus into

Hazrat: An honorific title meaning "respected"

Isa: The Arabic name for Jesus

a god, and so they dishonored Hazrat Isa and blasphemed Allah! That is why Allah sent Muhammad 襃 and Islam as the final message for all of mankind. It embodies all the messages that Allah sent through the prophets: Adam, Noah, Abraham, Ishmael, Isaac, Moses, David, Elijah ... all of them brought messages from Allah to their people, and although the people accepted their messages at first, later generations corrupted them all. Light gets dimmer the farther it gets from its source! That is why we cannot trust the Bible today; it is corrupted. Only the Quran is perfect. Only Islam is incorruptible. Allah will guard it until the message spreads and the world becomes Muslim. That is when the day of judgment will come. That is the day Islam will be victorious."

We were all entranced by Abba's love for the faith, embracing his vision for a global Islamic future. There was nothing violent about its victory. It was a romantic notion of vindication and destiny.

After processing for a few moments, Ammi brought us back to earth. "Challo, that's enough. We are going to arrive at the masjid in a few minutes. Let's get ready." And she was right. We were nearing the mosque. Time had felt suspended, and I hadn't even noticed getting off the ferry. I loved discussing matters of religion. The Quran, Allah, Muhammad, dates, names, places ... they all enthralled me. Even talking about Jesus and the Bible was fascinating. To me, it was all a part of Allah's plan for mankind, a plan that was finally enacted through the greatest man who ever lived, Muhammad 襃. He had our hearts, and he had our allegiance.

For much more detail on the Muslim view of Muhammad, read part 3 of No God but One, *titled "Muhammad or Jesus: Two Different Founders."*

Chapter Six

RIGHTEOUS THROUGH RITUAL PRAYER

THE GLASGOW MOSQUE was one of my favorite places in child-hood. It sat at an oddly angled intersection near the River Clyde, just off the main road. Made of red stone and capped with a green dome, it had many floors with irregularly placed staircases, doors, and hallways. It was the perfect place to play hide-and-seek with the other Muslim boys.

Apart from children's games, there were many congregational activities at the mosque. We came together for holy days, celebrations, funerals, weddings, picnics, parties, and pretty much anything we wanted to do as a community. The mosque is a very dear place to Muslims, especially expatriated Muslims who long for fellowship. But none of those are the primary purpose of a mosque.

The primary purpose is congregational prayer, *salaat*. These are the obligatory prayer rituals, offered five times daily by all Muslims. First standing, then bowing, then briefly prostrating with their foreheads to the ground before rising and sitting on their heels, Muslims recite prescribed Arabic supplications to Allah.

> *Salaat*: The Muslim ritual prayers

Each of the five daily prayers has its own name: *fajr*, *zuhr*, *asr*, *maghrib*, and *isha*. Although the words and postures are the same for all, the number of repetitions differs. Each repetition is called a *rakaat*. A Muslim is required to pray seventeen rakaat daily, and optional prayers can be offered alongside these. In our jamaat, all told, we were taught to pray thirty-one rakaat per day whenever possible.

The prayer times often become a schedule of sorts for Muslims, waking up with the adhan for fajr, taking a late morning break from work for zuhr, going home after asr, having dinner after maghrib, and preparing for sleep after isha. For each of these prayers, after hearing the adhan, Muslims perform an ablution called **wudhu**, a ceremonial washing of the arms, face, and feet. Often they recite memorized du'aas while performing the wudhu. Then they hurry to the congregation to pray.

Rakaat: Units of repetition in salaat, composed of standing, bowing, prostrating, and sitting postures

Wudhu: Ceremonial washing before salaat

Imam: A leader of Muslims, usually referring to one who leads prayer at a mosque

Muslims all around the world pray roughly the same way. In fact, they all face the same point, toward the *Ka'ba*, the Muslim holy shrine in Mecca, which looks like a black cube. It is Islamic lore that Abraham built the Ka'ba with his son Ishmael, and when Muhammad took refuge in Medina, he commanded Muslims to start facing the Ka'ba during salaat. They have done so ever since, whether standing in a circle in the Grand Mosque, which houses the Ka'ba, or in a line halfway around the world. In the West, you might see a zealous Muslim pull out a compass at prayer time to find the exact direction. I have even seen prayer rugs with compasses built into them.

The prayer is led by one man, called the **imam**. Men and women pray separately but in sufficient proximity so that the women can hear the imam's voice as he leads the prayer. While the imam leads, some portions of the prayer are recited silently and individually, and other portions he prays aloud. Sections of each prayer involve the recitation of the Quran, and the imam always recites these aloud from memory.

The process of reciting the Quran during prayer was an ingenious method to propagate the Quran in the mostly illiterate society of seventh-century Arabia, and it still works today. That is why the only criterion for an imam is that he knows the Quran well and is able to adeptly recite large portions of it. Every once in a while, an imam might make a mistake in recitation, and it is the duty of the Muslims in the front row to correct him. Thus, a hierarchy of piety is often found in the rows of salaat, with elder, respected Muslims toward the front.

With that minor exception, Muslims take pride in the equality found in salaat. From rich men to poor men, statesmen to workmen, all men line up side by side and pray as one. It is a solemn event, where no one speaks, no one crosses in front of those praying, and no one interrupts.

No one except, of course, a five-year-old brat from America. A few times, while running around the worshipers during salaat, someone would give me a swift spank to jar me out of my mischief. My parents were fine with this; it took a mosque to raise a Muslim child, and the members of our jamaat trusted one another deeply.

On one occasion during the salaat, I was restless and fidgety. Out of nowhere, I felt a swift spank on my behind. I turned around to see who it was, but there was no one behind me. I surmised it was my uncle, who was standing next to me, so after finishing the salaat, I tearfully accused him of the spanking. Without flinching, he pointed up to the sky and said, "No, it was Allah." My eyes went wide, and I thought, "If only I had turned around faster, I would have seen the hand of Allah!" Twenty years later, he confessed it was him, but in the meantime, I was honored to have been spanked by God Himself. I always stood with due solemnity in salaat after that.

Since the postures and words are memorized,[11] there is nothing extemporaneous—indeed, nothing personal—about salaat. For the vast majority of Muslims, it is simply an act of duty, not personal or heartfelt expression.

True, one can dwell on the meaning of the words that he is reciting and by doing so make it more personal, but rare is the worshiper who can do that for each of the seventeen required rakaat every single day. Even then, the words are exogenous to the worshiper, not the least because they are in a foreign language. This is true even for Arabic speakers. Arabs speak colloquial forms of Arabic that vary by region. If they want to learn a form of Arabic that approximates classical Arabic, they have to learn it at school. The language of the daily prayers is not personal to anyone.

Jumaa: The name for the Muslim Sabbath day

This may lead one to wonder why Muslims continue to pray five times a day. What is the point in reciting the same words five times a day, every day, when they don't mean anything personally? I wondered that myself when I was young, and when I asked Abba, he said "Nabeel, before Allah, we are all dirty, and we need His cleansing. Now imagine you bathed five times a day. How clean you would be! The salaat is the spiritual bath that Allah has given Muslims to keep us pure and clean. That is why we pray five times a day."

There is some variation in the prayers. On Fridays, the Islamic Sabbath day, the imam gives a sermon and Muslims pray a modified form of the zuhr prayer, called *jumaa* prayer. The word *jumaa* means "congregated," and it can be prayed only with three people or more. So important is jumaa prayer that the word *Friday* in Arabic and Urdu is named after it. Ammi and Abba told us that if we missed three jumaa prayers in a row, we would have a black scar on our heart that could never be cleansed.

Unfortunately, we could not go to the mosque on Fridays because of its distance from our home and because of Abba's schedule. Of course, we could also not go to the mosque for the five daily prayers either. So we usually prayed the daily salaat and jumaa as a family at home. If ever Abba was deployed and there was no male relative staying at our home, I would lead Ammi and Baji in prayer. That started at a young age, when Ammi felt I was mature enough.

Salaat solidified my father as my spiritual leader and indelibly chiseled the Quran into my heart.

Although I enjoyed leading prayer, and although some of the imams in our jamaat had melodious voices or commanding presences, Abba was always my favorite imam. His tempo, his voice, his melody, and his position in front of the rest of our family just seemed right to me. Even now, I can hear his voice reciting long portions of the Quran if I just close my eyes. That is why I know those portions, because I heard Abba repeat them so often. Salaat solidified my father as my spiritual leader and indelibly chiseled the Quran into my heart. That is the power of salaat.

Chapter Seven

DIVERSITY IN ISLAM

THE YEAR 1989 WAS IMPORTANT for our jamaat. It was the one hundredth anniversary of the Ahmadiyya sect of Islam, our sect, and people from all over the world were gathering in England to celebrate the centenary. Our family considered it Allah's special blessing that this momentous event occurred while we were stationed in the United Kingdom. We would be among tens of thousands of people in attendance.

The celebration was held in the English countryside at Tilford, where massive marquees served as meeting halls and trodden grass as paths. There were tents for praying, serving food, broadcasting by satellite, and selling memorabilia. Diplomats and other honored guests had been invited from all across the world to attend the sessions, and many came bearing messages of tolerance and multiculturalism.

The female diplomats were the only women allowed in the men's area. The women's area duplicated almost all of the men's venues, but the two were separated. I was still young enough that I could get into the women's section without raising any eyebrows, and I often did. It was far livelier than the men's area. The women wore colorful clothing, laughed loudly, and talked incessantly, completely ignoring the speeches being televised from the men's section. There, the atmosphere was always solemn, and as a six-year-old, solemn meant boring.

During one of the main sessions, I intended to go from the women's meeting hall to the men's bazaar, where they were selling specially designed centenary badges. On my way over, an elderly man firmly grabbed my shoulder as I tried to pass by him. That was never a good sign. He physically turned me around, placed his hand between my shoulder blades, and guided me to the men's main hall. He sat me down, very close to the front and too close to himself. He did all this without saying a word, but he gave me a very stern look that said all he needed to say: "Sit down and listen to the speech." To this day, I have no idea who he was, but I knew better than to disobey an elder at a jamaat gathering, so I turned my attention to the speaker. The badge had to wait.

The speaker was a missionary from Pakistan whose accent made him exceedingly difficult to understand. His native tongue was Punjabi, a language related to Urdu and spoken in rural Pakistani villages. He was importing his Punjabi accent and inflections, unabated, into the English language. The result was not pleasant. Fortunately, his message was a staple of high-profile gatherings in our jamaat that I had heard many times before.

He was defending the fact that we were Muslims.

"The other Muslims say we are not Muslim, but who are they to cast us out of Islam? According to Anas ibn Malik, Muhammad ﷺ said, 'Anyone who proclaims the **shahada** is Muslim.' And the shahada is clear: 'There is no god but Allah, and Muhammad ﷺ is His messenger.' Even today, all you have to do is recite the shahada and you will be accepted into the fold of Islam."

> **Shahada**: The central proclamation of Islam: "There is no god but Allah, and Muhammad is His messenger"

He seemed to say this directly to the diplomats, who shifted in their seats.

"Every person must recite the shahada to become a Muslim, and that is all he must do to be Muslim, according to this beautiful hadith of our beloved prophet Muhammad ﷺ."

The missionary was becoming more and more animated by the moment. Years later, I found out that he had seen his loved ones suffer terrible persecution at the hands of other Muslims. Some members of his congregation had even been killed. His rhetoric was cathartic, fire expelled directly from his heart.

"Neglecting the shahada makes you non-Muslim; reciting the shahada makes you Muslim; and we recite the shahada. That's it. We are Muslim! But why do I bother to clarify this, as if we are teetering on the border of Islam? Do we reject any of our Islamic obligations? No!"

In rapid-fire fashion, the missionary enumerated the fundamental practices required of all Muslims, the **Five Pillars of Islam**.

> **Five Pillars of Islam**:
> The fundamental practices required of all Muslims
>
> **Zakat**: Obligatory alms
>
> **Hajj**: The annual pilgrimage to Mecca
>
> **Six Articles of Faith**:
> The fundamental Muslim beliefs

"We recite the shahada; we pray the salaat; we pay *zakat* to the poor; we fast during Ramadhan; and we make pilgrimage to the Ka'ba to perform *Hajj*! These are the things we are commanded to do by Allah in the Quran, and we do all of them. Who can deny we are Muslim?

"And we explain this to them with clear proofs from the Quran and hadith, but they want to find a way against us, so they change their objections! They say to us, 'You pretend to be Muslims with your actions, but you do not believe what Muhammad ﷺ taught!' Tell me, what did he teach that we do not believe?"

The missionary transitioned from the fundamental practices to the fundamental beliefs, called the **Six Articles of Faith**.

"We believe in the one God Allah; we believe in the unseen spiritual beings; we believe that Allah sent prophets into this world; we believe that He gave sacred scriptures to His prophets; we believe that there will be a day of judgment; and we believe that Allah's decree is sovereign over the universe! What don't we believe?

"What we don't believe is falsehood! We don't believe, like the Shia do, that Allah made a mistake by allowing Abu Bakr to become khalifa! We don't believe, like the Sunnis do, that we can murder people in the name of Allah, let alone murder other Muslims! These are egregious beliefs, and were we to believe them, our ejection from Islam would be justified!"

Ahmadi missionaries were not known for cautious treatment of sensitive matters in moments of passion. His word choice was provocative, but there was some truth in it. He was referring to the main division among Muslims, the division between Shia and Sunni. There are three major branches of Shia Islam, and together the Shia make up approximately 10–15 percent of the world's Muslims. They believe that authority in early Islam passed through Muhammad's bloodline, so that when Muhammad died, his male next of kin ought to have borne the mantle of Islamic leadership. That would have been Ali. However, when Muhammad died, there was no appointed successor. The Muslims elected Abu Bakr as the first khalifa. For the most part, those that recognize Abu Bakr's caliphate follow one of the four schools of Sunni Islam, and they make up about 80 percent of the world's Muslims.

The remaining 5–10 percent are those who fit comfortably in neither category. That's where we stood.

"Muhammad 🕊 proclaimed that if we recite the shahada, we are Muslim. We do that. The Quran tells us we must perform the Five Pillars. We do that. Islam teaches us that we must believe the Six Articles of Faith. We do that! So why do they call us *kafir*?"

"They have the audacity to call us kafir because we do not interpret two words in the Quran the way they do. Two words! '*Khatam an-nabiyeen*, the seal of the prophets.' In the minds of

> *Kafir*: Infidel, non-Muslim

these violent and uneducated Muslims, disagreement over these words justifies murdering their brothers in Islam, astaghfirullah!"

The imam was referring to the controversial claim made by the founder of our sect, Mirza Ghulam Ahmad, that he was a subordinate prophet under Muhammad. Most Muslims argue that 33:40 precludes any prophethood after Muhammad, thereby making Mirza Ghulam Ahmad a false prophet and his followers non-Muslim. Because of this, hundreds, if not thousands, of Ahmadi Muslims have been murdered in countries like Pakistan and Indonesia at the hands of orthodox Muslims.

"They have taken the religion of peace and turned it into a religion of bloodshed and violence. But *inshallah*, Allah will restore

Islam through Ahmadiyyat. He has already sent the imam of our time, the Promised Messiah, and his successors are divinely appointed khalifas!"

Here was even more offense in Ahmad's claims. After claiming to be a prophet and running into the *khatam an-nabiyeen* argument, Ahmad partially defended himself by saying he was no new prophet at all. He argued that people of many faiths are waiting for their prophets to come back. Jews are waiting for Elijah, Hindus are waiting for Krishna, Buddhists are waiting for Buddha, and Christians are waiting for Jesus. Ahmad claimed to be all these figures wrapped up in one. To top it off, his successors claimed to have established a new caliphate, a claim that is very offensive to the Muslims around the world who are still waiting for a final caliphate.

Inshallah: A very common Muslim formula meaning "if Allah wills it"

"Who can outwit Allah? He is the best of planners, and He will revitalize the world through Islam and Ahmadiyyat! This inevitability not even Satan can alter!"

When the missionary said this, sporadic yells were emitted from the congregation, all calling the same proclamation: "Takbir!" The thousands of men gathered in the tent responded in one accord "Allah-hu-akbar!" The strongest voice won out and boomed again "Takbir!" With emboldened passion, the entire host of men erupted "Allah-hu-akbar!" Ahmadis tend not to clap in agreement, instead marshaling one another to praise Allah and invoke His blessings.

The man who had yelled "Takbir!" continued to rally the gathered Muslims, bellowing "Islam!" which was received by "*Zindabad*," long may it live. "Islam!" "Zindabad!" "Ahmadiyyat!" "Zindabad!" Time seemed to hang in the air as the unknown voice thundered call after call, leading an army of Muslims in praising Allah. That the army was made up of pacifist Muslims would do nothing to allay the trepidation of an uninitiated observer. The roar of thousands was heart-stopping.

With nothing further to add, the missionary thanked the assembly and concluded the speech. Considering it today, I realize that the issue of orthodoxy and heresy is multifaceted and complicated. It is true that many Muslims call each other non-Muslim at the slightest provocation. The label of infidel is all too readily doled out over minor disagreements. I doubt whether any of the dozens of sects in Islam have ever escaped the accusation of heresy.

That said, the founder of Ahmadiyyat made some very bold claims, offensive to many parties. Claiming to be the second coming of Jesus offends both Christians and Muslims. Demanding the veneration due to a prophet is no small claim for Muslims, and it is not difficult to see why some of the orthodox consider Ahmadiyyat a cult.

But to me, many things weigh in favor of Ahmadis being Muslims. As the missionary said, Ahmadis adhere to the central doctrines and practices of Islam. Based on their daily lives and applied beliefs, Ahmadis are virtually indistinguishable from Sunnis. Along a similar vein, when I was an Ahmadi, I saw myself tied to Islam far more than Ahmadiyyat. But perhaps most important, Muhammad himself would consider Ahmadis Muslim: "Do not excommunicate anyone who declares that there is no God but Allah."[12]

> A man is Muslim if he exclusively declares that Allah is God and Muhammad is Allah's messenger.

The lesson to be learned is that there is much division in Islam. The best determination of whether a man is Muslim is if he exclusively declares that Allah is God and Muhammad is Allah's messenger. Beyond this point, there is great diversity in Islam.

Chapter Eight

THE PATH
OF SHARIA

WHEN IT COMES to *sharia*, the diversity in Islam can lead to widely disparate views. Sharia is not a field that the average Muslim knows well. When I first heard the term, I was at an *ijtema*, a tournament that our jamaat held once a year.

The tournament events were both religious and physical in nature. The religious competitions included Quran memorization, Quran recitation, adhan performance, Islamic poetry recitation, speech competitions, hadith memorization, and general religious knowledge tests. I'm not too sure what the physical competitions included because Ammi had me tied up with the religious ones, especially the speech competition.

Sharia: Islamic law

Ammi was very thorough in preparing me for my speech. Not only did she write the whole script, she trained me to deliver it. During the nights before the competition, after isha salaat, Ammi would have me stand up and do practice runs. She stood behind me while I was speaking and moved my arms and hands at the appropriate times to make emphatic gestures, as if I were her marionette. She directed me where to pause for dramatic effect, when to turn my head, and how to raise my tempo and volume for maximum impact. I found out later that she had been the captain of her debate team in Pakistan, which explained the course of her conversations with Abba.

On the day of the ijtema, I competed in the six- to eight-year-old bracket. The topic of my speech was, "always tell the truth, no matter what the consequences may be." I won an award for my speech, along with a few other awards. Ammi and Abba also competed, but the adult competitions always seemed much more lighthearted than the youth sessions. The tournament as a whole seemed centered on propagating Islam to the younger generation. To this end, the adult events were staggered and finished after the youth competitions so that the young participants could be in attendance.

I decided to sit in on the men's extemporaneous speech competition. The prompts in this competition tested a wide array of topics, such as, "Outline the history of Ahmadi jamaat," "What must we do to raise our children in the Islamic way?" and, "How do we know Jesus is not the Son of God?"

A man that I called Uncle Faizan, a fluent English speaker in his early forties, drew the prompt, "Explain sharia, including its sources and application." He stood up and began his speech by greeting the audience with a formal salutation.

"Respected imam, revered elders, honored guests, and dear brothers, *Assalaamo alaikum wa rahmutallah wa barakaathu.*"

The room responded in unison, "*wa alaikum salaam.*"

Glancing down at his prompt, Uncle Faizan began. "The topic I have been given today is sharia. Sharia is Islamic law. The word *sharia* means 'the path,' as in the correct path we must walk according to Allah's will."

The elders who were judging the event looked impressed. For non-Arab Muslims, being able to accurately define Arabic terms was always worth bonus points, tournament or not.

Emboldened by their reaction, he continued. "There is no book of sharia. We must derive the law from a hierarchy of sources using a process of jurisprudence called *fiqh*. The first and greatest source is the Quran. Nothing can supersede the Quran

Assalaamo alaikum wa rahmutallah wa barakaathu: An extended Muslim greeting meaning, "The peace of Allah and His mercy and blessings be upon you"

Fiqh: Islamic jurisprudence

because it is the word of Allah. But the Quran is not comprehensive. As Muslims, there is much we must do and believe that is not found in the Quran. For this, we go to the second source, hadith."

Some of us in the crowd were taken aback by the blunt comment that the Quran was insufficient. Though technically true, it ought not to have been stated so crudely. It sounded almost shameful, as if the Quran were somehow less than it should be. But Uncle Faizan's eyes were set on the elders, who did not display any reaction, so he proceeded.

"The hadith elaborate and clarify what is found in the Quran, but they never contradict. There is no contradiction in Islam. If a hadith is found in any way to contradict the Quran, then it is inauthentic and must be disregarded. If no hadith can be found to clarify an issue, then we must turn to the third source of sharia: the *ulema*, Muslim scholars who are wise and experienced in Islam." Uncle Faizan smiled courteously at the imam, on whom the flattery was not lost.

Ulema: Muslim religious scholars

Mufti: A Muslim legal expert

"That is where sharia comes from, but where can we see it? We see it everywhere in a devout Muslim's life. It is how we pray, when to fast, whom to marry, what foods to avoid. All these basic matters are issues of sharia. There are also far more detailed matters, like whether we must pay zakat on appreciated home values." The elders chuckled and gave Uncle Faizan the signal to wrap up.

"That is a brief explanation of sharia, its sources, and its application. *Shukria*, thank you." With that, he sat back down on the ground as the elders nodded their approval.

As I would come to know later, it was a solid answer to the question, at least from an Ahmadi perspective. Ahmadis have very little choice in their authority structure, and so the jamaat leaders have full say in interpreting sharia for them. What the leaders say goes. This is not the case for most Muslims.

Other Muslims have options. For example, if a Sunni woman wants to obtain a divorce from her husband, she has to receive approval from an authority. This must be from a *mufti*, someone trained in at least the basics of sharia. If she were to present her case before a mufti, he would provide her with his decision, called a *fatwa*. Fatwas are nonbinding, though, and if she were to dislike it, she could decide to go to another mufti and see if he provides a more favorable fatwa.

> *Fatwa*: A decision or ruling by a Muslim authority

Muftis from different schools of thought have different precedents and therefore provide different fatwas. For example, some schools of Sunni thought insist on a woman's consent before she is given in marriage. Other schools do not, requiring that the woman abide by her family's wishes. Since no one is bound to any specific school, some women choose schools of thought based on the fatwas they prefer. Even though this practice of "fatwa shopping" is discouraged by Sunni scholars, it serves as a perfect example of the kind of thing Ahmadis cannot do because of their very strict authority structure.

There is another dimension to the complexity: each denomination differs on what hadith they consider accurate. Since the hadith are the second rung of sharia, these differences of opinion have real consequences. Many of the differences between the ways Sunnis and Shias practice Islam are over this very matter. Their books of hadith are disparate. This difference, combined with the Shia position regarding the authority of imams, results in a significantly different view of sharia.

Differences aside, it is worth noting that a great deal of overlap exists between the majorities of Muslims. For example, all four major schools of Sunni thought and all three major schools of Shia thought teach that people who leave Islam must be killed for their apostasy, disagreeing only on the details of qualifying circumstances and implementation. Only outlying groups, such as liberal Muslims and Ahmadis, disagree with this time-honored practice.

I did not learn all of these details at the ijtema, nor did I need to. In fact, most Muslims do not know these things. They know Islam to the extent that they practice it, and these are matters for the learned. More than anything else, the ijtema and other gatherings like it caused us to grow deeper in love with Islam and deeper in community with one another. They reassured us that we had religious leaders who had answers that we might not have. By meeting together regularly and discussing matters of our faith, we became a strong community.

> *For much more detail on sharia, read part 1 of* No God but One, *titled "Sharia or the Gospel: Two Different Solutions."*

Chapter Nine

DREAMS OF
THE FAITHFUL

IT WAS AFTER A SIMILAR GATHERING one night when we were driving back from Glasgow to Dunoon that Ammi and Abba were obviously worried about something. Our family had lost track of time, and the ferries over Holy Loch had stopped running for the night. To make it back home, we had to drive around the loch, which took no less than two and a half hours.

But that had happened a few times in the past, and Ammi and Abba had never been worried before. The next day was a Sunday, so Abba wasn't concerned about missing work. They were sitting in the front seats, not speaking loudly enough for us to hear in the back, but Baji and I could tell that their speech was pressured, and a shadow of concern was growing between them. Something was amiss.

Baji spoke first. "Abba, what's wrong?"

"Nothing, beytee. Check your seat belt, make sure the door is locked, and go back to sleep. It's past your bedtime. We'll be home soon, inshallah." Ammi turned a distraught glance toward Abba. They said nothing.

After a moment, I prodded them again. "What's going on, Ammi?"

"Did you hear Abba? Do what he says." Whatever it was, Ammi and Abba were not about to share it with us, and there was no way we could fall asleep now. But we didn't want to get in trouble, either, so Baji and I pretended to be asleep.

After a few more tense minutes, Ammi had made up her mind about something. She turned to Abba and said, "Does it still look the same to you?"

"Yes, it looks the same. Actually, it looks even more like it."

"Then let's turn around! Let's go back! Challo, this is enough!"

This seemed to be all the prodding Abba needed. He turned the car around and started heading back toward Glasgow. Still, Baji and I knew not to ask any questions. The tension was fading, but the mood hadn't improved.

"Should I find a hotel?" Abba asked.

"No, we can stay at the Maliks' home. They will understand."

If Ammi could have said one thing to instantly transform my fear into joy, that was it. The Maliks were the one family from the masjid that we were especially close to. I called Mr. and Mrs. Malik "Uncle" and "Aunty," not just because that is standard terminology in Pakistani culture for elders but also because they were like a second set of parents to me. Whether I was carrying myself with the utmost propriety or plumbing the depths of my mischief, they received me with warmth and love.

Uncle and Aunty had five children who were our good friends. The oldest son in their family was thirteen, and he was my childhood role model. I was thrilled at the prospect of spending time with him. For the time being, the unnatural ride home was forgotten.

What made this turn of events even more exciting was that this would be my first time spending the night at a friend's house. Unless we were traveling or visiting family, we rarely spent the night anywhere but our own home. Sleepovers were unheard of, not only because you need friends for that but because Ammi was uncomfortable with the idea of leaving us beyond her supervision overnight.

We spent the night utterly elated, playing board games and watching movies. When our parents went to sleep, my friends decided to pop a new scary movie into the VCR: *Predator*.

When I said I lived a sheltered childhood, I meant it. A few moments into the film, I was utterly terrified. Even my friends' teasing would not coax me back to the television. I went to my bed and tried to fall asleep. My dreams that night were fitful, full of man-hunts, red dots, and unbearable Austrian accents. I woke up more tired than when I had gone to bed.

The next morning, after a Pakistani-Scottish breakfast fit for kings, Ammi thanked Aunty as she stood by the door. They waited until Abba and Uncle were out of earshot, speaking furtively. Ammi didn't mind me being nearby because she knew I hadn't had much sleep, and I always clung to her when I was out of sorts.

Aunty spoke while looking toward the street, her tone very matter of fact. "It's daytime now. You can tell me what he saw."

"Some dreams you don't share even in the daytime."

So this was the answer to the riddle. Abba had seen a dream. In our culture, dreams are carefully considered because, as a well-known hadith teaches, "The dreams of the faithful are prophetic."[13] In fact, dreams are the only means I know of by which the average Muslim expects to hear directly from God.

There is good reason for this expectation: dreams often did come true. Abba had many prophetic dreams. One example was when he was enlisted, he had to take a test for purposes of promotion to petty officer first class. The day of his test, he had a dream that he and five of his friends were in a battle-field under heavy fire. There was a fence in the distance, and they had to make it over the fence to be safe.

> Dreams are the only means by which the average Muslim expects to hear directly from God.

All six of them took off running. Abba made it over the fence first, and another friend made it over after him. The other four didn't make it.

A few weeks later, when he got his successful test scores back, he found out that the same five friends had all taken the test, and the only other one who passed was the one who made it over the fence in the dream.

Nani Ammi once had a recurrent dream about her father shortly after he passed away and was buried. He was knocking on her door and asking her for help, totally soaked by the rain. After having the dream on three successive nights, she decided to visit his grave. When she arrived, she found that an animal had burrowed a hole into his grave, and the monsoon rains had flooded it.

In my family alone, people have had clairvoyant dreams of sicknesses, miscarriages, births, deaths, and a host of other events. A dream was no matter to take lightly, especially one that might portend an avoidable calamity.

Aunty could tell Ammi needed to share Abba's dream with someone, so she asked again. "I want to give *sadqa* and pray for you. Tell me what he saw."

Ammi relented. "Okay, I'll tell you, but I'm not sure what it means, and don't tell anyone else. Two nights ago, he had a dream. We were all in the car, driving down a dark road. The road was very narrow, and there was fire on both sides. It was a dark fire, one that emitted no light. He couldn't see anything at all. When he turned around to check on Baji and Nabeel in the back seat, they were gone."

Ammi fell silent and watched Abba and Uncle as they stood by the car. Still matter of fact, Aunty asked, "What do you think it means?"

Ammi responded "Astaghfirullah, I don't want to think about it!"

"Then what happened on the road last night?"

Sadqa: A voluntary offering, often to prevent misfortune

Alhamdolillah: A Muslim formula meaning, "All praise be to Allah"; it is the Islamic analogue of *hallelujah*

Ammi hesitated before sharing. "The long road to Dunoon is a treacherous drive, even in the daytime. We didn't think anything of it, though, until we were halfway home, when the streetlights went out. It was dark and too much like the dream. That's when we turned around. Whatever the dream meant, I think Allah saved us from it."

Finally, Aunty turned to Ammi with a smile. "*Alhamdolillah*. Let us thank Allah, do du'aa before you leave, offer sadqa, and think no more of this. Call me when you arrive home so that I know everyone is safe." Ammi smiled in return and hugged her. Aunty was a true friend.

As we gathered around the car, both families offered du'aa together, silently praying for our safe and swift return home. Although this was standard procedure, it took on added meaning that morning.

When we were in the car and out of the city, I asked Abba if he'd had a bad dream. He glanced at Ammi, but she didn't say anything. "Yes, beyta."

"I had a bad dream last night too, Abba jaan. It'll be okay."

Abba chuckled. "There are different types of dreams, Billoo."

"What makes them different?"

"When you have one that is from God, you will know."

"Does Allah give you dreams a lot?"

"Yes, beyta. Too many." That was the last we spoke of it. A few days later, Abba decided to pray to Allah and request that he stop seeing prophetic dreams.

It has been over twenty years since then, and Abba hasn't received many dreams. I, on the other hand, would reach a point in my life when I spent many prostrate hours begging Allah for guidance through dreams. And as it turned out, Abba was right. When I got one, I knew it was from Him.

Chapter Ten

THE MONTH OF BLESSING

MY YEARS IN SCOTLAND were enchanted. My heart was captivated with the land and the people. Our home was situated on a hillside that often resounded with distant bagpipes on cold mornings. The mountains around Dunoon seemed to be carved for that very purpose. Blackberry bushes grew around our yard, just out of the reach of sheep grazing beyond barbed wire fence. I started my formal education at Sandbank Primary, the only school in our part of town, and I developed a few close friendships at the mosque. On more than one occasion, we were invited to dinner by strangers while stopped at a red light. I loved Scotland, and my affirmations of fondness for the country came with a thick Scottish accent.

The Cold War was ending, however, which meant the nuclear submarine base was no longer needed. It was time for us to move again, and there was only one positive aspect to leaving Scotland that I could think of: Ramadhan would be a lot easier.

Ramadhan is the Muslim holy month. For thirty days, Muslims fast from sunrise to sunset, not allowing any food or water to pass through their lips. This practice is obligatory for all able-bodied Muslims, which is why it is the fourth pillar of Islam. At the end of the thirty days, Muslims celebrate one of their two main holidays, **Eid al-Fitr**.

Ramadhan was awfully difficult in Scotland because of the length of the days. Scotland is so far north that it is just south of Iceland. During Scottish summers, the sun rose as early as four thirty in the morning, and it set as late as ten o'clock at night. If Ramadhan happened to fall during the summer months, as it did while we lived there, then Muslims had to fast for about eighteen hours a day. Not being able to

Eid al-Fitr: One of two major Muslim holidays; it marks the end of Ramadhan

eat for that long is bad enough, but the prohibition from drinking water is the most difficult injunction. To endure that for thirty days in a row is a test of fortitude and faith.

But Islam is often not as rigid as some perceive it. For instance, there are exceptions to the fasting requirements. If a Muslim is sick, traveling, or otherwise incapable of fasting, he has options. One of them is to provide a meal for a poor person to meet his obligation, and then when he is able, he can make up the missed fasts.

As important as fasting is, it would be an unfortunate misunderstanding to think only about fasting when considering Ramadhan. To Muslims, the holy month means much more. It is a time to build community, restore broken relationships, strive for purity, and above all, strengthen one's faith. Relatives are invited, gifts are purchased, parties are prepared. Like a monthlong Christmas, it is an extended time of celebration in Muslim lands around the world.

The Islamic calendar is lunar, and it is difficult to predict exactly when Ramadhan will start. There is usually a night of uncertainty. Every year I stood outside the house with Abba, staring at the sky

It would be an unfortunate misunderstanding to think only about fasting when considering Ramadhan.

with anticipation and excitement, hoping for the clouds to clear so that we could catch a glimpse of the moon. If there was a new moon, we bowed our heads and recited a memorized du'aa. Abba would then

go to the kitchen and tell Ammi the verdict. I cannot recall a time when she waited outside with us, because she'd always be preparing the next morning's food. There was a lot to prepare.

We usually woke up an hour before sunrise. After wudhu, we

prayed up to eight rakaats of optional prayer before sitting down to eat. The meal before sunrise was called *sehri*, and it served the dual purposes of giving us energy for the day and starting our day in fellowship. Ammi would be singing in the kitchen while preparing our food, usually praise songs for Allah or Muhammad. She would have the table set with our food: yogurt and eggs were a sehri

Sehri: The meal Muslims eat before fasting

staple, but we could also expect chickpeas, lentils, chicken kebab, cereal, milk, juices, and whatever else Ammi felt would complement the morning meal.

When we came into the kitchen, she would start making *roti* or *parattha*, Pakistani flatbreads. She would insist that we eat our flatbreads fresh and warm. Ammi always loved serving food, but never was she happier than when she was serving her own family the sehri. She wouldn't sit down to eat until we were almost done, and she was sure there was enough fresh bread for everyone.

Throughout the sehri, we had our eyes on the clock. We placed on the refrigerator a Ramadhan calendar that had the exact times for sunrise, so we knew when to stop eating. Just before it was time for the sun to rise, I would go to the prayer rugs and call out the adhan. Our family would continue eating and drinking until the adhan was finished.

One morning, when it was time to give the adhan, Ammi half-jokingly said, "Billoo, call the adhan slowly today, I need more time to eat!" Even though the adhan is supposed to be solemn, I started it off as fast as I could, taking delight in Ammi's amused yelp from the dining table. "Nabeel! You should be ashamed of yourself, doing this to your mother!"

During the course of the day, Baji and I would be in school, and if Ammi had even the slightest concern that the fast would interfere with our schooling, she didn't allow us to keep it. When we pointed out that our Muslim friends were fasting at their schools, she'd answer, "Am I their mother? You don't have to fast until you're old enough, and you're not old enough. You're just practicing. Maybe their mothers think they are old enough, but never compare yourself with other children." Even if she pretended she was angry, we knew Ammi was never actually upset with our desire to fast.

This was especially true because, like most Muslims, she made an exerted effort to be happy during Ramadhan, and it worked. Ammi spent her days during Ramadhan reciting the Quran and praying, and that always seemed to revitalize her. She often read through the entire Quran twice during Ramadhan, reading two of the thirty parts during the course of a day.

In the evening, our family would often go to *iftar* dinners at the homes of people from our mosque. Iftar is the breaking of the fast, and this is the time when the whole community gathers and celebrates. In books of hadith, it says that Muhammad used to open his fasts by first eating a date, so Muslims all around the world do the same thing. Of course, we usually ate our dates in the car on the way to the iftar, because we were running late.

After opening the fast with just a date, the community prays the maghrib prayer before eating the full meal in communion together. After some time for socializing, the adhan is then called again for isha prayer, and after isha, there is often a series of optional prayers that people pray during Ramadhan called **taraweeh**. Iftars at the local mosque usually have as the imam a **hafiz**, a man who has the entire Quran memorized. It is the goal of the imam to recite the entire Quran over the course of Ramadhan during these taraweeh prayers, and so these prayer sessions can sometimes last an hour or two per night. During the majority of the session, the worshipers stand silent, hands folded, listening to the recitation. When taraweeh is over, everyone goes home, planning to wake again in just a few hours.

In many places, Muslims go to a different home for iftar every night of Ramadhan. It is generally the host's job to provide the meal, and that means that there will be more food than everyone can eat. The irony of Ramadhan is that, after binging on buffets every morning and every evening, people usually gain weight during the month of fasting.

Iftar: The meal Muslims eat after fasting, often in large gatherings

Taraweeh: Voluntary prayers offered at night during Ramadhan

Hafiz: A man who has memorized the entire Quran

It wasn't until after we moved away from Scotland that I was allowed to start fasting regularly during Ramadhan. We left Scotland in 1990 for a submarine base in Groton, Connecticut. There was no community mosque in Groton, and it never felt like home for me. I didn't make any good friends, and the most noteworthy occurrence was the tragedy of losing my Scottish accent. Scotland was where I learned all about being Muslim and where I had fallen in love with my Islamic faith.

We moved again three years later, this time back to Virginia. Abba was about to become Lieutenant Commander Qureshi, and he was never to be moved by the military again. Virginia Beach is where I made lasting friendships, where I came of age, and where I decided the direction of my future. It is where I first felt the sting of my Islamic culture clashing with my American environment. It was where I ultimately decided to leave Islam and everything I knew.

To read an expert contribution on growing up Muslim in America by Abdu Murray, a lawyer, apologist, former Shia Muslim, and author of two published books on Islam and other major worldviews, see page 318.

Part 2

AN AMBASSADOR FOR ISLAM

⋯

Surely You are the one who sent Muhammad as the final messenger for mankind and the Quran as our guide . . .

Chapter Eleven

THIRD CULTURE

IN SEVENTH GRADE, I finally made lasting friends. David, Ben, and Rick were like brothers to me, and we did everything together. Ammi reluctantly realized that I was getting older, and she gradually let me spend more and more time outside of our home. Usually, I was out for some kind of extracurricular activity, and sometimes she'd let me go to a friend's house for a few hours.

But before I launched into my teenage years, Ammi had a serious talk with me. Late one evening, just after our family finished praying the isha salaat, Ammi stopped me before I left the prayer rugs. "Nabeel, stay here for a moment."

Immediately, I sensed that this was not going to be a normal conversation. "What is it, Ammi?"

"Beyta, I wish there were some Muslim boys in your school so you wouldn't be alone in representing Islam and so you would have true companionship. But that was not Allah's will. Always remember this: no matter where you are or what you are doing, you are an ambassador for Islam. You will always be an ambassador for Islam."

I listened with care, drawn in by her sincerity and intensity. "When people see your face, they will think, 'He is a Muslim boy!' It doesn't matter what you do. You could be the valedictorian, and they will think, 'Look at the Muslim valedictorian!' You could be the president of the United States, and they will think, 'Look at the Muslim president!' In the West, Islam is foreign to people, and many of them are opposed to it. They will always see you first and foremost as a Muslim. That is your identity, and you must embrace it."

Ammi did not often speak like this. Her words imbued me with a sense of responsibility. I concentrated hard on her words, wrinkling my brows.

She embraced me and held me close. "Billoo, don't worry! This is a good thing. It is a blessing and an opportunity for you to represent Islam and to help people understand its beauty. Become the valedictorian, so people will think, 'Wow, Islam produces good students!' Become the president, so people will think, 'Islam makes good leaders!' But even if you become a janitor, be the very best."

I nodded in affirmation, despite my doubts that she would be okay with a janitorial career.

"Shabash, beyta. Whatever you do, be the most respectful, honest, and dignified one doing it, so that people will praise Islam. Treat your teachers with the utmost respect! Treat them like you would treat me. When I visit them, I want to hear them tell me that you are the most respectful student in the class. Drinking is not allowed in Islam, but you must also never curse and never spend time alone with girls. Be such a virtuous person that no one can even point a finger of blame at you. In their hearts, they will praise you because they will know you are honorable, or they will dislike you because they dislike themselves. Either way, they will know that Islam has made you the good person you are."

And that is what I did. At school, I shared my Islamic beliefs with people who would listen; I stood up for the things that mattered to me; and I worked hard to uphold my morals and reputation. I knew people in my grade who were drinking, doing drugs, and having sex, even though we were only seventh graders. Thankfully, none of my friends were engaged in these activities, and it was not too hard for me to continue representing Islam the way I always had.

But things were changing.

Adolescent years are difficult for everyone. Teens develop their own identities and gradually break away from the one that their parents built for them. Each circumstance presents its own set of challenges. The challenge in our family, both for Baji and me, was that the direction of pull was not just toward a different personality but toward an entirely different paradigm. We were left straddling a chasm, with our feet firmly planted in neither culture.

The first change I noticed was at family gatherings. Almost all of Ammi's siblings lived in the Northeast, and we met many times a year. As I came into my teenage years, my parents, aunts, and uncles expected me to act like a good Pakistani teenager, and I wanted to be a good Pakistani teenager for them. The problem was that I had never been intimately acquainted with a good Pakistani teenager, so I didn't know what one acted like. That wasn't something Ammi could teach.

I ended up trying to emulate my older male cousins and my younger uncle in their manner of speech, but apparently, I lacked some of the finesse required to walk the line between witty and rude in Pakistani culture. That was something I could do in American culture just fine, in fact charmingly so. I began getting in trouble with my parents fairly frequently on our way back from family trips for being disrespectful.

> My mind was being shaped to think critically, but that shape did not fit into our culture.

I also realized that I asked far too many questions for my relatives' tastes. In our culture, elders are simply to be obeyed. Obedience is what shows them that you respect them and, in certain contexts, love them. Questions are often seen as a challenge to authority. In school though, our teachers taught us critical thinking and that it was good to question everything.

My mind was being shaped to think critically, but that shape did not fit into our culture.

This is not to say I didn't have unsavory character traits of my own; I certainly did. I was a prideful and self-serving youth, and that got me into plenty of trouble too. Good parents help shape and guide their children beyond these flaws, as mine tried to do. But some of what my parents saw as impertinence was actually a culture clash; I was cut out of different cultural cloth than they were. They thought I was fine Pakistani linen, but I was more of an Asian-American cotton blend.

The same was unfortunately true at school. I was far too Pakistani to fit in well with my American friends. There was always a barrier, no matter how much we did together or how close we became. I will never forget the last week of middle school, when there was an end-of-the-year school celebration. We were receiving our "senior superlatives," and I was given the superlative, "most likely to invent the pocket computer and then leave it in his pants on wash day." The evening was good fun, until it was time to take pictures. When my friend Ben wanted a picture with his best friends, he asked to take it with just David and Rick. It was like an icy knife through my heart. It actually still hurts to think about that incident, but it wasn't his fault. I just couldn't fit in perfectly anywhere.

No one understood that, not even I. I was no longer of traditional Pakistani culture, and I was no longer of American culture. I had a third culture, and no one met me there.

Chapter Twelve

MUSLIMS IN
THE WEST

LYING FLAT ON MY STOMACH, I peered between railings at a secret meeting on the floor below. Our family had gathered earlier that day for my grandfather's funeral services. Emotions ran high, but an additional, unstated tension had been present throughout the day. Though the adults had sent me and my cousins to bed, I had snuck out. I needed answers.

An older cousin sat at the end of my uncle's living room, her face in her palms, the elders positioned around her in a semicircle. The atmosphere was thick with concern and melancholy. No one spoke.

Finally, my grandmother softly broke the silence. "Are you still pure?"

Like lightning, my cousin's mother interjected, "Of course she is!" But all eyes were trained on my cousin. Slowly, without lifting her face from her hands, she nodded.

Ammi began to berate my cousin in a tone that I had heard her use only on Baji, though in matters far less severe. "If you are pure, then forget him! Move on, and get married to a good Ahmadi Muslim before our reputation is tarnished any further. Or at least a non-Ahmadi Muslim. But a Hindu? Astaghfirullah!"

Through tears and fingers crossed over her face, my cousin whimpered, "But I love him."

One aunt snickered and spoke under her breath, "I can't believe her mind could be so dysfunctional." Turning to my cousin, she chided, "You don't know what love is! Don't become Americanized. Listen to your elders!"

There was another break in the conversation, and the silence intensified the emotions. The men in the room did not speak. Their presence served simply to validate the gravity of the discussion and to anchor the women's emotions.

After a few moments, my cousin's mother added, "Your grandfather was a missionary. Can you imagine how he must have felt when he found out his own offspring dishonored our heritage? Dishonored Islam?"

"We don't have to imagine," my grandmother suggested, looking directly at my cousin. "It is because of what you've done that he isn't here anymore."

This was the only personal accusation I ever heard my grandmother make. It was spoken out of an Eastern sense of tough love, but to this day, it haunts my cousin.[14] She was not the only one, though, who collided over these matters with the extended family. The culture clash of immigrant parents with their Western-born children is especially common during the emotionally stormy teenage years, and it serves to illustrate a vital fact: Muslim immigrants from the East are starkly different from their Muslim children born in the West.

People from Eastern Islamic cultures generally assess truth through lines of authority, not individual reasoning.[15] Of course, individuals do engage in critical reasoning in the East, but on average, it is relatively less valued and less prevalent than in the West. Leaders have done the critical reasoning, and leaders know best. Receiving input from multiple sources and then critically examining the data to distill a truth is an exercise for specialists, not the common man.

Muslim immigrants from the East are starkly different from their Muslim children born in the West.

This phenomenon creates stark dichotomies in the minds of Muslims raised in these cultures. An entity is either a source of authority or it isn't. It is either trustworthy or suspect. It is either good or it is bad. Shades of grey are far less common among authority-based cultures.

For the most part, Eastern teachers have taught the Muslims that the West is Christian, that its culture is promiscuous, and that the people oppose Islam. So the average Muslim immigrant expects people in the West to be promiscuous Christians and enemies of Islam.

When they come to America, their cultural differences and preconceptions often cause them to remain isolated from Westerners. Like Ammi, many develop relationships only with other expatriates from their country, so their perspectives are never corrected. What is worse, some Muslims do receive poor treatment from Westerners and Christians, and this only serves to bolster their notions that all Westerners and Christians are the same way.

On the rare occasion that someone does invite a Muslim to his or her home, differences in culture and hospitality may make the Muslim feel uncomfortable, and the host must be willing to ask, learn, and adapt to overcome this. There are simply too many barriers for Muslim immigrants to understand Christians and the West by sheer circumstance. Only the exceptional blend of love, humility, hospitality, and persistence can overcome these barriers, and not enough people make the effort.

That explains why our families fight hard to keep us from becoming "Americanized." The term had nothing to do with nationality; it had everything to do with their perception of the culture. To be Americanized was to be disobedient to your elders, to dress less conservatively, and to spend more time with your friends than your family. Cursing, drinking, and dating were simply unfathomable.

> There are simply too many barriers for Muslim immigrants to understand Christians and the West by sheer circumstance.

One of the greatest travesties of all is that Muslim immigrants often associate Western immoralities with Christianity, and correlation becomes causation in the minds of the uncritical. The West is Christian, the West is Americanized; ergo, it is Americanized because it is Christian. Christianity, in the minds of many Muslims, has produced this promiscuous, domineering Western culture. Christianity, therefore, must be ungodly.

I remember pointing out to Ammi and Abba that the people dressed provocatively on television might not be Christian, and their response was, "What do you mean? Don't they call themselves 'Christian'? Don't you see them wearing crosses?" If I argued that some of them may be Christian in name only and might not even believe in God, they responded that this simply meant they were Christians who don't believe in God. They did not categorize religion with belief but with cultural identity. The tragedy here is that no one has given them a reason to think otherwise. If they were to intimately know even one Christian who lived differently, their misconceptions might be corrected, and they might see Christianity in a virtuous light.

> If they were to intimately know even one Christian who lived differently, their misconceptions might be corrected.

All of this is different for their children, for second-generation Muslims in the West. The second generation is as varied and disparate as their peers. If anything can be said of them, it is this: almost universally, they see the world as Westerners and yet still align themselves with Islam.

Some may be, as I was, raised to think critically and yet still love Islam. I have many highly educated female cousins who wear the burqa and are willing to defend that choice with thoughtful reasons. Others, like a few of my male cousins, have rejected everything about Islam and their culture, with the exception of the title "Muslim."

Whether a young Muslim stays connected with his culture or becomes nominal often has to do with pressures in the culture clash. If the parents are extremely devout, as mine were, then there is far more of a chance that the child will try to live a traditional lifestyle. If the parents are nominal, there is little chance the child will care more than nominally for Islam.

Who the child's friends are and what they believe is also highly influential, as well as what they learn in school. Baji grew to see things differently from me. She still wears a burqa and loves Islam, but she has blended Islam with Western pluralism. She believes that Allah can lead people to Christianity, Hinduism, Judaism, or any other religion, and they can still attain salvation because all paths lead to Allah. She believes this even though we were raised in the same house. Her experiences outside the home shaped her quite differently from me.

As for my cousin, though she eventually "came around" and did not marry the Hindu boy, it is unlikely that she will ever fully recover from that episode. One of my male cousins was reprimanded when he tried to marry a Filipina, but he "came around" and fully recovered, ultimately marrying a Pakistani girl. Another of my male cousins wanted to marry an American girl, was reprimanded, and then went ahead and married her anyway.

All of these second-generation American Muslims are my relatives. They all trace their lineage back to the same town in Pakistan, they were raised in the same jamaat, and they are roughly the same age. Yet they all see the world and process it extremely differently.

Perhaps most significant of all, none of them see the world as their parents do, not even close. Yet they all call themselves Muslim and identify themselves with their parents' faith.

What, then, does it mean to be Muslim in the West? It can mean anything. If you really want to know what someone is like and what they believe, you have to get to know them and ask them personally. But the best we can do before getting to know someone is to determine whether he is an immigrant or a second-generation Muslim. This one factor often makes a huge difference.

Chapter Thirteen

SWOONS AND SUBSTITUTIONS

MY PARTICULAR BLEND of East meets West was shaped by Islamic apologetics. I did not have to wrestle long with some of the postmodern relativism that captures my generation. To me, it was self-evident that truth exists. What's the alternative? If truth doesn't exist, then it would be true that truth doesn't exist, and once again we arrive at truth. There is no alternative; truth must exist.

Traditionally, Muslims and Christians have shared this understanding. Each believes in truth, not the least because they believe their faith is true. But their common perspective extends much farther. They have roughly analogous beliefs in monotheism, spiritual and physical realms, angels and demons, good and evil, a final judgment, heaven and hell, the inspiration of scriptures, and many more peripheral beliefs.

Commonalities perhaps also serve to sharpen disagreements between the two faiths.

These commonalities are a double-edged sword. They build a common platform for dialogue such that the two can often understand each other and see the world from a similar perspective. But the commonalities perhaps also serve to sharpen disagreements on the most sensitive difference between the two faiths: their views of Jesus and Muhammad.

Christians believe Jesus is God incarnate, and this is a necessary belief for orthodox Christianity.[16] Muslims believe that Jesus is no more than a prophet, and to consider him God incarnate would be blasphemy and would cause one to be condemned to hell eternally, according to the Quran.[17]

Muslims believe Muhammad is the messenger of Allah, and this belief is so important that it makes up half the shahada, the primary proclamation of Islam. Christians believe that those who teach contrarily to the gospel of salvation through Jesus are false teachers.[18]

This difference in beliefs is why dialogue between Muslims and Christians has mostly focused on Jesus and Muhammad. As a young teenage Muslim, to be an effective ambassador for Islam, I thought it was my duty not only to have an unimpeachable reputation but also to have a command over these points of contention.

Regarding Muhammad, Westerners rarely knew anything. I could say whatever I wanted about him and others would believe me. Of course, I did not try to deceive anyone, but it was not hard to make a case for Muhammad to the average Christian, simply because of their ignorance. I shared with them all the things I learned in my early childhood about Muhammad, especially his mercy upon returning to Mecca, and I was able to leave people with a much more positive impression about Muhammad and Islam than they had before.

Regarding Jesus, there are two issues on which Muslims particularly disagree with Christians: that Jesus died on the cross and that Jesus claimed to be God. The Quran specifically denies both of these beliefs.[19] To be a good ambassador, I just had to master these two issues and persuasively argue that Jesus never claimed to be God, nor did he die on the cross. For the latter, the founder of our sect had written a small book to equip the jamaat. It was called *Jesus in India*, and I had read it many times.[20]

My first opportunity to argue what I had learned was on a school bus in front of our middle school while we were waiting to go home. It was shortly before Easter, and I was discussing my plans for the upcoming school break with my friend Kristen. Our class had let out early, so we got on the bus before it was crowded. We were some of the oldest kids, so that secured us seats toward the back.

We sat down across the aisle from one another as she told me her plans for Good Friday.

"Good Friday?" I had no idea what that meant.

"Good Friday is the day Jesus died on the cross."

"What's good about that?"

"That's how he took our sins, by dying on the cross." Her answer was straightforward, but I was amused. I had been told this is what Christians believed, but no one had ever said it to me before.

"How does his death on a cross take away your sins?"

"That's what they told us at church. I don't know. We don't go to church a lot. I never asked." Kristen wasn't being defensive; she was being honest. That was one of the reasons I enjoyed talking with her. She was brutally honest and intimidatingly intelligent. I later developed a little crush on her, but I wouldn't admit it to myself. To do that, I would have had to compromise my culture, and that was not an option. I was an ambassador. But I did allow myself to be mean to her boyfriend.

I decided to redirect the conversation. "Well, I don't think he died on the cross anyway."

"Why's that?" She was intrigued, so I started with my trump card.

"Because of the Bible."

"What do you mean?"

"Well, first, we know that Jesus didn't want to die on the cross. When he was in the garden of Gethsemane, he prayed that God would take the bitter cup away from him. Obviously, the bitter cup was his impending death on the cross, and Jesus prayed all night that God save him, to the point where he was sweating drops of blood." I paused and waited for her affirmation. She nodded.

"I don't know about you, but I think God loved Jesus. There is no way that God would let Jesus' prayers go unheard. In fact, I think the book of Hebrews says that. Anyway, when Jesus was put on the cross, if you do the calculations, you can see that he was on the cross for only three hours. Hanging on a cross for three hours doesn't kill you.

People lasted on the cross for days at a time. He was taken down too quickly." She looked like she was processing everything, and I paused a moment to see if she would ask the obvious question. She did.

"So why was he taken down?"

"Exactly why the Bible says! Pilate commanded that he be taken down. Pilate's wife had seen a dream and begged her husband that he not allow Jesus to be killed. She must have been able to persuade her husband to save him after the Jews were convinced that he was crucified. So Pilate gave the order to take Jesus down from the cross. That's when Jesus was placed in the tomb." I stopped, because it was clear Kristen had an objection.

"But his disciples saw him afterward, and they thought he had risen from the dead. How could they have thought that if they took him down?"

"I didn't say the disciples took him down. It was Joseph of Arimathea and Nicodemus. Pilate couldn't be seen working with the disciples, because that would make it obvious he was helping Jesus. So he worked with Joseph of Arimathea and Nicodemus. Joseph took Jesus' body and put it in the tomb, and Nicodemus brought one hundred pounds of aloe and other medicines, along with linen bandages, to heal Jesus. God used the medicines to heal Jesus while he was in the tomb for those three days."

Kristen interjected with a question that I hadn't thought of. "But why would God do all this to save Jesus? Couldn't He have just taken Jesus up to heaven a few days earlier if He didn't want Jesus to die on the cross?" That was pretty sharp. I hadn't seen it from that angle. But our jamaat had given me an answer for the reason why Allah wanted Jesus to live.

"Jesus himself says he was sent for the lost sheep of Israel. The lost sheep were the tribes of Jews who were scattered over Asia during the Jewish Diaspora. Allah saved Jesus from death on the cross so he could go to the lost sheep and reform Judaism there, as he did in Israel."

We had been so engrossed in conversation that we hadn't noticed the students filing into the bus. In the seat in front of me, a boy who was one grade behind us had been listening attentively, apparently reaching his threshold. He caught our attention with a noisy grunt of contempt and, after looking at me, turned around angrily toward the front and said, "Disgusting."

I thought to myself, "If he had an argument, he'd share it. Truth silences falsehood."

Kristen had seen him too and looked at me to make sure I wasn't offended. I wasn't, but she went ahead and said loudly, "I think it's a very interesting perspective. Thanks for sharing."

The argument I shared with Kristen, often called "the swoon theory," is shared by Ahmadi Muslims and non-Ahmadi Muslims alike. It is a favorite among Muslim debaters, like Ahmad Deedat and Shabir Ally. It originated at the end of the eighteenth century when the age of enlightenment began generating naturalistic theories to account for Jesus' apparent resurrection. Muslims like Mirza Ghulam Ahmad had added a theistic twist to it, making it more plausible that Jesus could survive crucifixion. The argument goes: "If God can do the large miracle of raising Jesus from the dead, why can He not do the much smaller miracle of keeping him alive on the cross?"

The swoon theory is not the original Muslim explanation for Jesus' apparent death, though, nor is it the majority view. Most Muslims believe "the substitution theory." Early in Islamic history, it was argued that Jesus was substituted before being placed on the cross. Allah put Jesus' face on someone else, and that person was crucified in Jesus' place. This is how they interpreted the Quranic verse, "Jesus was neither killed nor crucified, but so it appeared."[21]

The question naturally arises: Who was killed in Jesus' place? Different people have been suggested. Some say it was a devout young volunteer who wanted the honor of dying for Jesus. Others say that when Simon of Cyrene carried the cross for Jesus, they crucified him instead. Yet others say that Allah put Jesus' face on Judas's body for poetic justice. The last view seems to be the most popular today.

Another majority view regards Jesus' ascension. The Quran teaches that "Allah raised Jesus to Himself," leading Muslims to believe in the ascension and eventual return of Jesus.[22] So, like Christians, most Muslims are waiting for the return of the Messiah. Our jamaat challenged this view, because Ahmad claimed to be the Messiah. Appealing to the Bible, he argued that the Jews were mistakenly waiting for the return of Elijah from the sky. Jesus said

John the Baptist was the return of Elijah. In the same way, the world was waiting for the return of Jesus, but Ahmad was he.

Of course, I vehemently argued whatever my jamaat had taught me, so I provided the swoon theory and the position that Jesus traveled to India where he died at an old age instead of ascending.[23] The more I shared my views, the more I felt confirmed in my faith, and the conversations occurred with increasing frequency when I realized no one had anything substantial to rebuff my views. I felt I had mastered half of the arguments I needed to be a good ambassador for Islam, and I felt that the other half was going to be even easier to argue. And I was right, it was.

For much more detail on the Muslim view of Jesus'
crucifixion, read part 6 of No God but One,
titled "Did Jesus Die on the Cross?"

Chapter Fourteen

THE FATHER IS GREATER THAN JESUS

BY THE TIME I WAS IN TENTH GRADE, my personal life was changing significantly. I began to spend far more time with friends, both on the phone and at school during activities. I was much more concerned with my clothing, which Ammi was still picking out for me. I started to ask Ammi if I could wear contact lenses instead of glasses in an effort to combat the "nerd" reputation that I had acquired. No success.

The tug of Western culture was becoming difficult to resist. I was still not allowed to go to sleepovers, nor was I allowed to go to school dances. My friends and I had grown close, and that made my absence from these events all the more difficult.

But I still represented Islam proudly, especially when my beliefs were directly addressed, as they were one day while I was in Latin class.

At Princess Anne High School, Latin was taught by two teachers, both of whom were thrilled when their students enjoyed the class. The teacher who taught Latin 2, Mrs. Earles, was far more kind and lax with me than she ought to have been. I loved Latin, and I loved her class. But I was getting more mischievous by the day, goaded by a lack of reprimand. I was the kind of student who forgot to do his homework quite often, and upon remembering a few hours before it was due, I tried to squeeze in a way to get it done. Mrs. Earles' class was right before Spanish, and I often did my Spanish homework while she was lecturing. I would hide my Spanish textbook under my Latin textbook, working on it whenever she turned her eyes to the chalkboard, thinking that she was oblivious. Halfway through the year, I realized she wasn't oblivious at all, just highly tolerant of my shenanigans.

I was working on my Spanish homework on one of these occasions when the girl in front of me turned around and said, "Nabeel, can I ask you something?" Her name was Betsy, and she was the outspoken Christian in our grade. Everyone knew she was an evangelical Christian, and she often stood up for her faith. Despite her kindness and desire to help others, she had a soft yet adamant demeanor that made the rest of us uneasy. We thought she was a bit loony.

"Yeah, sure." I had no idea where this was going. Had she wanted a pencil, she wouldn't have asked to ask me something, she would have just asked for the pencil. Nor would I have been the one she'd ask, for that matter. I always forgot my pencils.

She paused for a moment, steeling herself before asking, "Do you know about Jesus?"

Now I knew she was crazy. We were in the middle of Latin class. All the same, I immediately gained respect for her. Why had other Christians never asked me this question? They did think I needed Jesus to go to heaven, right? Were they content with letting me go to hell, or did they not really believe their faith?

I considered how to approach my response in the present context. I looked up from my Spanish homework to assess the situation. Mrs. Earles had apparently stepped out for an indefinite period, and most of the students were chatting around us. I didn't know how far I wanted to go, because I knew I could quickly get passionate and carried away. I decided to keep my answers short.

"Yes."

Her eyes went wide. That was clearly not the answer she was expecting. "Really? What do you think about him?"

"Well, I'm Muslim, right? Muslims believe that Jesus was sinless and born of the Virgin Mary. He cleansed the leprous, gave sight to the blind, and raised people from the dead. Jesus is the Messiah, the Word of God."[24]

Betsy was stunned. I must have gone off script, because she did not know where to go from there. So I proceeded for her.

"But Jesus was not God. He was just a man." I had drawn the battle lines for her and waited to see how she went to war.

"Wow, you know a lot more about Jesus than I thought. That's great! I believe a lot of the same things, but I don't agree completely. Would you mind if I shared my view?" She responded softly yet adamantly, employing the very sneaky maneuver of being herself.

"Sure, go ahead." This was getting interesting.

"Well, I don't know if you know, but I'm a Christian."

"Yeah, I thought so." I smiled, thinking to myself, "the whole world knows you're Christian, Betsy." She beamed, genuinely happy that I knew she was Christian.

"We believe that Jesus is the Son of God, and that's very important to us. Because he was the Son of God, he had no sin and was able to take our sins upon himself."

I had many problems with that statement, but I had already drawn the battle lines, so I stuck with the issue of Jesus' deity. I decided to take a concessionary approach.

"Betsy, I don't think the Bible we have today is the word of God. It's been changed too many times throughout history. But for now, let's just say I did think so. Where does Jesus say, 'I am God'?"

Betsy thought for a moment. She didn't seem too troubled, but it was clear to me she couldn't remember him saying it. After an uncomfortable moment passed, which she seemed totally comfortable with, she said, "In John's gospel, Jesus says, 'The Father and I are one.'"

That was the one I expected her to go for, and I was ready. "Yeah, but also in John, Jesus prays for his disciples to be one just as he is one with the Father. So he clarifies exactly what he means by 'one.' He means unified in spirit and will. If he meant 'one' as in 'one being,' would he be praying for his disciples to be 'one' in the same way? He's not praying for his disciples to all become one being, is he?"

"That's a good point," she said thoughtfully. Good point? I was in the process of dismantling her worldview, and she was being congenial? Did this girl ever get agitated?

"Well, I can't think of it right now, but I'm sure it's there. I can look it up and get back to you."

"I'd love for you to, Betsy, but you won't find anything. Jesus never said he was God," I argued. "He made the opposite quite clear to us. He felt the pangs of hunger, thirst, loneliness, and temptation. He cried, and he bled. He didn't call himself 'the Son of God,' he called himself 'the Son of Man.' He was very obviously human."

Betsy was nodding along, "Yes, I agree. Jesus is a man, and he is God too."

"How can someone be man and God? Man is mortal, God is immortal. Man is limited, God is infinite. Man is weak, God is omnipotent. To be man is to not be God, and to be God is to not be man."

This seemed to give her some pause. She was off balance, so I decided to push a bit harder.

"When Jesus went to Galilee, Mark's gospel tells us he could do no miracles. Not that he chose not to, but that he couldn't. Can God not do miracles? When a woman in a crowd touched him, he had no idea who it was. Would God not know something that simple?" After pausing to let her process, I continued.

"When a man called him 'good,' he said that he is not good, only God is good.²⁵ He draws a distinction between himself and God. He does it again when he said he didn't know when the world will end, and that only God knows. He's making it very clear that he is not God."

Betsy said nothing. She had not thought of this before. I decided it was time for the coup de grâce.

"Betsy, in case there is any question, in the gospel of John, Jesus said, 'The Father is greater than I.' And I agree with Jesus. God is greater than he is. I think you ought to agree with him too."

Betsy didn't know what to say. I waited.

"Well, I don't know what to say." She was sticking with her signature maneuver. "I'll tell you what, I'm going to look into these things. In the meantime, I'd like to invite you to a play at our church that I'm a part of. Would you like to come?"

"Sure, sounds like fun. But I don't have a driver's license yet. Mind if my dad comes along?"

"Of course not. Bring as many people as you'd like. Here's the information. Let me know what day you're coming when you get a chance." Betsy handed me a flyer for the event and smiled.

I saw something behind the eyes of her smile that I hadn't seen in her before. She was agitated. I smiled back.

For much more detail on the Muslim view of Jesus, read part 8 of No God but One, *titled "Did Jesus Claim to Be God?"*

Chapter Fifteen

HEAVEN'S GATES AND HELL'S FLAMES

I WAS VERY EXCITED TO BE INVITED to a church. I had been to one before—a Catholic church—and I remember that day as an exciting, Latin-infused blur. Honestly, it was so confusing that I could not figure out why I had been invited. I recall that some of my friends were there, including Ben and his family, but they weren't Catholic either. At one point, while our row was standing, everyone started walking to the front to get something from the priest. I didn't know what to do, so I started going with them. Ben's mom grabbed my arm and sat me back down into my seat. Startled, I looked over at her. She was emphatically shaking her head no. The priest, who had been rather solemn until then, was trying to hold back a laugh.

No one had told me Protestant churches were any different, so I was expecting something similar. To me, the sanctuary of First Baptist Norfolk looked like an auditorium of sorts. I guessed that all the church stuff happened elsewhere, but I couldn't see where.

I sat with Abba in the balcony, toward the back. Even though neither of us knew what the play was about, Abba was glad I had accepted the invitation. He said it would have been rude not to and that it was a good way to keep the door of conversation open with Betsy. He was proud of me for sharing my beliefs, and he was hoping to help me process the play we were about to see.

The play was called "Heaven's Gates and Hell's Flames," and it turned out to be a performance of the Christian salvation message. It was during the play that I learned Christians called this message "the gospel." I had thought that the word *gospel* only referred to the four books about Jesus. Throughout the play, the message came across loud and clear: accept Jesus as your Lord, and you will go to heaven. Otherwise, you will go to hell.

Different scenarios were performed, each one ending with some-one's death and his reception into heaven or damnation to hell based solely on whether he had accepted Jesus. The imagery in the play was not subtle. When someone was sent to hell, red and yellow lights flashed through the room, a thunderous cacophony played over the loudspeakers, and Satan came rampaging through the set, dragging the sinner off the stage.

On the other hand, if someone had accepted Jesus, he would be ushered by radiant angels into a bright door, ecstatic with joy. In the final scenario, a man was driving a car and his passenger was talking to him about Jesus. The man said he had done many bad things and ignored God his whole life. The passenger was able to convince the driver that he was a sinner and needed Jesus, so the driver prayed a prayer. No sooner had he prayed than a terrible accident occurred. Both men died, dramatically depicted by turning off the lights. When the lights came back on, beautiful music was playing, and the driver was escorted into heaven.

I'm not sure if it was intentional, but it was ingenious to end the play with that scene right before we all got in our cars to drive home. We started our follow-up discussion as soon as we put on our seat belts. "Nabeel, what did you think of the play?"

"I think it was silly, Abba. They were obviously trying to play on people's fears and emotions."

"Yes, I agree, beyta, but sometimes that's not bad. We should be frightened of hell, and we should be frightened of Allah's wrath."

I was nonplussed. "So you think the play was good?"

Abba laughed. "I didn't say that! I think there was something much worse than their attempts to scare people."

"Well, the message is all wrong," I started, collecting my thoughts. "What they're teaching people is they can do whatever they want their whole lives, and all they have to do is say a prayer and they'll go to heaven."

Abba nodded. "Right. And what's wrong with that? What's the purpose of religion?"

"The purpose of religion is to make good people and a good society. If people can do whatever they want, they will indulge their sinful desires and society will fall apart. They have a blank check to sin. Even Hitler could go to heaven just by accepting Jesus."

Abba prompted me on. "And that's why ..."

"And that's why America is the way it is. Christians teach that there is no accountability for their deeds."

"Good. Very good, beyta. So when your friend at school asks you what you thought, make sure you share that with her. But don't leave her with just that. You need to sweep away falsehood with the truth. What is the truth about judgment?"

"Allah judges us based on our choices in this world. Everything we do is recorded by angels: one on our right shoulder recording our good deeds, and one on our left shoulder recording our bad deeds. When we stand before Allah, our deeds will be read aloud. No one will be able to intercede for us; not our family, not Jesus, not even Muhammad ﷺ. Allah will weigh our good deeds and our bad, and if our good deeds are greater than our bad deeds, Allah will give us paradise."

"What about Christians, Billoo. Can Christians go to heaven?"

"Yes. The Quran says that if Christians and Jews believe in one God and do good deeds, they can go to heaven."[26]

I was referring to a Quranic verse that is a point of controversy among Muslims. Some Muslims argue that this verse was abrogated by a later Quranic verse that says, "If someone comes to Allah with a religion other than Islam, it will not be accepted from him."[27] Other Muslims, our jamaat among them, reconcile the two verses by arguing that "Islam" here does not refer to the faith-system, but to the broader meaning of the word, *peace*.

The latter interpretation is obviously more tenuous, but only if one believes in the **doctrine of abrogation**. Surah 2:116 and 16:101 of the Quran both apparently teach that Allah can cancel older sections of the Quran with newer ones. Traditionally, Muslims developed a field of Quranic exegesis called "the abrogator and the abrogated" in which they strove to determine the criteria and history of Quranic abrogation. Some Muslim scholars taught that up to five hundred verses of the Quran no longer apply because later verses abrogated them. Other Muslim scholars taught that as few as five verses were abrogated. Regardless of the exact number, most orthodox sects of Islam believe in the doctrine of abrogation.

> **Doctrine of abrogation**: The belief that teachings and verses of the Quran have been repealed, usually by later Quranic revelations

A few Muslims dissent on this view, and the Ahmadi jamaat is among them. These Muslims argue that if any part of the Quran could be canceled, then it would not be the eternal word of God. They resort instead to harmonization of apparently abrogated verses, like the tenuous interpretation above. The difficulty for this view, though, is that the hadith are full of accounts of abrogation.

But I didn't know these things at the time. All I knew was what our jamaat taught about salvation and that anyone who believed in one God could go to heaven, as at least one verse of the Quran clearly stated.

"And how many gods do Christians believe in, Billoo?"

"Some believe in one, some believe in three."

"Yes, and the Quran says it would be better for them if they stopped saying 'three.'"[28] That is why I'm glad you're having these conversations with your friends. They at least need to hear that there is only one God. If you can bring them to Islam and Ahmadiyyat, that would be even better."

Before wrapping up our conversation on salvation, he quickly added, "But don't spend too much time with this girl! Girls are dangerous for you, especially at this age. You are like a fire, and they are like oil. Even if you are not attracted to each other, after time, just being close to each other causes you to start burning. That is how you were made."

"Okay, Abba, gosh! I got it. Can we talk about something else?"

Ammi and Abba were only too willing to give me the "fire and oil" talk. It served to remind me that, when the time was right, we would come together as a family and discuss whom I would like to marry. If I had a girl in mind, my parents would then talk to her and try to arrange the marriage. If not, my parents would find a suitable wife. I would not date anyone at all, let alone a Western girl. To do so would be to depart from tradition.

Chapter Sixteen

TREASURED TRADITIONS

TRADITION IS THE OUTWARD STRUCTURE of Islam, the body animated by the soul of Islamic teaching. It seeped into us through immersion in the Muslim lifestyle; every single day was imbued with tradition. I strived to pray the salaat five times a day, recited many detailed du'aas, followed intricate instructions for ceremonial washings, and regularly looked to Muhammad's example for guidance. More than a billion Muslims joined me in adherence to traditions, whether praying about whom to marry, determining the appropriate length of a beard, or deciding whether to wear gold.

But these traditions did not come from the Quran. They are found in hadith. From marital rites to martial restrictions, commercial laws to civil suits, the vast majority of sharia and the Islamic way of life is derived from the hadith.

There is no overestimating the importance of hadith in the Islamic world.

There is no overestimating the importance of hadith in the Islamic world.

As Baji and I grew older, Ammi and Abba considered it very important that we learn hadith and their precepts. They often read from hadith collections, urging us to memorize the Arabic and understand its meaning. The first time they asked us to memorize a hadith was immediately after maghrib prayer one evening, while our family was still on the prayer rugs.

"Beytee, beyta, we want you to memorize this short hadith. Hazrat Umar narrates that Muhammad ﷺ said 'Deeds are judged by their intentions.'"[29]

After we recited the Arabic a few times, Ammi and Abba were satisfied that we had memorized it. They asked if we had any questions.

I had a few. "Abba, what book of hadith does this one come from?"

"This one comes from *Sahih Bukhari*. What can you tell us about Sahih Bukhari?"

"It is the most trustworthy book of hadith, compiled by Imam Bukhari. The hadith were not collected into books until a long time after Muhammad ﷺ's death. Many false hadiths had been fabricated, and it was difficult to determine which ones were accurate. Imam Bukhari sifted through five hundred thousand hadith and picked out the five thousand most accurate."

> *Sahih Bukhari*: A classical collection of hadith, often considered by Sunnis as the most trustworthy accounts of Muhammad's life

Ammi followed up, asking, "And how did he do that?"

"When Imam Bukhari heard a hadith, he assessed whether the person telling the hadith was trustworthy or not. If he had a bad reputation, if he had ever gotten in trouble, or even if he treated animals poorly, Imam Bukhari ignored that hadith. If he found the person trustworthy, he would ask him from whom he heard the hadith, and who that person heard it from, and who that person heard it from, all the way back to Muhammad. Imam Bukhari assessed the reputation of each individual in the chain, and if they were all trustworthy, then Imam Bukhari recorded the hadith in his book."

The chain of transmission was called the *isnad*, and it was immeasurably important to classical Muslim scholars. Islam arose in an authority-based society. When they asked the question, "Is this hadith authentic?" they answered by deferring to the authorities who transmitted it. Without the isnad, the hadith was considered worthless. Muslims put less stock into sirah literature than hadith specifically because sirah does not record isnad.

Ammi continued. "Very good. Beytee, what is the next most trustworthy book of hadith?"

"I don't know, Ammi." Baji was now eighteen years old and in college. She did not enjoy these detailed questions like she once had, but Ammi wouldn't let her off that easy.

"Yes you do. Challo, just answer this one, and that will be it. What is next after Sahih Bukhari?"

"Sahih Muslim?"

"Shabash. Nabeel, do you know any others?"

"I know Sunan Abu Daud, and I know that there are six that we consider authentic, and the rest are a mix of reliable and unreliable hadith. The six are called **Sahih Sittah**, and the first three are Sahih Bukhari, Sahih Muslim, and Sunan Abu Daud."

Abba continued the list for me, "And the other three are Sunan Tirmidhi, Sunan Ibn Majah, and Sunan Nisai.[30] These are the best six books of hadith, but among them, Sahih Bukhari and Sahih Muslim are the most trustworthy."

Ammi quickly added, "But even the most accurate ones are the word of Muhammad ﷺ, not the word of Allah. We must not equate the hadith to the Quran."

I pushed on this clarification. "But if Muhammad ﷺ said it, don't we have to obey him?"

Abba interjected, "Of course! But still, Muhammad ﷺ is not God. The Quran is the only uncorrupted, perfect book in the world. The books of hadith are more like the Bible because they are the works of men. There is divine truth there, but we have to be careful of corruption. We always have to check the truths we get from other sources against the Quran. Challo, that's enough for tonight. Don't forget the hadith you learned today. We'll ask you to recite it tomorrow!"

I was very interested in the hadith, not so much in their content

Isnad: The chain of transmission for a particular hadith

Sahih Sittah: The six books of hadith that Sunni Muslims consider most authentic as much as in their history and the ways Muslim scholars assessed them. I wanted to become adept at recognizing authentic hadith from fabricated ones. I started asking Ammi and Abba more about the systems of grading hadith, and I quickly came against the boundaries of their knowledge in these matters. In order to learn more, I would have to wait until our next jamaat gathering, when I could ask the experts about the right books to buy to find out more.

It so happened that Ammi and Abba decided to go back to the United Kingdom during the upcoming summer to attend a jamaat gathering. I decided to do some research while there. What I didn't plan, though, was to experience God in a very personal way. God was going to perform a miracle that changed my life forever.

Chapter Seventeen

SIGNS IN THE SKY

IT WAS MY FIRST TIME BACK in Britain since we had moved to Connecticut eight years prior. I could hardly contain my excitement. Abba did not even have a chance to get us out of Heathrow Airport before I managed to get a bottle of Irn-Bru and a bag of Hula Hoops crisps.

We headed back to the Tilford countryside, the same site where we had attended the centenary nine years earlier. As we drove past quaint English towns, I felt like I was taking a tour through my past. The narrow roads, clustered buildings, and smaller vehicles all brought back memories of a childhood I loved. Even the thought of English food didn't bother me.

This jamaat gathering was called *jalsa*. Our family attended the United States jalsa every year in Washington, D.C., and we usually attended the Canadian jalsa as well. But the United Kingdom jalsa was different. This is where the leader of our jamaat lived, and it always felt special to be in his presence. Because of him, tens of thousands of Ahmadis attended the United Kingdom jalsa.

As much as I anticipated seeing him, the people I most longed for were my friends from Scotland, the Maliks. Apart from one letter that I received from the youngest brother while I was in seventh grade, I had not heard from any of them. Public email was still in its nascent phase, and international phone calls were too expensive to justify.

But when I arrived at the jalsa, I realized I did not know if my friends would even be there. As special as the gathering was, there were myriad circumstances that could preclude their attendance. It would be nearly impossible to look for them by walking through the jalsa too. Apart from the sheer number of people to search through, we had all grown up over the previous seven years, and I was not sure I would recognize them even if I saw them. I sorely wanted to reunite with them, but I did not know where to start.

So I turned to God.

From a very early age, Ammi had trained me to respond in dire moments with prayer, but I knew of no du'aa for finding people. I had memorized a prayer to recite when looking for lost items, but given that it was the same prayer we recite when we hear the news of someone's death, I decided it would not be apt for the occasion. Instead, I just prayed from my heart, bowing my head and closing my eyes.

"God, can You please help me find my friends?" I had nothing else to say, so I said nothing else.

When I opened my eyes, what I saw stunned me stock-still. In the air before me were two streaks of color, one gold and one silver, as if whimsically painted onto the sky by an ethereal brush. They trailed into the distance, obviously leading me somewhere.

I still remember the words I spoke in shock: "You're kidding. I'm supposed to follow those, right?"

Whether I was speaking to God or myself, I am not sure. What I intrinsically knew was that no one could see the stripes but me. They were not so much in the sky as they were in my perception of the sky. They were neither a mile away, nor a foot away, nor anywhere in between. They just were. And they were waiting for me.

The jalsa was crowded, and everyone was outside the tents because there was no speech currently in session. I followed the streaks into swarms of people, sifting my way through the crowd as if in a Pakistani bazaar.

And in fact, the streaks swirled over the jalsa marketplace, the same area where I wanted to go for a badge almost a decade prior.

This time, I was not intercepted by a surly senior citizen. Instead, the streaks funneled downward, dissipating over a space next to a clothing tent. When I weeded my way to the clearing, I saw two men standing there, chatting and trying on skullcaps. It took a moment, but I recognized them: they were the older Malik brothers.

I ran to them and grasped their arms. When they recognized me, we rejoiced together. They were incredulous at my height, incessantly repeating, "You were just a wee boy!" And so they dragged me through the jalsa, reintroducing me to everyone from Glasgow whom I once knew. We were overjoyed. For the time being, the streaks in the sky were forgotten.

Later that evening, as I considered the day's events while lying in bed, I could not get past the gold and silver streaks. To me, there was nothing else for it: they meant God must exist.

Of course, I already believed that God existed. I had seen answered prayers, prophetic dreams, and rational argumentation pointing toward the existence of God, but there was always room for doubt. Perhaps the answered prayers were coincidences, or maybe the prophetic dreams were exaggerated over time to fit reality, or it was possible there were flaws in the logic of the arguments. Sure, I was 99 percent certain that God existed, but that shadow of doubt was always there.

But now, there was no remotely plausible alternative. How else could I explain what happened that day? I had no idea where my friends were, and when I prayed, I was supernaturally led to them.

I began to consider alternative explanations. Maybe I had imagined the streaks? No, that couldn't work, because I went straight to my friends. Maybe I subconsciously knew where my friends were? No, that was impossible. I did not even know if they were at the jalsa, let alone at that exact spot in the marketplace. Perhaps while I lived in Scotland I developed extrasensory connections with my friends that remained dormant until I called on them that afternoon, whereupon our psychic bonds were able to manifest themselves in my visual sensorium? Honestly, that was the best naturalistic explanation I could come up with, but not only did it skirt the boundaries of naturalism, it totally blew past the boundaries of plausibility.

"No," I told myself. "There is no alternative. God is real, and He hears my prayers, even the little ones like wanting to know where my friends are." That day, I no longer just believed that God was real. I knew God was real. And I knew God cared for me.

The timing could not have been better. When I returned to Princess Anne for my junior year, one of my mandatory classes was "Theory of Knowledge" (TOK), and it served as an introductory course to general philosophy and epistemology. Our textbook was called *Man is the Measure*, and one of the first discussions we had in class was, "How can we know whether God exists?" The discussions were deep and shook the faith of many theists in the class.

That day, I no longer just believed that God was real. I knew God was real.

Although our conversations focused on objective argumentation, as they should have, I came to realize that subjective knowledge can be far more powerful. I would never be able to convince anyone that I actually saw the streaks in the sky or that they actually led me to my friends. But I did not need to. It was a sign for me, and I went from being 99 percent sure that God exists to 100 percent certain.

Four years later, when my world started falling apart, that 1 percent made all the difference.

Chapter Eighteen

HONOR AND AUTHORITY

TOK WAS ONE OF THE MANY CLASSES that I had with my best friend, David. We had grown closer and closer since seventh grade, and by the time we were upperclassmen, we were inseparable. We had six of our seven classes together, became co-captains of the academic trivia team, and entered into the forensics team as a duo. David and I won fifth place in the state competition our junior year, surprising everyone because we were both rookies. During senior year, we won the state championship.

David and I had a few discussions about religion and the existence of God. He and I did not see eye to eye, and it was clear that our upbringing had a lot to do with it. He was hesitant to move past agnosticism, and my starting point was Islam. The discussions in TOK seemed to bolster his hesitance, and although it did not shake my conviction in God's existence, it did bring some critical differences between Eastern and Western cultures into sharp relief.

When my parents taught me to examine my beliefs, I was essentially expected to build a defense for what they had taught me. In TOK, we were ostensibly doing the same thing—examining our beliefs—but in practice, it was the exact opposite. We were critically probing our beliefs, challenging them, testing them for weak points, pliability, and boundaries. Some students were even replacing them.

This difference between Eastern and Western education can be traced to the disparity that divides Muslim immigrants from their children: Islamic cultures tend to establish people of high status as authorities, whereas the authority in Western culture is reason itself. These alternative seats of authority permeate the mind, determining the moral outlook of whole societies.

When authority is derived from position rather than reason, the act of questioning leadership is dangerous because it has the potential to upset the system. Dissension is reprimanded, and obedience is rewarded. Correct and incorrect courses of action are assessed socially, not individually. A person's virtue is thus determined by how well he meets social expectations, not by an individual determination of right and wrong.

Islamic cultures tend to establish people of high status as authorities, whereas the authority in Western culture is reason itself.

Thus, positional authority yields a society that determines right and wrong based on honor and shame.

On the other hand, when authority is derived from reason, questions are welcome because critical examination sharpens the very basis of authority. Each person is expected to critically examine his own course of action. Correct and incorrect courses of action are assessed individually. A person's virtue is determined by whether he does what he knows to be right or wrong.

Rational authority creates a society that determines right and wrong based on innocence and guilt.

Much of the West's inability to understand the East stems from the paradigmatic schism between honor-shame cultures and innocence-guilt cultures. Of course, the matter is quite complex, and elements of both paradigms are present in the East and the West, but the honor-shame spectrum is the operative paradigm that drives the East, and it is hard for Westerners to understand.

This reliance on positional authority explains some characteristics in parts of the Muslim world that confound many Westerners, such as the continued practices of honor killings, child brides of six or younger, and blood feuds. For one reason or another, the prevailing sources of social authority in these regions deem these customs acceptable, perhaps even preferable. No amount of sheer reason is going to change these practices, nor will externally imposed prohibitions. The change will have to be social, internal, and organic.

But honor killings and blood feuds are generally not struggles for children raised as second-generation Western Muslims. We wrestle with the honor-shame principle that tells us, "It's okay as long as you don't get caught." If there is no dishonor, it is not wrong.

I saw this principle play out many times while I was growing up, though I am obliged to share only innocuous accounts. The most innocent one I can think of has to do with free refills. Many of my Muslim friends thought it was perfectly acceptable to order water from fast-food restaurants and then go to the dispenser and fill up on soda. We rarely blinked an eye at this, and I myself did it regularly.

But at a Taco Bell in Virginia Beach one day, one of my friends was caught getting Mountain Dew Code Red instead of water. A young employee had glanced over the counter and seen my friend filling up on soda. Without much tact, he pushed my friend's hand away from the fountain drinks and said loudly, "You ordered water. You can't get soda!"

At this, many people turned to see the commotion, and my friend immediately blushed. It was obvious that the employee was correct, since the cups for water were transparent and the cups for soda were opaque. The employee caught him literally red-handed. The soda was clearly visible to all.

For my friend, this was the moment that made his actions a poor choice. He had suffered dishonor in front of many. Stealing the soda was not an issue for him before being caught. In fact, it was still not the issue after being caught. As strange as it might sound to Westerners, it was more dishonorable for him to be called out by a minimum-wage employee than to be caught stealing soda. So he denied it, asserting firmly, "I am getting water!" He filled the rest of the cup with water and walked away from the counter, as if it were perfectly normal for water to be a deep, bubbly pink.

On another occasion, one of my cousins was receiving some lighthearted ridicule from the rest of my family for having been caught committing minor insurance fraud. To help alleviate the shame, my cousin turned it into a funny story for us all.

He started by telling us that, as he was getting quotes for auto insurance, he found he would save a lot of money if he lied and told the insurance companies he was married. So he made up a long back-story about meeting his wife, what she did for a living, and even the mnemonic he used to remember her birthday. He planned to tell the agent that he unfortunately did not have any papers since she was still in Pakistan. When he had invented enough details, he called a company, convinced them he was married, and secured the lower rate.

Only one other family member and I chided him for this, and we were both American born. The elders laughed and told us to lighten up, asserting that the insurance companies had enough money as it was. My cousin boisterously agreed.

As the story went, over a year later, he had a fender bender and needed to make a roadside claim. While sharing details of the accident on the phone, the insurance agent asked him if he was with his wife. His mind on the accident, he responded that he did not have a wife. Unfazed, the agent asked him if he had ever been married, and my cousin replied "no." Shortly thereafter, my cousin received an adjusted insurance rate well over twice what he had been paying.

By the time the story was through, the family was roaring with laughter. For having told such a good story, he was able to transform the shame of being caught lying into the honor of being a good storyteller. Actually doing the right thing did not even enter into the equation, and neither did guilt.

These are relatively harmless examples of how an honor-shame culture might see things differently from a Western culture of guilt and innocence. Of course, there is a highly developed notion of morality in Islam, so we must take care not to oversimplify the matter and assume that Muslims do whatever they wish if they believe they will not be caught. All the same, it is safe to say that guilt is less of a determining factor in the East than is shame.

Coming back to second-generation Muslim Westerners, it might now be easier to see just how difficult it can be to straddle these two cultures. When engaged in something less than socially acceptable, the young Muslim will be tempted to hide it and will begin to struggle with internal guilt. The natural Eastern tendency to hide shameful truths exacerbates the Western tendency to feel guilty.

For me, this became a major problem as I progressed through high school. All my friends knew that I was Muslim and that I was not allowed to date. I had done my best to be an ambassador for my culture by telling others I was happy about the idea of an arranged marriage. And it truly didn't bother me—until I started developing a real interest in girls.

In my senior year, I developed a crush on a girl who also confessed she was interested in me. By anyone's standards in the West, it was a very innocent relationship, holding hands and speaking romantic words. But still, I kept it secret because it went against my Eastern standards, and I felt very guilty. I called it off after a matter of weeks, even though I still had feelings for her. Not long after, she started dating my best friend, David. My feelings for her were unabated, and after a while, I felt very guilty for having a crush on my best friend's girlfriend. I confessed to David that I had had a secret relationship with her before they started dating and that I still had feelings for her.

None of my friends understood why I had hid this from them, least of all David. From his perspective, I had utterly betrayed him by not being open with him and for harboring feelings for his girlfriend. There was a falling out between David and me just days before graduation, with everyone on one side and me on the other.

Once again, I was friendless, but this time I was deeply hurt and utterly confused. What had happened? Why did I always end up alone? I knew I had done something wrong, but was it so wrong that I deserved to lose all my friends? I went to no graduation parties, I was no longer invited to any of the precollege trips we had planned, I did not get to see my friends off as they went to college, and I was unable to reunite with everyone when they returned home for breaks.

Had I understood the way I was acting at the time, I might have done things differently. Had they understood me, they might have been less hurt by my secrets. Had we only known, I might still have my childhood friends today.

Some believe that cultural differences between East and West do not exist, that people all see the world the same way. Others consider the Eastern and Western paradigms as a curiosity to consider. But for me, and for others like me, the schism between East and West shapes the very course of our lives. Because of it, I had no friends in my early childhood, and because of it, I was launched into adulthood alone once more.

But for me, and for others like me, the schism between East and West shapes the very course of our lives.

Thankfully, the worst of the pain lasted only the summer. I started college a few months later, in August of 2001, looking forward to the prospect of reinventing myself and finding new friends. But just three weeks into college, a new crisis hit, and this one affected our entire nation. The world would never be the same again.

Chapter Nineteen

THE RELIGION OF PEACE

IT WAS THE BEGINNING of my fourth week at Old Dominion University. Baji and I both attended ODU for the same reason: it was the best school close to home, and Ammi and Abba would not let us go any farther. We often went to school together, but on Tuesday mornings, Baji would come after me to avoid waiting in traffic. I had to be at my anatomy lab by eight o'clock.

That Tuesday morning started like any other. I finished in the anatomy lab at ten thirty and headed toward Webb Center, the student union at ODU. I was free until the afternoon, when the forensics team met for practice. I had joined the team the first week of school and was excited to see if I could carry my high school success into college.

As I strolled through the entrance of the student union, the captain of the forensics team strode out hurriedly. I had no idea anything was amiss, so I asked, "What's going on?"

Without stopping, she said, "The second tower just came down." Confused, I saw a crowd by the televisions in the lounge behind her, so I made my way there.

The news stations were playing and replaying footage of the north and south towers of the World Trade Center collapsing. Over and over, they played the images of a plane crashing into one of the towers and each tower successively crumbling. It felt like a scene out of a movie, but we were transfixed by a very real horror.

No one moved, and no one spoke. After a few moments, my phone rang. It was Abba, his voice uncharacteristically pressured. "Nabeel, where are you? Why haven't you been picking up your phone?"

"I'm at school, Abba. I didn't have reception in the anatomy lab."

"Come home now! Is Baji with you?"

"No, is she okay?"

"She's not picking up her phone either. Find her, and come home right away."

Still reeling from the previous few minutes, I tried to fit the pieces together. "Abba, what's wrong? Why do I have to come home?"

Surprised, Abba asked, "Don't you know? There has been an attack."

"Yes, but why does that mean I have to come home?"

"Nabeel! They're blaming Muslims! People will be emotional, and they could take it out on you or Baji. It's your job to find her, make sure she's safe, and come home."

"But Abba, I ..."

Abba wasted no more time. "Nabeel! Do as I say! I have to call Baji. Keep your phone close." With that, he hung up.

I looked around at the people watching the televisions. Were these people my enemies? Could they really want to hurt me? Slowly, the danger shifted from being on the television to being all around me. I was now a part of this macabre movie, and I had a role to play. I left quickly and called Baji.

To my great relief, she picked up. "Assalaamo alaikum?"

"Baji, do you know what's going on? Where are you?"

"Yes, I'm in my car. I'm going home."

"Why weren't you picking up your phone when Abba called?"

"I was at 7-Eleven watching the TV, and a policeman pulled me aside. He told me it might not be safe to stay out because I am wearing a burqa. He offered to escort me back to my car, and now I'm going home."

"Really? That was nice of him. Okay, drive safely. I'll see you at home soon."

For the rest of the day, we stayed glued to the television. Abba made arrangements to take the week off, and he told us to do the same. We left the home only to buy American flags, which were quickly selling out. We displayed flags prominently on each car, in our yard, and kept a few in the garage, just in case.

We wanted people to know that we weren't the enemy, no matter what they were hearing on the news.

This was not paranoia on my father's part. During Operation Desert Storm, members of my family had been targeted and victimized. Nani Ammi was refused service at a gas station in New York because she wore a burqa. Nani Ammi, my sweet little grandmother. A distant aunt of ours had even been assaulted in a parking lot, punched in the stomach while getting groceries. Indeed, not long after the September 11 attacks, the mosque that sat at the outskirts of ODU was vandalized, all of its windows broken. I knew the people who paid to repair the mosque. They were good, hardworking people.

As the days progressed, it became clear that the hijackers were indeed Muslim and that this attack on our nation had been carried out in the name of Islam. But what Islam was this? It was clearly not the Islam I knew. True, I used to hear of Muslims in distant lands committing atrocities in the name of Allah, but those accounts were too remote to create any cognitive dissonance. This hit much closer to home. This hit us in our hearts.

Over the following weeks, news stations mercilessly looped footage of the crumbling towers. Again and again and again, I witnessed thousands of innocents massacred in the name of my God. It finally became too much. I had to learn the truth about my faith once and for all. I had to figure out how to reconcile my Islam, a religion of peace, with the Islam on television, a religion of terror.

In the twelve years since that day, I have learned that the question is far more complex than it first appears. The most important consideration is the definition of *Islam*. If by *Islam* we mean the beliefs of Muslims, then Islam can be a religion of peace or a religion of terror, depending on how it is taught.

> It became clear that the hijackers were indeed Muslim. But what Islam was this?

In the West, Muslims are generally taught a very pacific version of Islam. Just like Baji and I, Western Muslims are taught that Muhammad fought only defensive battles and that violent verses in the Quran refer to specific, defensive contexts. *Jihad* is here defined as primarily a peaceful endeavor, an internal struggle against one's baser desires. When asked about their religion, Western Muslims honestly report what they believe: Islam is a religion of peace.

In the East, though, Muslims often have a less docile view of Islam. They are taught that Islam is superior to all other religions and ways of life and that Allah wishes to see it established throughout the world. They often define *jihad* as a primarily physical endeavor, a struggle against the enemies of Islam. When asked about their religion, these Muslims will honestly report what they believe: Islam will dominate the world.

So if we define Islam by the beliefs of its adherents, it may or may not be a religion of peace. But if we define Islam more traditionally, as the system of beliefs and practices taught by Muhammad, then the answer is less ambiguous.

The earliest historical records show that Muhammad launched offensive military campaigns[31] and used violence at times to accomplish his purposes.[32] He used the term *jihad* in both spiritual and physical contexts, but the physical jihad is the one Muhammad strongly emphasizes.[33] The peaceful practice of Islam hinges on later, often Western, interpretations of Muhammad's teachings, whereas the more violent variations of Islam are deeply rooted in orthodoxy and history.[34]

Of course, like all people, Muslims in the East and West generally just believe what they are taught. Rarely is there much critical investigation into historical events, and the few that invest the effort usually do the same thing I had done in my TOK class: attempt to defend what is already believed, potentially ignoring or underestimating evidence that points to the contrary. This is only natural, since it is extremely difficult to change beliefs that are dear to the heart.

Such was the case with me. In my heart of hearts, I wanted to know the truth about Islam, but it would be nearly impossible to challenge my childhood beliefs just by investigating them. I would keep finding ways to ignore difficult truths. What I needed was something that would not let me get away with my biases. I needed something that would mercilessly loop my bad arguments before my eyes, again and again and again, until I could avoid them no longer.

I needed a friend, an intelligent, uncompromising, non-Muslim friend who would be willing to challenge me. Of course, not only would he have to be bold and stubborn enough to deal with the likes of me, but I would have to like and trust him enough to dialogue with him about the things that mattered to me most.

Little did I know, God had already introduced us, and I was already on a path that would change my life forever.

To read an expert contribution on East meets West by Mark Mittelberg, a bestselling author and primary creator of the evangelism course Becoming a Contagious Christian, *see page 321.*

Part 3

TESTING THE
NEW TESTAMENT

O Allah, the Bible couldn't be right, could it?

Chapter Twenty

BECOMING BROTHERS

THERE IS A SIMPLE REASON I never listened to street preachers: they didn't seem to care about me. It wasn't that they were annoying. I found their passion admirable, and I appreciated people who stood up for what they believed. Rather, it was that they treated me like an object of their agenda. Did they have any idea how their message would impact my life? Did they even care?

Sure, there are street preachers who share their message while still greeting people kindly, getting to know others' troubles, and praying over personal pains, but I never saw them. What I saw were men who would stand on street corners accosting the public with their beliefs. No doubt they reached a few, but they repelled many more.

Unfortunately, I have found that many Christians think of evangelism the same way, foisting Christian beliefs on strangers in chance encounters. The problem with this approach is that the gospel requires a radical life change, and not many people are about to listen to strangers telling them to change the way they live. What do they know about others' lives?

On the other hand, if a true friend shares the exact same message with heartfelt sincerity, speaking to specific circumstances and struggles, then the message is heard loud and clear.

Effective evangelism requires relationships. There are very few exceptions.

In my case, I knew of no Christian who truly cared about me, no one who had been a part of my life through thick and thin. I had plenty of Christian acquaintances, and I'm sure they would have been my friends if I had become a Christian, but that kind of friendship is conditional. There were none that I knew who cared about me unconditionally. Since no Christian cared about me, I did not care about their message.

> Effective evangelism requires relationships. There are very few exceptions.

But that was about to change.

It took a few weeks after 9/11 for life to regain a semblance of normalcy. Baji and I started attending classes again, Abba was back at work, and Ammi felt safe enough to run errands. Although Islam was in the hot seat on the news and a general mistrust of Muslims still hung in the air, the wave of emotional attacks was not as bad as we had expected. True, our community mosque was vandalized, and we frequently heard of anti-Muslim sentiments, but we knew of no physical attacks against Muslims. We felt safe to return to our lives, and not a moment too soon.

The first forensics tournament of the year was upon us. Unlike the tournaments in high school, collegiate forensics tournaments were multiday affairs, often in other states. Our team's first tournament was slated for West Chester, Pennsylvania.

On the day of our departure, Ammi decided to drive me to ODU so she could see me off. When we arrived at the Batten Arts and Letters Building, one of the other students on the forensics team came out to greet us. I had spoken with him a few times at practice, but we were still getting to know each other. He rushed over to us and starting helping with my bags while introducing himself to Ammi.

"Hi, Mrs. Qureshi. I'm David Wood."

Ammi was glad to meet someone from the team before sending me off to who-knows-where. "Hello, David, very nice to meet you. Are you going with Nabeel on this trip?"

"Yeah. He told me you might be concerned, but we'll take good care of him. Don't worry."

Nothing David could have said would have made Ammi happier. "Nabeel, I can tell this is a good boy. Stay close to him!"

"*Acha*, Ammi, I will."

"Keep your phone on you, okay Nabeel? Call me when you get to the hotel so I know you're safe and so you can give me your hotel room number."

"Acha, Ammi, I will. I'll be okay. Don't worry."

Telling Ammi not to worry was like telling her not to breath, so she just ignored me. "And don't forget to call Abba, too, so he knows you're okay."

"Acha, Ammi!"

Ammi then looked to David. "Remind Nabeel to call us. He's very forgetful."

David couldn't hide his smile. "I'll make sure of it!"

Ammi was finally satisfied. "Thank you, David. I'm so glad I got to meet one of Nabeel's friends. After the trip, you should come over to our house for a meal. I'll cook you real Pakistani food."

There was no hesitation in David's voice. "You don't have to say that twice. Thanks, Mrs. Qureshi!"

"Okay boys, have fun. Be good! Nabeel, call me. And don't forget to pray the salaat!"

Ammi took my face in both her hands and kissed me on the cheek, just as she used to do when I was four years old, except now I was the one bending over. David was almost beside himself with repressed glee, expecting me to be embarrassed by Ammi's show of affection. But this was normal for our family, and I rather enjoyed receiving this much love from her.

As she started to get back in the car, she called out a traditional Pakistani valediction. "*Khuda hafiz,* beyta." May God protect you.

"Khuda hafiz, Ammi. Love you."

As she drove out of the parking lot, David just stared at me, a comical smile painted on his face.

"What?"

"Oh, nothing, nothing. She does know you'll only be gone for three days, right?"

"Yeah, but I don't leave home very often." I picked up some bags and starting walking into the building to meet our team.

"Uh-huh." David picked up the rest of the bags and followed, his silly smile unrelenting. "Hey, you know what? It's been a while since you talked to your mother. You really should call her."

I stopped and glared at David, then turned around and looked out at the main road. Ammi was still there, waiting at a red light to take a left turn. She was watching us walk into the building.

Out of playful spite, I turned back to David and said, "You know what? I will. Thanks, David, for your heartfelt concern about my relationship with my mother." I pulled out my cell phone and called Ammi. David chuckled to himself.

And so our friendship was off to a flying start, skipping right past the niceties and straight into brotherly teasing. In the days to come, many would comment that David and I were foils of one another. We were both exactly the same height—six feet, three inches—but I had dark skin and black hair, while David had light skin and blond hair. I was a slender 175 pounds, while David easily had forty pounds of muscle over me. I was very meticulous with my appearance and image, while David preferred jeans and T-shirts. I had a pampered childhood, while David came out of trailer parks and a gritty past.*

But what I did not know about David was to be the starkest contrast of all. David was a Christian with strong convictions who had spent the previous five years of his life studying the Bible and learning to follow Jesus. Even though the gospel was his passion, he did not bombard me with his beliefs straightaway. The discussions arose much more naturally, after we became friends, and in the context of a life lived together. In fact, I was the one who brought it up.

---

* I could not say much more about David's past when this book was first published for two reasons: (1) David hadn't yet made his testimony available to the public at that time, and (2) his testimony is so powerful that had I shared the details myself, it would have derailed my story. I am thankful to say, though, that he has since gone public with his testimony, and at this point you're too far into this book to be derailed! So please, buckle up and watch his testimony. It is one of the most powerful stories I know. You will find it here: *www.youtube.com/watch?v=DakEcY7Z5GU.*

Chapter Twenty-One

OPENING
MY EYES

THE TRIP UP TO WEST CHESTER was a blast. All the team-
mates were getting to know one another, practicing their forensics
pieces, sharing life stories, and just laughing together. It was a very
eye-opening experience for me, since it was my first time becoming intimately acquainted with people who had widely divergent
lifestyles and thoughts. One girl on the team advocated legalizing
drugs, one of the boys lived with his girlfriend, and another boy lived
with his boyfriend.

"Welcome to college," I thought.

We stopped for dinner at an Italian restaurant in Maryland. After
the staff arranged a table large enough for all of us, they sat us down
next to the kitchen where we had a clear view of all the cooks. David
and I had spent the past few hours getting to know more about each
other. We decided to sit together over dinner and split a pizza.

David can read people pretty well, and he quickly realized that
I do not get offended by playful comments. Far from it, I always
appreciate when people let down their guard with me and speak
completely unfiltered. Political correctness is for acquaintances, not
friends.

So as we read through the menu, he turned to me with mock
concern and said, "Nabeel, since you're probably feeling homesick, I

was looking for a pizza that might cheer you up. But they only have a Mediterranean pizza, not Middle Eastern pizza."

Unfazed, I replied, "But lucky for you, they do have a white pizza. My guess is that it'll be bland and tasteless. You'll love it."

David laughed. "You're on. I hope this place is authentic. There's a way to test that, you know."

"Oh yeah?"

"Yeah, watch this." With that, David turned to the kitchen and yelled, "Hey, Tony!"

Immediately, three of the cooks looked over at us, and we started laughing hysterically. "David, next time you pull a stunt like that, wait until after they've made our food!"

So the night continued in lighthearted frivolity. When we finally made it to the hotel, our coach told us there were two rooms to be shared among the four guys on the trip. It was a no-brainer for us, and before long, David and I were getting settled.

The rest of the team wanted to go out and celebrate. Most members left to go drinking or dancing at a nearby bar, while some of the others went looking for a suitable place to smoke various things. I had never engaged in any of these activities, and I was not looking to start. David also decided against joining them, which intrigued me. I wondered what made him different from the rest of the team and more like me.

I did not have to wait long to find out.

While I was unpacking, David sat down in an armchair in the corner of the room and kicked up his feet. He pulled out his Bible and started reading.

It's difficult to express just how flabbergasted I was by this. Never in my life had I seen anyone read a Bible in his free time. In fact, I had not even heard of this happening. True, I knew Christians revered the Bible, but I figured they all knew in their hearts that it had been changed over time and that there was no point in reading it.

So in the same moment I found out David was a Christian, I also concluded that he must be especially deluded. Since there were no barriers between us, I just asked him.

"So, David," I began, still unpacking my clothes. "Are you a ... hard-core Christian?"

David looked amused. "Yeah, I guess I am."

"You do realize that the Bible has been corrupted, right?"

"Oh yeah?"

"Yeah. It's been changed over time. Everyone knows that."

David looked unconvinced but genuinely interested in what I had to say. "How's that?"

"Well, it's obvious. For one, just look at how many Bibles there are. You've got the King James Version, the New International Version, the Revised Standard Version, the New American Standard Bible, the English Standard Version, and who knows how many others. If I want to know exactly what God said, how am I supposed to know which Bible to go to? They are all different."

"Okay. Is that the only reason you think the Bible isn't trustworthy?" David's calm and controlled response was surprising. People were usually caught more off guard.

"No, there are tons of reasons."

"Well, I'm listening."

Breaking away from my suitcase, I collected my thoughts. "There have been times when Christians take out whole sections of the Bible that they don't want anymore, and they add stuff that they wish were there."

"Like what?"

"I don't know the exact references, but I know that they added the Trinity into the Bible. Later, when they were called out, they removed it."

"Oh, I know what you're talking about. You're talking about first John five."

I had no idea what "first John five" meant, but I practically jumped him for admitting the flaw. "So you've known all along!"

"I know what you're referring to, but I don't think you're seeing it right."

"How am I not seeing it right?"

"It's not that Christians are just adding and removing things, as if there is some grand conspiracy with people controlling the text of the Bible. I mean, let's just imagine for a second that someone did want to add stuff. Do you think he could just change all the Bibles in the world?"

"Well, maybe not all," I admitted, approaching my bed and sitting across from David, "but enough."

"Enough to what?"

"Enough to effectively change the text."

He looked unimpressed. "Nabeel, are you telling me that Christians the world over would just let someone change their holy texts ... and that this massive change would not be recorded anywhere in history? Come on."

"Not the world over, but I can imagine someone getting away with that in a specific region."

"So you agree, then, that if there were an interpolation in a specific region, we would find copies of the Bible without that interpolation elsewhere in the world?"

"I guess so."

"Well, there you have it," he said with an air of finality. "That explains the multiple versions of the Bible and the issue with first John five."

"Umm, what?" I felt as if I had been playing a game of chess with David, and he had unexpectedly declared "checkmate."

"The fact that there are **manuscripts** of the Bible all over the world means we can compare them and see where changes have been introduced. It's a field of biblical study called 'textual criticism.' If anything is changed, like the verse about the Trinity in first John five, then we can easily find the alteration by comparing it to other manuscripts. That explains the major differences between various versions of the Bible. But don't get the wrong idea; there are only a handful of major differences between them."

> **Manuscript**: A physical copy of a text, whether in part or in whole

"What about all the minor differences?"

"Well those are just stylistic differences in translation, for the most part. There are different translations of the Quran, aren't there?"

"Yeah, but they're all using the Arabic text to translate, not foreign language transmissions."

"Well, it's the same with the Bible. Most of the differences between Bible versions are just matters of translation, not the underlying Hebrew or Greek."

I let all this new information sink in, and I looked at David in a new light. Where did he get all this information? Why hadn't I heard it before? I found it all hard to believe.

My incredulity won out. "David, I don't believe you. I've got to see this for myself."

He laughed. "Good! You'd be letting me down if you didn't look into this further. But if you're gonna do this right, you better bring it!"

I got up and started walking back toward my suitcase. "Oh, don't worry. It's been brought."

> Where did he get this information? Why hadn't I heard it before?

After I finished unpacking, we focused on final preparations for the tournament. All the while, I kept thinking about our conversation. I was still fully convinced that the Bible was corrupt, but I had to deal with more advanced arguments than I had previously heard. I was excited to return home and dive more deeply into these matters.

For much more detail on the Muslim view of the
Bible, read part 4 of No God but One, *titled "The*
Quran or the Bible: Two Different Scriptures."

Chapter Twenty-Two

TEXTUAL EVOLUTION

BEFORE LONG, we were back at school, catching up on classes. David was a double major in biology and philosophy, and I was pre-med. It turned out we were in a few of the same classes: chemistry and evolutionary biology.

Sometimes, being in classes together was a good thing. David and I studied chemistry together regularly with the mutual understanding that it was all out war. We were trying to outdo one another. After every exam, our professor posted the grades outside the lecture hall, and David and I would clamber over one another to see them. Because of our friendly competition, David and I always had the highest grades in the class.

Other times, being in classes together was not a good thing. In evolutionary biology, David and I could hardly pay attention. The teacher made no attempt to hide her atheism, and we were often distracted by her side comments. Being strong theists, we found most atheist arguments petty and unconvincing. Whenever our professor said something with an atheist bent, we would turn to one another and make jokes about it ... or about her. We were college kids, after all.

One particular day, after a brief pro-atheism tirade, she returned to teaching us about taxonomy, the classification of all living things into kingdom, phylum, class, order, family, genus, and species. I leaned over to David and whispered, "After much observation, I've concluded that her hair has a life of its own. I'm trying to figure out what phylum I'd put it in."

David responded with a serious tone, "That's a tough call, Nabeel. It appears to have developed self-defense mechanisms reminiscent to those of scorpions. What do you think?"

"Very astute, David. I would have said it looks more like moss or lichen, but now that you mention it, it could very well be a sentient being."

The next few moments were spent stifling laughter, and this kind of impertinent banter ultimately led me to drop the evolution course. We just couldn't focus when we were there together.

As I went through college, I learned that evolutionary theory had crept into many fields: biology, sociology, anthropology, communications, psychology, and even religious theory. Indeed, there were notes of evolutionary theory in the arguments I used against the Bible. I asserted that the Bible had changed over time, altered in transmission by those in power according to their aims. Later, I would come to argue an evolutionary model for the gospels, that the earliest gospel, Mark, had a much more human view of Jesus than the later gospels, and that Jesus' divinity in the gospels gradually evolved.

But for now, David and I were focused on the first point, the textual integrity of the Bible, specifically the New Testament. Like most Muslims, I was not concerned with the Old Testament nearly as much as I was with the New Testament. The way I saw it, the Old Testament mostly agreed with the Quran: it named many of the same prophets,

> There were notes of evolutionary theory in the arguments I used against the Bible.

it showed prophets going to war against polytheists, and it did not say anything about the Trinity. The New Testament is what really offends Muslim beliefs, so this is what we discussed.

It was after chemistry class one day that David and I continued our discussion about the New Testament. "Alright, David, I've been looking into textual criticism some more, and I've found problems."

"What do you have?"

"Looks like I was right about whole sections of the Bible being interpolations. Bible scholars are saying that the end of Mark is not original, and neither is the story in John about the woman caught in adultery.[35] You know, the story where Jesus says, 'Let he who is without sin cast the first stone?'"

"Yeah, I know that story. You're right, they're not original to the text. What's your point?"

I was surprised he so readily conceded this point. "You don't see this as a problem? I mean, whole portions of the Bible are not actually God's word."

"I know what you're getting at, but no, this isn't a problem. Don't you see? The very fact that we can identify these additions means that we can detect alterations."

"True, but regardless of whether you can detect it, it means the Bible was altered."

"Later manuscripts, yes. But so what if a later manuscript had alterations? It's not like anyone would consider a later copy more accurate over an earlier copy. The early manuscripts are the ones that matter, and we have many early copies of the New Testament without those interpolations."

I considered his suggestion carefully. "How many, and how early?"

"Well, we have many manuscripts from the second century in the original Greek and dozens more in the third century. In our possession today, we still have two full New Testaments from the early fourth century.[36] If you want to see how much the Bible has changed from the fourth to the twenty-first century, all you have to do is pull out manuscripts and compare."

This was an interesting proposition. It took all of the conjecture out of the debate. I had to make sure I heard him clearly. "So you're telling me that we actually have whole Bibles from the early 300s?"

"Yup."

"And how different are they from today's Bibles?"

David looked me square in the eyes. "Nabeel, modern translations of the Bible are based on those manuscripts."[37]

I considered his words, but the very fact that there were multiple versions continued to bother me. It meant that the words of the Bible were not agreed upon. "Aren't the exact words important, David?

As a Muslim, I believe that the Quran is exactly the same as it was dictated to Muhammad. Not a single word has ever been changed.[38] From what you are telling me, it seems like you think the exact words of the Bible do not matter."

"The words do matter, but they matter because they constitute a message. The message is paramount. That's why the Bible can be translated. If the inspiration were tied to words themselves as opposed to their message, then we could never translate the Bible, and if we could never translate it, how could it be a book for all people?"

I didn't know if David was challenging my view of Quranic inspiration, but what he said made sense.

As I silently contemplated his perspective, he continued. "Nabeel, I think we should take a step back for a moment and look at this a little more broadly. You are trying to argue that the Bible has been irretrievably changed. But first, you need to be more specific. There are sixty-six books in the Bible; what part are you talking about? When was it changed, and how? Was it changed in any significant way?"

I continued to sit in silence. My teachers had never taught me any specifics. They just repeatedly proclaimed that the Bible had been changed. I said nothing.

"If you think there has been a significant change, you should provide evidence of that. Conjecture is not enough. You need proof."

Even though David was making plain sense, I didn't like being in a corner. "I already told you, the end of Mark, a story in John, and the interpolation in first John five about the Trinity are all examples of how the Bible has been changed."

"And I told you, virtually no scholar considers those segments as parts of the Bible anymore. You need to show me a major change in something we actually consider a part of the Bible."

I continued to fight. "What if there are other parts like those three that we just haven't found yet?"

"That's conjecture again, Nabeel. 'What if' does not constitute much of an argument. What's the claim? Where's the evidence? If there are no specifics, there's no argument."

It was clear I was flailing. David leaned back and made his concluding point. "When the books of the New Testament were written, they proliferated quickly. They were copied many times, with copies being sent far off to other Christians so they could read them as well. After reading them, those Christians often copied the books before sending them on. How exactly can this kind of proliferation of texts, without any central control, be uniformly and undetectably altered? How can someone corrupt the words? No one had control over Christendom until hundreds of years after Christ. We have dozens of manuscripts from before that time, and they are the same as today's Bibles. There is just no conceivable model for the New Testament to have been changed in any significant sense, no model that's consistent with the facts of history, anyway."

"There is no conceivable model for the New Testament to have been changed in any significant sense."

I relented for the moment. "Alright. Let me sit on this for a while." David hadn't changed my mind because I knew in my very core that the Bible had been altered. Yet, for some reason, I couldn't figure out how. I began researching the matter in earnest.

In the meantime, I decided to try a different approach: denying that the Bible was ever trustworthy in the first place.

Chapter Twenty-Three

REVISITING
RELIABILITY

IT WASN'T LONG before David was over at our house, taking Ammi up on her offer. When I opened the front door for him, he made a beeline for the refrigerator, which amused Ammi tremendously. She found it endearing.

But had he used his nose first, he would not have bothered with the fridge. Ammi loved cooking for guests, and as was her custom, she had a feast waiting for us on the table. She had prepared lamb korma, goat biryani, chicken makhani, beef nihari, and much more. I'm sure there must have been vegetables on the table, but I always ignored those.

When we sat down to eat, David looked happily confused. We were starting with the nihari, a rich beef curry, but there was no silverware on the table. I showed David how to eat with roti, using my fingers to tear the flatbread and scoop up chunks of food. David gingerly followed suit. He made it through the meal without any mishaps, which made me wonder if God was with him after all.

Soon we were in the living room, lazing on sofas and basking in the afterglow of our feast. David was lying on his back, staring at the ceiling. Though he had come over to study chemistry, I realized his guard was down and this was the perfect time to push him on the reliability of the New Testament.

"For the sake of argument," I postulated from my chaise, "let's just say I agree that the New Testament hasn't been changed."

"Hallelujah," he mumbled, not moving a muscle.

"Even if it hasn't been changed, that doesn't automatically make it trustworthy. In other words, how do I know that what it says is accurate?"

David turned to me in mock surprise. "But, Nabeel! How can you ask such a thing? Doesn't the Quran say the **Injil** is the word of Allah?" It was clear that David had been studying Islam so he could understand me better. And he was right. My position was not common among Muslims, who often believe that the gospels of the New Testament are the Injil.

> **Injil**: The book that Muslims believe Allah sent to Jesus, often considered to be the gospels of the New Testament

"I'm not convinced the Quran was talking about the gospels in the New Testament. Maybe it was referring to another book given to Jesus, one that we don't have anymore." I was proposing a view that I had heard espoused by Muslim debaters.

David considered this. "Well, I'll address your question, but I wonder if you're searching for ways to doubt the New Testament. The only gospels that even come close to being from Jesus' time are the gospels of the New Testament."

"Wait," I interjected. David was making a bold claim, and I wanted to make sure we were clear. "Are you saying that the gospels of the New Testament are earlier than all other accounts of Jesus' life?"

"Yes. All the other accounts of Jesus' life came much later."

"But I heard that there were many other gospels, and these were just the ones Christians chose to put into the Bible."

"There were other gospels, to be sure, but they all came much later, in the mid-second century or afterward. The four gospels in the New Testament are all first century, right after Jesus. That's one reason why the early Christians chose them."

I tried advancing my case. "But what if the Injil was another gospel, one revealed to Jesus, and it was lost after his death?"

"There are at least two critical problems with that, Nabeel. First, it's pure conjecture. 'What if' is not much of an argument if there is no evidence. Second, you know the Quran tells Christians to 'judge by the Injil.'[39] That means they still had it in Muhammad's day. The Injil is not a lost scripture."

I tried to respond, but I could not immediately see how to vindicate my position. The more I thought about his argument, the more it left a sour taste in my mouth. Gone was my afterglow.

David continued. "As objective investigators, if we are going to learn about Jesus' life, we must turn to the gospels because they are the most likely to be accurate. Where else would we go?"

I sat up to consider this point. "Well, even if they're the best, that doesn't mean they're any good."

"True, but these books were written shortly after Jesus' crucifixion, in the lifetime of the disciples. That's far better than most other biographies. For example, the main biographies about Alexander the Great were written around four hundred years after his death.[40] If we are confident we know anything about Alexander, we should be exponentially more confident in what we know about Jesus."

> "If we are going to learn about Jesus' life, we must turn to the gospels because they are the most likely to be accurate."

"Yeah, but being better than other biographies doesn't mean that the gospels are trustworthy."

"You're not getting me. It's not just that the gospels are temporally closer to Jesus than other biographies are to their subjects, but they are so close that eyewitnesses were still alive at the time. Given that the gospels were circulating within Christian communities, the eyewitnesses must have heard them and contributed to them."

I smiled. "That sounds like conjecture to me, David. Where's the evidence?"

"Well, early church fathers record that this is exactly what happened. According to Papias, an author writing around AD 100, the gospel of Mark is based on Peter's eyewitness testimony.[41] Papias also refers to John and Matthew as disciples.[42] So it's more than conjecture that eyewitnesses contributed to the gospels; it's recorded history that they actually produced them."

"What about Luke?"

"Luke was Paul's traveling companion, so he wasn't a disciple. But he says at the beginning of his gospel that he interviewed eye-witnesses, and given that most of what he says agrees with Mark and Matthew, that makes sense."

That sounded weak. "I don't know. You're admitting Luke wasn't an eyewitness, which is problematic. Plus, I've heard there are many historical inaccuracies in his gospel."

David was ready with a response. "Luke has given us the most historical data, which means he gives people more opportunities to question him. But the more we find archaeologically, the more he is proven accurate. For example, some scholars used to conclude that Luke 3:1 inaccurately named Lysanias the tetrarch of Abilene. They argued that Lysanias existed fifty years prior and that Luke mistakenly said he lived during Jesus' time. Christian scholars argued that there very well might have been a second Lysanias, but the skeptical scholars deemed that to be apologetic speculation.

"It turns out that during an excavation, archaeologists found an inscription dating from the time of Jesus that mentioned a second Lysanias, one who was the tetrarch of Abila. This proved that skeptics are sometimes too quick to criticize Luke and that Luke was a reliable source of ancient information."

This was all news to me, and it was fascinating. But I did not want to admit, even to myself, that the gospels were trustworthy. My whole life, I had been told I could not trust them, and it would be shameful for me to admit my teachers were wrong. So I continued to push. "Can we be sure about all this, David? I mean, I haven't seen these inscriptions, and even if I had, I would not be able to test them for authenticity. Plus, I'm not sure how much I can trust church records. They're biased, after all. There's just too much room for doubt."

This seemed to annoy David. "Look, Nabeel, you've studied epistemology. You know that, if you wanted to, you could doubt that we're having this conversation, or even that we exist! It's like the *Matrix*. We could all just be brains in jars, being fed stimuli by mad scientists. You can't disprove that.

"So it all depends on how skeptical you're willing to be. Feel free to be as skeptical as you want, but just don't be inconsistent. If you're going to be this skeptical about the Bible, I want you to be equally skeptical when we take a look at the Quran."

Rallied by the mere hint of a challenge to my faith, I perked up. "The Quran can take the highest levels of skepticism, David. It's easy to prove that the Quran has never been changed and comes from Allah through Muhammad himself."

Insistent, David responded, "Nabeel, with the level of skepticism you're proposing today, I'm not sure you could hold to any beliefs. We'll see when we get there, but for now, do you realize we're just working with levels of probability? There's no such thing as absolute certainty, not in the real world."

"Yeah, that's true."

"Good. So, the best explanation by far is that the gospels are a reliable source for Jesus' life, unquestionably more reliable than anything else we have. Can you at least agree to that?"

A rift was beginning to form between my heart and my head. What I wanted to believe was fighting a battle with the evidence for the New Testament. I was torn.

Stalling, I glanced over at our chemistry assignment, which was on electronegativity and bond strength. "It's too bad religion isn't like science. Then we could just demonstrate which claims are true in a lab."

> A rift was beginning to form between my heart and my head. I was torn.

"I don't know, Nabeel. Even science is inductive, relying on observations and best explanations, not always deductive conclusions. I don't think what we're discussing is too conceptually different."

I stared at him incredulously. "Now you're just arguing for the sake of arguing! You just want to disagree with me on everything, don't you?"

David laughed. "I hate to say it, but I disagree with that too! Let's just agree to disagree for now." I nodded in affirmation, and with that, we turned our attention to chemistry for the rest of the evening.

But in the recesses of my mind, I did not disagree with David ... not really. If his facts were accurate, then his arguments made sense. I could not get myself to concede it, though, because there would be a cost to pay. I'd have to admit that my parents and teachers were wrong about the Bible. But they were so adamant, so devoted to God, so genuine. Could they really be wrong?

So I did not admit to David that his arguments made sense. In fact, I did not even admit it to myself.

To read an expert contribution on the New Testament by
Dr. Daniel B. Wallace, a professor of New Testament studies
at Dallas Theological Seminary and a senior editor or consultant
on five Bible translations, see page 324.

Part 4

COMING TO
THE CRUX

—————— •:• ——————

To have to eat, to grow fatigued, and to sweat and spill blood, and to be finally nailed to a cross. I cannot believe this. God deserves infinitely more.

Chapter Twenty-Four

LITMUS TESTS

OVER THE NEXT COUPLE OF YEARS, I grew deep roots at ODU. I joined many organizations and honor societies, hoping to get a vibrant college experience and beef up my resume. Apart from membership in a handful of clubs, I became president of the forensics team, overseeing practices and functioning as a liaison with the office of student activities. I also worked in the admissions department, where I made PowerPoint presentations and filled in for tour guides when there were not enough around. Because of my flurry of extracurricular involvement, I made many good friends and was never lacking in companionship.

But there was no question about it, David was my best friend throughout college, and I was his. When I was between classes and had nothing to do, or if it was time to grab a meal and no one was around, David was the one I called first. Though I could goof around with most of my other friends, there was no one I connected with as deeply as David. My faith mattered to me, and David's faith mattered to him. That was the level we connected on, a level deeper and more personal than most friendships.

Plus, it helped that David and I both spent most of our time in either the science buildings or the Arts and Letters Building. We regularly saw each other and often planned to walk together from our science classes, which tended to be earlier in the day, to our humanities courses.

One such route was after chemistry lab. David and I had lab in different rooms, so whenever we met afterward, we would share stories about our exploits. We started off with mere exaggerations, but soon we were weaving impossible tall tales with the goal of outdoing each other's story. The one-upmanship was meant to be grandiose.

On one specific occasion, I had to come up with an impressive feat of acid–base titration. I really enjoyed this topic and grasped it intuitively, probably because we could visually test our progress. In the process of our titrations, if we did not know whether our liquid was acidic or a basic, all we had to do was dip litmus paper into it. If the paper came out pink, it was an acid. If the paper came out purple, it was a base. The litmus paper made it easy to know where we were in the process of our overall experiment.

After the lab, I waited for David in the courtyard outside. He was late. When he finally walked out of the building, I wasted no time giving him my story.

"Dude, it only took me fifteen minutes to do my titrations. I didn't even need litmus paper. I just eyeballed it, and *bam!* I was done. I've been waiting for you ever since."

"Oh yeah? Well, when I got to the lab, I got a beaker of acid and a beaker of base, and I put them next to each other and commanded them to titrate themselves. They obeyed out of fear and awe. So it took me only one minute."

"Uh-huh. So why are you late?"

"It took me an hour to sign autographs for all the professors."

"That's why you're late?"

"That's why I'm late."

I picked up my backpack, and we started heading toward the Arts and Letters Building. We began inventing one whopper after another, trying to get the last word on whose chemistry skills were the most legendary. The walk was short and relaxing, taking us past the large glass windows of the library and a calming fountain by the new broadcasting building.

When there was finally a lull in the banter, David's visage slowly grew serious. It seemed to take on a hint of concern. My friend's concern was my concern, so I grew serious too.

"Yo, Dave. What's on your mind?"

"I was just thinking of something. I wanna know what you think, but I'd like you to answer me honestly."

David didn't usually talk like this, so he had my attention. "Yeah, man. What's going on?"

"Right now we're goofing off and arguing about who's better at chemistry. It's pointless fun. Don't get me wrong, we're having a blast and that's great. But the laughs are what we're after; the argument itself is pointless."

I nodded.

"It's also really fun when we talk about the Bible and Christianity, but I wonder if we're not just goofing off and trying to outdo each other there too. You see what I'm saying? I guess I'm wondering if our conversations about faith are more than just fun arguments."

"What do you mean? Of course they are."

"Let me put it this way. Let's just say Christianity were true. Just for a moment, imagine with me that Jesus really is God and that he really did die on the cross for your sins and that he rose from the dead. He loves you, and he wants you to live your life following and proclaiming him."

"Okay, I'm imagining it. It's hard for me, but I'm trying."

"Alright. Now, if it were the case that Christianity were true, would you want to know it?"

"I'm sorry, what?" I didn't understand what he was asking.

"If Christianity were true, would you want to know it?"

"Why wouldn't I?"

"All kinds of reasons. For one, you'd have to admit to yourself that you were wrong all these years, and that's not easy. It would also mean you'd have to go back through your entire life and sort out everything you ever thought you knew about God and religion. That's tough, man. I can easily imagine not wanting to do that."

I did not answer immediately but kept on slowly walking with David.

The trees along the path were thinning out as we approached the Arts and Letters Building. Squinting as we came out of their shadows, we decided to put our backpacks down by the fountain and take a break. I looked past David, out over the water.

After a moment, I responded. "Yes and no."

I looked over at David. He waited.

"Yes, I would want to know because I want to know the truth, and I want to follow God. He is the most important thing there is. But, no, I wouldn't want to know because it would cost me my family. They'd lose the son they've always wanted, and they'd lose all the respect they have in the community. If I became a Christian, it would destroy my family. I'm not sure I could live with that. After all they've done for me? No."

The silence that followed was pregnant. The sound of flowing water washed over any awkwardness, and we stood for another few moments, saying nothing.

Finally, David asked, "So who do you think would win: God, or your family?" It was a blunt question, but that's how I needed to hear it.

"God."

Even as I spoke, a wave of defiance swept over me. I came to my senses and turned to David. "But it's not like any of this speculation matters. Christianity is not true. Islam is the truth. Will you be willing to admit it when you realize it, David?"

David looked at me incredulously. "Nabeel, you're doing it again! I hate to say it, but it seems like when we talk about our faiths you just try to win the argument instead of honestly looking for the truth. It's as if you presuppose that Christianity is false."

If anyone else had made these accusations, I probably would have walked away and avoided further discussion. But this was my best friend, and I knew he cared about me. I considered his words carefully.

"Maybe you're right. I don't think Christianity could even possibly be true."

> If anyone else had made these accusations, I probably would have walked away. But this was my best friend.

"Why not, Nabeel? You haven't been able to defend your position in any of our discussions. You thought the Bible had been altered over time, but you weren't able to defend that. You thought it might not be trustworthy, and you weren't able to defend that."

"Well maybe it's because I'm not well versed in these things. I'm no scholar, I don't know all the answers." In saying this, a hidden reality was revealed: Western though my upbringing was, it was built upon the Eastern bedrock of authority.

David remained focused. "What would it take for you to begin to think that Christianity is possibly true?"

I reflected on this for a moment before responding. "My dad taught me everything I know about religion, and he knows way more than I do. If I saw that even he could not answer objections, then I would begin to look into things more carefully."

"Then you'd think that Christianity is possibly true?"

"Just possibly."

David considered this. "Do you think your dad would be up for a conversation?"

"Of course," I answered, without hesitation.

"I've got a friend named Mike who holds meetings at his house once a month, where people from all kinds of backgrounds get together and talk about religion. We call them 'Dream Team' meetings. I know he would be willing to have a conversation with your dad. You think that'll work?"

"Yeah, definitely. I'll check with my dad, but I don't think he'll have a problem with it. Count us in."

"Okay, good. Let's pick a topic, so we don't go all over the map. What should we discuss?"

"Well, if there's a litmus test between Islam and Christianity, I think it's the issue of whether Jesus died on the cross."

"Alright. We'll talk about Jesus' death on the cross. That settles it." David and I turned back to look over the water, considering the implications of what had just happened.

Years later I would find that this was a major turning point for David. If I had said that I didn't want to know if Christianity was true, David would not have pursued our conversations any further. He had long before realized that people who wanted to avoid the truth usually succeeded.

It was a turning point for me too. Convinced that Abba would be able to deftly handle anything that was thrown his way, I was not prepared for how the conversation would go.

Chapter Twenty-Five

CRUCIFYING THE SWOON THEORY

SHORTLY AFTER THE CANDID CONVERSATION by the fountain, I asked Abba if he would be willing to go to meet with Mike and talk about Jesus' death. As expected, Abba responded enthusiastically. Like me, he loved talking about matters of religion because he was convinced of the truth of Islam. He saw every opportunity to discuss our beliefs as an opportunity to honor and glorify God.

But because of final exams, family trips, and other obligations, there was no opportunity in the near future for us to go to one of Mike's meetings. It wasn't until my sophomore year that the stars aligned.

David and I were taking genetics together, and he told me in class one day that a friend of Mike's was coming to town, someone who had studied the **historical Jesus**. If we wanted, the five of us could meet over the weekend. It sounded like the perfect opportunity, so I made sure Abba and I were available. Before long, the day we had been waiting for finally arrived.

Historical Jesus: Jesus as he can be known through historical records

It turned out the meeting was not far from our house, practically in our own neighborhood. The man hosting the event, Mike Licona, had been a friend of David's for some time. Formerly a Tae Kwon Do instructor and insurance salesman, he had been studying the New Testament for the past few years. He had recently finished a master's degree in religious studies and was considering a doctorate.

When we arrived at his home, he greeted us warmly. At 6' 4", he had a rather striking figure, but despite his formidable height and martial arts training, he had kind eyes and a soft voice.

Mike introduced us to his friend, Gary, who was also rather imposing. He appeared to be about five years older than Abba, with sharp blue eyes and a well-trimmed beard. He looked like a mix between Santa Claus and an offensive lineman. Gary extended his hand to me.

"Hi, my name is Gary Habermas. I'm a friend of Mike's, one of his former professors."

"Nabeel Qureshi. Good to meet you. Thanks for coming to the meeting. I hear you're familiar with the historical Jesus?"

Gary chuckled. "I guess you could say that. I've written a few books on the topic."

This was my first indication that things might not go so well for Abba and me that night. I decided to ask him some more questions, to see whom exactly we had stumbled upon. "David told me you knew the subject well, but I didn't realize you've written books on it. How long have you been studying the field?"

"Well, my dissertation was on the historicity of Jesus' resurrection. I wrote it in 1976, and I've been studying the historical Jesus ever since, so that's over twenty-six years."

Smiling and nodding, I decided to let Abba do most of the talking for the evening.

The five of us continued getting to know one another as we seated ourselves in Mike's living room. Mike sat with his back to the window and Gary at his left. I sat in a recliner facing Mike, with Abba to my right. David sat farther away from us, in an armchair toward the corner of the room. He reined us in when it was time to begin.

"Well, I'll quickly give some background and then hand it over to Nabeel and his dad. We wanted to talk about the crucifixion of

Jesus. Nabeel and Mr. Qureshi believe Jesus did not die on the cross, whereas the rest of us know that's just not true."

Gary's mouth dropped, and I just shook my head. But Abba had met David a few times and knew he was a bit cheeky, so he chuckled, and Mike lightheartedly chided David. "Now play nice, David!"

"Alright, alright. But you guys think Jesus was crucified, right? Crucified, but not killed on the cross?"

Abba responded, "That's right."

Mike stepped in. "Well, why don't we just start there? Tell us why you think that."

With that, Abba and I had the floor. Abba did the lion's share of the talking, mostly arguing the case found in Mirza Ghulam Ahmad's book, *Jesus in India*. It was the same case I had shared with my friend Kristen years earlier on the school bus, except Abba wove in supplementary arguments.

Mike and Gary listened attentively, asking questions only for the sake of clarification. They did not disrupt Abba or interject with refutations, much to David's chagrin. After about half an hour, there was a subtle shift in the mood of the room. Mike and Gary were looking for an opportunity to start responding.

When Abba mentioned the **Shroud of Turin**, Gary piped up, "Wait, you think the Shroud of Turin is real? You think Jesus' image is on that shroud?"

Abba doubled back and considered his claim more carefully. "Yes, I do. Why, what do you think?"

"Well, I think there's a lot of good reason to agree with you, but I'm surprised that you think it's Jesus. It's pretty clear the man in the shroud is dead."

Shroud of Turin: A controversial relic, it is often believed to be the burial cloth of Jesus himself, supernaturally bearing his image

The imams in our jamaat proclaimed the authenticity of the shroud, but they argued that Jesus was alive when the shroud was placed on him. Having heard some of their arguments, Abba replied, "But blood coagulates when a man dies, and the man in the shroud has blood flow."

"You're right, but the blood flow on the shroud demonstrates a separation of serum and clotted blood, which only happens after death. You also see evidence of rigor mortis, another indication the body is dead."

Not being overly familiar with the details of the shroud, Abba decided to stick with the gospel accounts. "But even in the Bible, it says that when Jesus' side was pierced, blood and water gushed out. That means that his heart was still pumping. Otherwise, how would blood gush out?"

Gary shook his head. "If his heart was still pumping, what was the water? What the author of the gospel calls 'water' is either the serum after it has separated or it was fluid from around the heart. Either way, Jesus had to be dead in order for there to be 'blood and water.'"

Mike had a New Testament in hand and added, "The Greek word you're translating as 'gushed out' is the same word for simply 'coming out.' It doesn't mean the heart was pumping. Besides, if you're going to quote John, you've got a bigger problem: John says explicitly that Jesus was dead. See? 19:33, 'He was already dead.'"

Abba asked Mike to show him the Bible, and Mike pointed out the verse. It was in Greek, so it couldn't help Abba too much, but Abba continued to look at it, switching back and forth between Mike's Greek New Testament and his own King James.

After giving him a moment, Gary spoke up again. "I don't think a man could survive the kind of spear wound dealt to Jesus. The very reason they stabbed him in the chest was to make sure he was dead. The spear would have gone into Jesus' heart, killing him instantly."

"But the Bible doesn't say it went into his heart," Abba pressed, "just that it pierced his side. Plus, he was only on the cross for a few hours; he could easily survive that."

"Well, I wouldn't be so sure. There's an entire history of the practice of crucifixion, and I can assure you of this: it wasn't gentle enough to survive. As far as we know, no one in history ever survived a full Roman crucifixion.[43] The Romans designed it to be a humiliating, torturous, surefire method of execution. Are you familiar with the flogging process and the rest of the crucifixion?"

Abba shook his head.

"They used what's called a flagrum, a whip that was designed to rip skin off the body and cause excessive bleeding. After just a few lashes, the victim's skin began to come off in ribbons and their muscles tore. After a few more lashes, the muscles became like pulp. Arteries and veins were laid bare. Sometimes the flagrum would reach around the abdomen and the abdominal wall would give way, causing the victim's intestines to spill out. Obviously, many people died during the flogging alone."[44]

This was all news to me, and I was horrified. I knew the Bible said Jesus was flogged, but it gave no details. If this was truly the kind of torture Jesus underwent, I was going to have a harder time defending the idea that Jesus survived the cross. But Gary was not done.

"After the flogging, victims were nailed through their arms to a crossbeam. The nails would go right through the median nerve, causing extreme pain and incapacitating the hands. A seven-inch nail would then be driven through both feet, and the crucifixion victim would be made to hang from his arms, a position that makes it nearly impossible to breathe. He would have to use his little remaining energy to push against the nail in his feet so he could breathe out.

> If this was truly the kind of torture Jesus underwent, I was going to have a harder time defending the idea that Jesus survived the cross.

He could breathe in as he sagged back down, but he would have to push back up before breathing out again. When all his energy was drained and he could not push up any longer, he would die of asphyxiation."

Mike quickly added, "Which is why they broke the legs of the robbers next to Jesus. Without their knees, they couldn't breathe out, so they died."

Gary continued, "And that made it pretty easy for the guards to tell when someone was dead; all they had to do was see if the victim stopped pushing up. But the guards developed ways to ensure the victims really were dead. Other than breaking the knees, sometimes they'd crush the victim's head, sometimes they would feed the body to dogs, or, as in the case of Jesus, sometimes they would pierce the victim's heart."

With each point, I felt our position become more and more

problematic, but Abba was not through. "Jesus prayed for the bitter cup to be taken away from him in the garden of Gethsemane. Clearly, he did not want to die! Would God not honor that?"

Mike answered, "Yes, but he also said to God, 'Let Your will be done, not mine.' So, on the human level of experiencing pain, of course Jesus did not want to be crucified. But on a deeper level, Jesus wanted God's will to be done, and so he was willing to be crucified. He made this clear when he turned back to Jerusalem much earlier in his ministry, prophesying his death and willingly walking toward it."[45]

Gary added, "And that's something that I wanted to clarify about your position. It looks like you quote the gospels to help build your case but that you do not take verses into account that might oppose your view. For example, you quoted the dream that Pilate's wife had, even though it appears only once in one of the gospels,[46] but you ignore the times Jesus prophesies his death, even though that occurs multiple times in each gospel.[47] Why is that?"

Abba answered honestly, "Because it's not possible that Jesus died on the cross. He was beloved of God, and he cried out to be saved. If there are verses that say he prophesied his death on the cross, those verses must have been added by Christians."

I felt my face flush. From my earlier conversations with David, I knew arguing against the textual integrity of the New Testament was difficult, but that was not what I found embarrassing. Rather, it was clear to me that Abba was cherry-picking verses to defend his views. I decided to speak up.

"Abba, I think they're saying that, unless we have good reason to discredit a specific verse, it might be inconsistent to use ones we like and ignore the ones we don't like."

Abba turned to me, utterly stunned that I would contravene his authority. He looked betrayed, and I regretted my words. From that point on, he did not say much. I took over the remainder of the conversation, which turned out to be rather brief.

"Okay, I hear your case, guys, but I also see there's room for doubt. Are there scholars that agree with Abba and me that Jesus did not die on the cross?"

Mike responded, "Well, in the 1700s some scholars started suggesting that Jesus did not die on the cross, but the theory was short-lived. David Strauss, a highly respected non-Christian scholar, argued a key point: not only was Jesus' survival of the cross highly implausible, it would have nipped the Christian movement in the bud.[48]

"You see, the disciples went from being afraid of associating with Jesus in the garden of Gethsemane to being willing to die for proclaiming him the Risen Lord. If Jesus had just barely survived the crucifixion, he would have come to them broken and on the verge of dying. That is not the kind of appearance that would inspire a total transformation and a disregard for death. That boldness was the ethos of the early Christian movement, and without it, there would be no Christianity."

Gary added, "These are just some of the reasons why virtually no scholar in the field denies Jesus' death on the cross. In fact, the opposite is true: most scholars agree that they can be more assured of Jesus' death by crucifixion than of anything else in his life."

I pushed. "You're talking about Christian scholars, right?"

"Christian, non-Christian, you name it. And, like I said, there are other reasons, all compelling. For example, there are multiple non-Christian sources from the first century after Jesus who testify to Jesus' death on the cross, and there are many more Christian sources that confirm it. Plus, there's no tradition to the contrary, not for a long time. But to answer your question, I'm talking about virtually everyone."

Mike added the last word. "Scholars are virtually unanimous: the death of Jesus on the cross is among the surest facts of history."

I let these words sink in. Soon, Abba indicated that it was time to leave. I wanted to stay and talk some more, but Abba was firm. The silence during the ride home served to echo Mike's concluding words. It seemed to me that if I wanted to hold onto an Islamic version of Jesus' crucifixion—whether through the substitution theory or the theistic swoon theory—I would have to discard history. The Quran required me to close my eyes to the evidence and believe solely on faith.

> There were no shades of grey: the Christian claim aligned with the evidence 100 percent.

Here were the results of our litmus test, and there were no shades of grey: the Christian claim aligned with the evidence 100 percent.

But what was worse, I had seen Abba refuted. For one reason or another, he had elected to ignore an obvious truth during our conversation, and that did not sit well with me at all. I realized I could no longer uncritically trust what my parents had taught me. I did not doubt their sincerity, their devotion, or their love, but I was beginning to doubt their grasp of the truth.

It was as if, rather suddenly, a veil of certainty was lifted, and I was seeing the potential of the world in a new light. It was like I had been wearing colored glasses my entire life, and they had been taken off for the first time. Everything looked different, and I wanted to examine it all more carefully.

Maybe, just maybe, I should start considering it a remote possibility that the Christian message could possibly be true.

For much more detail on the Muslim view of Jesus'
crucifixion, read part 6 of No God but One,
titled "Did Jesus Die on the Cross?"

Chapter Twenty-Six

A MUSLIM
AT CHURCH

WHEN WE ARRIVED HOME, Ammi met us at the door. She was curious to know how the meeting went. I debriefed her on our conversation, emphasizing that we were able to get our point across. But given that Abba was still hesitant to speak and that I was anxious to leave the room, I doubt she was convinced. As soon as I could, I excused myself and made my way upstairs.

The room at the end of our upstairs hallway was originally designed to be a large closet or laundry room, but when Abba had the house built, he asked the builders to extend it into a full-size bedroom. He made it his library, lining the walls with bookcases, each full to the brim. Whenever I wanted to study literature on religion, I would go to the appropriate section of Abba's bookcase, pick out some books, and flop down on my stomach to start reading. It was something I often did for fun.

But I was not thinking about fun that day. I was on a mission to resolve the tension that was growing in my heart and mind.

I pulled out the books we had about Jesus, almost all of which were written by Muslim authors and scholars. I began systematically sifting through the literature, looking for information that I could use to respond to what I had just heard.

It was then that I noticed something for the first time: the books

Abba had on Jesus' life were all polemical. They started with a conclusion, found facts that supported their position, and then made their case. As Gary had pointed out about Abba's argument, the treatments were not careful or fair. They did not grapple with counterarguments, which left the cases they made untested and brittle.

Even though I had seen our arguments fail multiple times, I now became convinced it was because we had poor methodology. Eastern authors were able to make passionate cases that compelled the heart, but Western authors thought more systematically and linearly, equipping themselves with excellent counterarguments and more tempered positions. Perhaps if I employed Western methodology with Eastern passion, I would be able to craft the most compelling and defensible case of all.

It was time to become more systematic about my approach, but I had no idea how to start. Just then, David called. I flipped open my phone.

"Nabeel!" he started, cheerfully. "What'd you think of the conversation?"

"I'm still processing it. I think I need to learn about methodology."

"Oh yeah? How?"

"I dunno. You got any ideas?"

"Actually, yeah. I noticed you didn't want to leave at the end of the conversation, so I asked Mike and Gary if they had another opportunity to talk. Turns out they were planning on doing lunch tomorrow, and they wouldn't mind having us along. It'll be after church, where Gary is the guest preacher. Wanna join us? You could ask them all about historical methodology, and ..."

"Whoa, wait." My brain did not compute his suggestion. "You want me to come to church with you?"

"If you want."

"And what would I tell my parents?"

"What do you mean?"

I tried to talk some sense into him. "You think they're going to let me just go to church with you? So I can talk with Mike and Gary? Not after today."

"Take your thumb out of your mouth, grow some chest hair, and just tell them. You're an adult, for crying out loud."

I sighed, exasperated. "You don't understand. It's much more complicated than that."

To my parents, a second meeting could indicate that I was beginning to give Mike and Gary a place of authority in my life. This would be especially true if I did not bring Abba with me to the meeting, but bringing him was out of the question. I wouldn't be able to speak freely if he were to come along.

I did not want to give them cause for undue concern, and honestly, I did not want to give them the opportunity to tell me I couldn't go. I decided to tell my parents I was going to hang out with David, which was the truth, but not the whole truth. Over the following years, there were a few more occasions when I had to test my moral compass by navigating between full and partial truths for the sake of a higher good. I never liked it, but I otherwise felt stuck between a rock and a hard place.

I went to David's house the next day, and he drove me to his church. It was a college church called "Campus Impact," and it was a totally new experience for me. They had what they called a worship team on stage: singers and a band that played guitars, drums, and other instruments as people clapped and sang along. There were humorous announcements, a brief break during which people seemed coerced to greet one another, and a bucket that people passed along to collect money.

I had never seen any of this before, and it all seemed very irreverent to me. Worship was supposed to be a solemn, reflective time of bonding between man and God, yet these people were banging on drums and asking for money. At the mosque, no one was allowed to stand in front of you while you worshiped so that you could focus on worshiping God. That there were girls on stage during a worship service seemed to border on sacrilege.

So the worship service disturbed me and left a sour taste in my mouth. I thought, "If this is what it means to worship God as a Christian, I want nothing to do with it."

For me, the sermon was the main event. When it came time for

Gary to speak, he delivered a sermon on immortality. He argued that Jesus' resurrection was a historically verifiable event and that the implications were tremendous. It meant that life does not end when we die, that we are immortal. This was cause either to rejoice or to be gravely concerned, depending on what life after death might hold.

I thought, "If this is what it means to worship God as a Christian, I want nothing to do with it."

But, according to Gary, Jesus' resurrection also answered this question. It meant that the Christian message was true and that we could know we would be in heaven forever with God if we trusted Jesus as our Lord and Savior.

That is where my Muslim mind took issue with Gary. Yes, God makes us, in a sense, immortal. Though our bodies will die, our souls will never cease to be. But even if Jesus had already been raised from the dead, that didn't make everything else about Christianity automatically true.

After church, we went to a restaurant called "The Max," and I made that very point between bites of salad.

"Gary, let's say the resurrection of Jesus actually happened. That doesn't all of a sudden mean that we ought to accept him as our Lord and Savior. That just means he was raised from the dead."

"Yes, but you have to start asking the question, 'Why?' Why did he die on the cross, and why was he raised?" Gary paused to let me process, then continued, "Plus, you have to grapple with the fact that this man is obviously telling the truth about himself."

"What truth?" I asked, breaking away from my food.

"That he is divine."

"Wait a minute. That's a whole separate issue. I don't think Jesus claimed to be God."

Gary gave a slight nod. "Fair enough, but you'd at least agree with this: if Jesus was raised from the dead, then that means God has His stamp of approval on Jesus."

"Yes, of course, but I already believe that God approves of Jesus."

David interjected, "Nabeel, just yesterday you said you wanted to learn methodology, which means you want to be more objective in your research and argumentation, right?"

"Absolutely."

"Then 'I already believe something' is not a good reason to continue believing it. You need better reasons, ones that are grounded in objective facts. If the resurrection happened, we have good reason to believe that God approves of Jesus. That's the point."

I turned back to Gary. "Okay, I get it. But so what? What does that mean for me?"

Even though the question was directed at Gary, David continued, "It means you should look and see if Jesus really did claim to be God."

"Okay, I want to do that. But how? And that's my main question here: how can I investigate this stuff more or less objectively? How should I go about this methodologically?"

Mike, who had been mostly listening up to this point, perked up. "I've actually been working on a book, one that Gary and I will be publishing together, where we address that very question in regard to Jesus' resurrection.[49] Historians carefully use criteria and techniques when investigating the past. Their systematic approach is called the **historical method**."

Mike began to lay out some of the basic criteria of the historical method, such as the **criterion of multiple attestation** and the **criterion of early testimony**. What I began to notice was that the historical method is mostly about being fair, careful, and using common sense.[50]

Wrapping up the discussion, Mike had one final point. "Nabeel, the most important thing is that you have to be consistent when you do your research.

Historical method: Criteria and techniques used by historians to systematically investigate the past

Criterion of multiple attestation: A principle of the historical method that posits that a recorded event is more likely to be historically accurate if it is recorded in multiple independent sources

Criterion of early testimony: A principle of the historical method that posits that early accounts of an event are more likely to be accurate than later accounts, all else being equal

Read both sides of an argument. Don't agree with any theory before you test a few. See which argument addresses the most facts and issues, how well it addresses them, and how important those facts and issues are to the overall argument. Ultimately, that's how we find the best explanation of the past."

This term intrigued me. "The best explanation?" I asked.

"Yes, that's what studying history is all about. There will always be competing theories, and no theory about the past is ever perfect. But there is often a best explanation, and sometimes it far exceeds all the others. In the case of the events surrounding Jesus' death, the best explanation is that he rose from the dead. And this far exceeds all other theories."

I was processing this information in my head, determining how I would apply it. "Alright, I think it's coming together. Here's what I want to do: I want to put the main issues of Christianity and Islam into historically investigable terms so that I can determine which one is more likely to be true. So tell me if you agree with this: if we can determine that Jesus claimed to be God, that he died on the cross, and that he rose from the grave, then that would be a good case for Christianity."

"If we can determine that Jesus claimed to be God, that he died on the cross, and that he rose from the grave, then that would be a good case for Christianity."

The three of them nodded.

I continued, "But if we can determine that Jesus did not die on the cross, that he did not rise from the dead, or that he did not claim to be God, then I would have good reason to think Christianity is false. Do you agree?"

David asked for clarification. "Are you saying all three must be false in order to disprove Christianity?"

I shook my head. "No, if any one of those three arguments is not compelling, the whole case is not compelling. For example, so what if Jesus claimed to be God and then died on the cross? There are many people who claim to be God and end up dying. But if he rose from the dead after that, now that's something."

At that, Gary asked, "Well, we talked about Jesus' death on the cross yesterday. What do you think? Do you think the case is strong?"

"I think it's strong enough that I am going to look into his resurrection and his deity for now. I might revisit his death on the cross later."

Mike smiled, "I'm really glad you're using your mind to be careful and intentional about your faith. Too many people stick with what their parents taught, or go with the flow, or worse, become bitter. You give me hope, Nabeel. I'm glad to know you."

I smiled back. Mike and Gary were nice guys. They didn't try to push me to believe one thing or another, nor did they seem to think of me as an outsider, as "that Muslim boy." I was like them, someone who was pursuing God and truth with all his heart and mind.

And now I had found the path of my pursuit: assess the historical case for Jesus' death, his deity, and his resurrection. If these three arguments were strongly evidenced, then there would be a strong case for Christianity. If not, then the case would be poor. Other factors, like my opinion of church services, were irrelevant.

We finished our lunch, said our goodbyes, and parted ways. I would not see Gary or Mike again until a great Muslim debater came to town more than a year later. His objective was to argue against Jesus' resurrection in front of hundreds.

His opponent? My new friend Mike.

Chapter Twenty-Seven

DEBATING THE RESURRECTION

THE DEBATE HAD BEEN REQUESTED by Muslim organizations, so it was heavily advertised at the Norfolk mosque. Posters had been up for weeks, flyers were distributed, and a buzz of excitement permeated conversations. This was going to be a great opportunity to see a Muslim scholar, a **sheikh**, challenge Christian arguments. That Mike himself was the debate opponent made this scenario almost too good to be true. Would the arguments he shared with me and Abba for the death of Jesus hold up under the scrutiny of a Muslim scholar?

> **Sheikh**: A Muslim leader, usually with graduate-level education in Islamic theology

The Muslim debater was a well-known apologist who hailed from Toronto named Shabir Ally. He had a congenial stage presence that made me especially appreciative of him. His gentle demeanor helped combat the violent post–9/11 stereotype of Muslims, which I felt was the best approach. All the same, he boldly wore his Muslim skullcap, a thick black beard, and flowing garb typical of Muslim cultures. Even though he was not Ahmadi, he espoused some Ahmadi arguments, making him the perfect debater in my estimation.

David had the privilege of chauffeuring Shabir around town

before the debate. Shabir asked David if they could watch Mel Gibson's new movie, *The Passion of the Christ*, so the two of them watched it together before David brought him to the venue for that evening's debate at Regent University.

Since Shabir had to freshen up, David arrived extra early and reserved the best seats in the house. Gary was back in town for the debate, and I bumped into him in the foyer before the event started. Soon, with David on my left, Gary on my right, and seven hundred spectators surrounding us, the debate was under way.

Mike was an engaging speaker, and he started by sharing that he went through a period of time where he tested his beliefs, not simply accepting what his parents believed but rather seeking to find the truth about life and God. The information he was about to present was what persuaded him that Christianity was true. This teaser had me at the edge of my seat because I was right there with him, at that very phase in my life.

He continued his opening statement by emphasizing the importance of the resurrection. "The reason Jesus' resurrection is so important is because the truth of Christianity hinges on this event. Jesus' atoning death and resurrection have been bedrock doctrines of Christianity since its inception. Therefore, if Jesus did not rise from the dead, the foundation collapses and Christianity is false. On the other hand, if Jesus did rise from the dead, then there is good reason to believe Christianity is true. That's why this evening's debate is much, much more than an academic discussion. The eternal destiny of our souls may very well hinge on what we do with Jesus and his resurrection."

I thought to myself, "You're right, Mike. Christianity hinges on the resurrection, and there are souls in the balance. Your case better be compelling!"

Two things were undeniable about Mike's argument: it was historically grounded, and it was concise. He laid out his argument clearly. "Tonight, I want to present

"If Jesus did not rise from the dead, the foundation collapses and Christianity is false."

three facts for you that are strongly evidenced and granted by a large majority of scholars. Combined, the best explanation for these three facts is that Jesus rose from the dead.

"Fact number one: Jesus' death by crucifixion. That Jesus was crucified and died through the process is granted by virtually 100 percent of scholars who study the subject."

As he would do after stating each fact, Mike provided evidence. For the fact that Jesus died by crucifixion, he delved into the arguments that he and Gary had shared with me some eighteen months prior, including the excruciating process of flogging and the multiple attestations of Jesus' death by crucifixion. He added that the expert opinion of modern medical professionals was that Jesus must have died, given the historical process of crucifixion.

Having argued sufficiently for the first fact, Mike proceeded to the next. "Fact number two: The empty tomb. An impressive 75 percent of scholars who study the subject acknowledge the empty tomb."

Mike explained that there were multiple reasons to believe that Jesus' tomb was empty a few days after his crucifixion. First, the Christian movement was founded on the principle that Jesus had been raised and was no longer dead. Christianity began in Jerusalem, and if Jesus' body had still been in the tomb, the Jewish authorities in Jerusalem could have easily ended Christianity by parading Jesus' body throughout the city. That they didn't do it lends weight to the position that the tomb was empty.

Another reason to conclude the tomb was empty was the Jewish concept of resurrection. Most Jews believed in a bodily resurrection, that the very body that died and was buried would be raised on the day of resurrection and transformed into an immortal body. It would seem that if the disciples were proclaiming Jesus' resurrection, they envisioned his very body having been raised, and that implies the empty tomb.

The final reason has to do with the position of the Jewish leadership. When asked about Jesus, they said that the disciples had stolen his body, implicitly agreeing that the tomb was empty.

To sum up this point, Mike quoted William Wand, a former professor from Oxford University: "All the strictly historical evidence we have is in favor of [the empty tomb], and those scholars who reject it ought to recognize that they do so on some other ground than that of scientific history."[51]

That brought Mike to his final piece of evidence: "Fact number three: Testimony to the resurrection of Jesus. On a number of occasions, we see that the disciples of Jesus believed that he had been resurrected and appeared to them. Not only the disciples testified to this but foes of Jesus as well."

Mike referenced multiple early sources to defend this point. He argued that the early church was built on the teaching that Jesus was risen and the fact that the disciples were willing to die for their belief that Jesus rose from the dead. In fact, not only were the disciples willing to die for this belief, but so were a couple people who had been opposed to Jesus' message during his life, namely, Paul and James.

This point seemed problematic to me. So what if people were willing to die for their belief that Jesus appeared? That does not mean he did. But Mike anticipated this and clarified that, at the very least, it meant they truly believed he had appeared to them, and they weren't lying about their beliefs. His point was pithy: "liars make poor martyrs."

Finally, after presenting the three facts, Mike made his argument: "Let's go ahead and build a case now based on those three facts. We've seen that these facts are strongly evidenced historically and that they're granted by an impressive majority of scholars, if not virtually every scholar who studies the subject, including skeptical ones. We can see Jesus' resurrection easily explains all of these facts without any strain. In the absence of any plausible alternate theories to account for these facts, Jesus' resurrection can be accepted with confidence as an event that occurred."

In other words, Mike was arguing that Jesus' resurrection was the best explanation of the known facts, and other theories required investigators to strain, twist, or ignore the facts.

I leaned back in my seat and considered the argument. There seemed to be something wrong about this. Could it be so simple?

I considered alternative explanations. "What if the people who thought they saw the risen Jesus had just hallucinated?" Well, the tomb wouldn't be empty, would it? Plus, how likely is it that so many people would hallucinate about the exact same thing on multiple occasions? Mike quoted 1 Corinthians 15 during the debate, which said five hundred people saw Jesus risen at the same time. Was there such a thing as mass hallucinations? Plus, that still doesn't explain why enemies of Jesus like Paul would have seen the risen Jesus. He would have no reason to hallucinate Jesus' return.

"What if it wasn't Jesus they saw, but someone else?" I considered this for a moment, but it also did not work. As before, the tomb would not be empty. Plus, was it really possible that the disciples would confuse someone else with Jesus? They had been with Jesus for a thousand days or more. It was not a good explanation.

"What if Jesus did not die on the cross?" That was the Ahmadi position, and Mike and Gary had refuted all those arguments. But when Shabir began his opening statement, it was clear he was going to argue that position. A surge of excitement overcame me; would this celebrated champion vindicate our position after all?

Shabir began speaking, and it was immediately obvious he was quite comfortable on stage and well acquainted with the information. "The fact that I am a Muslim may be a bias that precludes me from appreciating the evidence for the resurrection of Jesus. I want to first acknowledge that, then put it aside and look clearly at the facts. I do not find the evidence for the resurrection persuasive. If someone said to me that a man had died and was then seen alive three days later, I would have to ask, 'Are you sure he was really dead?'

"Scholars who have combed the gospels have asked, 'What caused Jesus' death?' Doctors who have read the accounts cannot agree as to what caused his death. If we take just the narratives the way they are in the text, one would not be sure Jesus actually died on the cross."

Shabir had much more to say, but this was the heart of his defense. As the debate proceeded, though, it became clear that Shabir had to deny and ignore far more than an objective investigator would. He denied that the usual crucifixion process was meted to Jesus, though he gave no reason why; he denied the validity of John's crucifixion account, even though he admitted that John's account was more true to the historical process of crucifixion; he accepted that non-Muslim scholars universally conclude Jesus died by crucifixion, but he paradoxically denied that the crucifixion played any significant role in their assessment; he ignored clear statements from all the gospels that Jesus died; on and on, he denied and ignored very important bits of data to make his case.

As enraptured as we all were by Shabir's oratory and rhetorical prowess, focusing on his arguments led to two conclusions: his skepticism of the data was unwarranted, and he applied nowhere near the same level of skepticism to his own position. This inconsistency had to be the result of his bias, one that I could see even as a Muslim who wanted to agree with him.

After the debate, Mike and Shabir went to different rooms to meet with audience members and answer their questions. I slowly rose from my seat, disappointed and processing what it all meant. I paced around the hall and contemplated the debate for about an hour, until Mike, David, Gary, and I finally headed toward the parking lot together. It was dark and cold, and we could see our breath crystallize in the pale streetlights as we spoke.

Mike turned to me and said, "Nabeel, I'm really interested to hear what you think. If you could assign one hundred points divided between me and Shabir, how would you assign them?"

"That depends on what I'm assigning the points for," I began. "If we are talking stage presence and oratorical persuasiveness, I'd have to give Shabir eighty points and you twenty."

Mike shrugged his shoulders. "Well, thanks for being honest. I did stumble over some of my words, and my slides weren't working right, so I can see that. But I guess I'm more interested in the argumentation. What did you think of the overall case?"

I thought for a moment. "I think you won in that department, Mike. I'd give you sixty-five and Shabir thirty-five."

Gary gave a shout for joy. "Hey, that's great, Mike! That's a two-to-one ratio in favor of the resurrection, from the perspective of a thoughtful Muslim. So, Nabeel, you think the argument is pretty good, huh?"

Now I shrugged. "There's still room for doubt, but objectively speaking, it seems to be the best explanation."

David couldn't resist taking the opportunity to jab me. "So, Nabeel, are you a Christian yet?"

"In your dreams!" I laughed, punching David in the shoulder. "We still haven't looked at whether Jesus claimed to be God, which is a bigger issue to me. Plus, when it comes time to investigate Islam, you'll see how strong arguments can be. It's untouchable. As far as arguments go, the only thing Christianity has over Islam is the resurrection."

Gary looked at Mike as if he couldn't believe what he had just heard. "The only thing we've got is the resurrection? Buddy, that's all we need!"

All four of us discussed the debate in the parking lot for a few more minutes until the freezing cold overcame our desire for further fellowship. I hugged Gary, not knowing when I'd see him again. Mike invited me to the monthly discussion meetings at his house, and I told him I'd try to come.

"The only thing we've got is the resurrection? Buddy, that's all we need!"

David walked back with me to my car, and we ended up sitting in it and discussing Christianity and Islam for another two hours.

When I finally left Regent University for home, I had clarified some points in my mind. It was clear that they had gotten me with their strongest arguments first, and they certainly were strong. The historical evidence categorically pointed to Jesus' death on the cross, and the best explanation for the events surrounding his death was that Jesus was raised from the dead.

But now it was my turn. I was going to put together the best argument to prove that Jesus never claimed to be God. In my heart, I knew that this next issue would be the decisive battle, and I was ready to go to war.

For much more detail on defending Jesus' resurrection to Muslims, read part 7 of No God but One, *titled "Did Jesus Rise from the Dead?"*

To read an expert contribution on defining moments by Dr. Michael Licona, Associate Professor of Theology at Houston Baptist University and author of The Resurrection of Jesus, *see page 329.*

Part 5

JESUS: MORTAL MESSIAH OR DIVINE SON OF GOD?

. . .
—————·—————

*Did You enter into this world? Did You become a man?
And was that man Jesus?*

Chapter Twenty-Eight

GENETICS
AND JESUS

MGB 101 WAS AN AMPHITHEATER-STYLE auditorium, the third largest room on a campus of twenty thousand students. Immensity notwithstanding, David and I sat as far away as possible from the professor and the other students for one very good reason: we found the professor's manner of speech hilarious and often could not keep from outbursts of laughter.

Dr. Osgood was an excellent teacher, so adept at imparting knowledge that neither David nor I needed to study outside of class to ace the material. But he used quirky terminology, and over time, we had been sensitized to his choice of words. A staple of his parlance was the word *cartoon*, which he used to refer to anything from a graph to a video. That was comedic gold every time, but the coffers were about to overflow.

He motioned to the projected image at the front of the room. "Class, your next topic to master is DNA replication. On their paths to inevitable death, cells divide hundreds or thousands of times, undergoing a precise process of copying their genetic information through each generation of daughter cells. 'DNA replication' is that process. If the process were not virtually flawless, species survival would be impossible. In order to understand the mechanics of DNA replication, we must revisit the DNA molecule. Here we have a cartoon of DNA."

I stifled a snigger by clearing my throat.

"I have already noted that DNA is a double helix comprised of two sugar-phosphate strands connected to each other by nucleotide bases. Notice now that the carbon to phosphate bonds in each strand of DNA run from 5' to 3'. This is the basis for the directionality of each strand."

Leaning over to me, David commented under his breath, " 'Directionality'? Is 'direction' not noun enough for him that he has to add a suffix?" We burst into giggles.

But Dr. Osgood wasn't done yet.

"Due to the conformation of the nucleotide bases, each strand runs in opposite directions. Taking the two strands together, DNA has antidirectionality."

David and I turned toward each other, eyes wide in stunned disbelief. This was too much fodder for us. It took our brains a moment to confirm that, yes, he really just said 'antidirectionality.' As if Dr. Osgood had lobbed a canister of concentrated laughing gas at us, David and I were overtaken by paroxysms of silent laughter. We shook for minutes, unable to stop. Finally, when other students began shooting deadly looks at us, we were forced to find a way to stop laughing. I bit my cheek as hard as I could.

Regaining control of my body before my judgment, I wrote out the word *antidirectionality* on a sheet of loose-leaf paper and passed it to David. After another fit of laughter, David scribbled something on the paper and handed it back to me. It now read, *pseudoantidirectionality*. The fits resumed. When I was able, I took my turn and passed the paper back. A few minutes and a couple hundred calories later, we had the word *quasipsuedoantidirectionalityeousnessificationism* scrawled across the page. We had laughed so hard in our seats that the bolts were coming loose.

The class had just begun, but we decided it would be best to leave. Neither of us could pay attention, and we were not gaining any popularity points by sticking around. We quickly slipped out of the class, yet another benefit of sitting in the back.

We joked and laughed as we made our way to the forensics room, arriving a full hour before practice. Pausing to catch my breath, I slipped my backpack off my shoulder and sat down at the front of the classroom. David took his normal seat at the back. We were coming off our high, each deciding how best to use this newfound time.

I was considering studying the information in the genetics lecture we had just left when a thought struck me. "You know, David, genetics is a major problem for the Christian faith."

David looked characteristically amused. "Oh yeah?"

"Yeah. Think about it. Why do we have children? In fact, why does any species reproduce?"

David said nothing, but waited. By now he had learned that, to really interact with my thoughts, it was best to let me talk it out first.

"Reproduction is for survival. It's just like Osgood said: cells are going to die, so they replicate themselves as much as they can first. The problem is obvious: why does God need a son if He is immortal?"

After pausing for dramatic effect, which seemed lost on David, I continued. "Jews understood this, so they never said God begot a son. And Jesus was a Jew. It must have been after Jesus that Roman culture mixed with the early church. Romans have plenty of stories of gods impregnating women, producing god-men."

David asked a clarifying question. "Is that what you think Christians teach?"

"Isn't it? You say that the Holy Spirit visited Mary, making her pregnant. It would only be logical for the Christian Jesus to be a demigod, since he was born of a human and a god. But let's face it, the Bible describes a fully human Jesus. That explains his hunger, his thirst, his bleeding, his ignorance, and his death."

Although I was assembling my arguments on the fly, these thoughts were hardly new, nor even my own. Two decades of Islamic teaching, daily bolstered by the repetition of the Quran's words, "God begets not, nor is He begotten,"[52] were combining with a critical intellect and an ardent desire to advance the faith of my fathers. My battle against the lordship of Jesus was an organic outgrowth of everything that defined me. It was here I would make my stand, and I was not backing down without a fight.

> My battle against the lordship of Jesus was an organic outgrowth of everything that defined me.

But whether by preoccupation, a stroke of intuition, a leading of the Holy Spirit, or unfamiliarity with the subject, David didn't fight back. "Nabeel, have you read any books by Christians on the deity of Jesus?"

"No, but I've talked to a bunch of Christians about it."

"Well, let's do this. I'll give you a book tomorrow, and you read it when you get a chance. Then we'll talk."

I was taken aback. David rarely turned down a tussle. "Why not talk now?"

"Because I need to study the stuff we missed in genetics."

"And whose fault is that, David?"

"As much yours as anyone else's, buddy!"

"Hey, you were the one who started the whole 'suffix' business!"

And so we bickered our way through the hour, neither studying genetics nor arguing theology. It was all for the best, though. My Islamic identity was so strongly forged as a reaction against the deity of Jesus that a discussion at this point invariably would have been counterproductive and divisive.

What was needed first was a small inroad, a route past the Islamic knee-jerk reaction against Jesus' deity. The book David planned to give me would get me asking the right questions and start me on that path. It proved to offer significant headway, especially considering how small it was.

For much more detail on Muslim arguments against Jesus' deity, read part 8 of No God but One, titled "Did Jesus Claim to Be God?"

Chapter Twenty-Nine

JESUS CREATES CARPENTERS

I LOOKED DOWN AT THE BOOK David slid across the table toward me. The lunchtime din of the student union forced me to focus extra carefully, taken aback as I was by the book's title and compact size. Furrowing my brow, I rifled through its pages before sending it back across the table. "I already know Jesus is more than a carpenter."

David was in an exceptionally playful mood. Fridays had a way of doing that. "Yeah, but he's way more than a carpenter. He actually creates carpenters."

I smiled. "I know that's what you say, but that's not what the Bible says."

"Yes it does. The Bible says that all carpenters were made through Jesus."

"Come on, David, I'm serious." I faked a frown for emphasis.

David's smile grew. "So am I. What do you think it means when the Bible says, 'All things came into being through Jesus'?"

"It says that?" The frown wasn't fake anymore.

"Yup."

"Not in the gospels, though. I need to see it in the gospels."

"Last I checked, the ..." he inserted an egregiously fake cough before loudly exclaiming, "GOSPEL OF JOHN," he coughed again, "is a gospel."

"That's in John?"

"Yup." He smiled, feigning innocence.

This ran counter to everything Muslim teachers taught about Jesus in the Bible. Was it possible that a gospel actually said Jesus was the Creator? Why hadn't I heard this before? None of the Christians I had spoken with mentioned this, and I had challenged so many. Come to think of it, had anyone other than David told me this, I would not have believed him, assuming instead that he was fabricating things. But I knew David well, and he would not go that route with me. Maybe David was distorting something? I did not know, but I was intrigued.

David saw my gears turning and slid the book back toward me, but this time, dramatically, in slow motion. When I reached out to take it, he quickly pulled it back. "But you already know Jesus is more than a carpenter," he said, still smiling.

I leaned forward and snatched the book away from David. "Quit gloating."

Later that weekend, I flopped onto the ground in Abba's study, examining the book more carefully. *More Than a Carpenter* was very compact, the size of my hand and only about one hundred pages.[53] The author's name was Josh McDowell, and I had seen his name before. Abba owned a book called *The Islam Debate*, a transcript of a 1981 dialogue between McDowell and celebrated Muslim apologist Ahmed Deedat. I had not yet read it because it was a full-size monograph and seemingly dealt with defending Islam. I was more concerned with defeating Christianity.

But here was a book on Christianity by Josh McDowell, a booklet really, so small it was begging me to read it. I dived in, checking all McDowell's Bible references for accuracy. It is hard to believe, but despite having dozens of Bible verses memorized for the sake of refuting Christianity, this was my first time actually opening a Bible. All the Bible verses I had read before were in Muslim books.

I devoured McDowell's book in a matter of hours. Most of it encouraged people to take Jesus and their faith seriously, but I already did that. The chapter that affected me most was chapter 2, "What Makes Jesus So Different?" Here, McDowell defended the claim that the New Testament presents Jesus as God. When I finished the book, I decided to revisit that chapter with a more critical eye.

I found many of McDowell's arguments insufficient. There were alternate explanations he was not considering. For example, he quoted Matthew 16:16, where Peter exclaims that Jesus is "the Son of the living God," in order to show that Jesus is divine. But I had been taught a counterargument early in childhood: many people are called sons of God in the Bible, such as Adam, Solomon, even unnamed strangers.[54] The Bible actually teaches that we can become sons of God, even going so far as to say that humans are gods.[55]

Elsewhere, McDowell quoted Matthew and Luke to argue that Jesus had characteristics of God, like omnipotence, but none of his references were convincing for me.[56] They all showed Jesus doing miracles, to be sure, but the Muslim explanation for Jesus' miracles was simple: they were all done by God's permission, not by any power intrinsic to Jesus. This is what the Quran said,[57] and I had long before memorized Bible verses that showed Jesus' works were actually from the Father and that he could do nothing without God.[58] As a Muslim trained to counter Christianity, I found nothing new in most of McDowell's statements, and I had long been adept at turning these arguments back at Christians.

But McDowell did succeed in convincing me that even if there were verses in John's gospel that I could use to refute the deity of Jesus, there were others that painted Jesus in an undeniably divine light. For example, Jesus said, "all will honor the Son just as they honor the Father."[59] In addition, a disciple addressed Jesus as "God," only to be praised by Jesus.[60] I had not heard these quotations before, and they did not fit into my mindset. They could not. There was no way Jesus would say or allow these things, at least not the Jesus I knew.

I began processing these new verses, struggling to harmonize them with the contrasting verses I had memorized as a child. I paced across the study, wondering, "How does it all fit together? I know there are verses in the Quran that apparently contradict one another, but Abba or an imam can usually resolve them. Is there anyone in the jamaat who knows the Bible as they know the Quran?"

A thought that had been simmering in my mind since I started reading McDowell's book suddenly came to a whistling boil. Like a man finally stepping back for the first time after inspecting a mosaic piece by piece, I realized I had missed the big picture:

The Bible and the Quran were nothing alike. Not in the slightest. Why was I trying to interpret them in the same way?

Muhammad dictated the contents of the Quran to his scribes over a period of twenty-three years. Only after his death was the Quran collected into a book. Verses that had been dictated years or decades apart are frequently found side by side in the Quran, often with no obvious connection. The result is that Muslims place relatively little weight on surrounding passages when trying to interpret sections of the Quran. For context, they turn instead to historical commentaries, hadith called *asbab-an-nuzul*.

> I realized I had missed the big picture. The Bible and the Quran were nothing alike.

So fractured are narratives in the Quran that only one story has a clear beginning, middle, and end: the story of Joseph. All the other stories pick up in the middle, or else they are never carried to their conclusions. It was no wonder I had to turn to my teachers in order to understand the Quran.

But as I read through the Bible in conjunction with McDowell's book, I realized that the gospels were coherent narratives, each serving as its own context. There was no need for any commentary in order to understand the gospels. Anyone can understand the Bible.

Conversely, I could not just focus on individual verses to make a point about a gospel, as we often did with the Quran. I needed to read the whole gospel, understand the author's intent and themes, and let the book speak for itself.

> *Asbab-an-nuzul*: A body of Islamic literature purporting to detail the circumstances of specific Quranic revelations

Armed with this new perspective, I decided to read the gospel of John from the beginning before trying to interpret it. I sat back down on the ground and opened Abba's Bible to John 1.

What I found did not sit well with me.

"In the beginning was the Word, and the Word was with God,

and the Word was God. The same was in the beginning with God. All things were made by him; and without him was not any thing made that was made."[61]

There it was. Full stop. I pored over these verses, reading them and rereading them. There was no other explanation. The verses were saying that God created the world by means of the Word, that the Word was coeternal with God, and that it was God Himself, yet in some sense separate from Him.

It was obvious that "the Word" was Jesus, not just because John's gospel was ostensibly about Jesus but also because the Quran calls Jesus the "Word of God."[62] Besides, verse 14 left little doubt: "And the Word became flesh, and dwelt among us, and we saw His glory, glory as of the only begotten from the Father." It had to be Jesus.

Incredulous, I put the Bible down and began pacing the room once more, assembling the pieces in my mind. This was John's first chapter, his prologue. Like an introduction in modern books, it gives us the lens through which to read the rest of the book. It was as if John were saying, "As you read this gospel, keep in mind that Jesus is coeternal with the Father, His partner in creating the world."

Here was the context I needed to resolve the tension in other parts of the gospel. Whatever difficulty I might have while reconciling verses, I had to keep John's prologue in mind: Jesus is God.

If Jesus truly did claim to be God, then the Quran is wrong and Islam is a false religion.

As the inevitability grew in my mind, I stopped pacing and stared at the Bible, still open to John 1. I could not believe it. It simply could not be true. Jesus could not be God. There must be some other explanation, or else I was deceived. There must be some other explanation, or else my family and everyone I loved was caught in a lie.

If Jesus truly did claim to be God, then the Quran is wrong and Islam is a false religion.

There must be some other explanation. I did not yet know what that explanation was, but it had to be there. I had faith that it was there, and I did not doubt that Allah would show it to me.

I immediately went to our living room, where we offered our congregational prayers. I approached the prayer rug, raised my hands to my ears, recited "Allah-hu-akbar," and offered Allah two rakaats of *nafl* prayer.

I was ready to recommit myself to this battle, and I was invoking the help of Allah.

Nafl: Optional prayers designed to invoke the help of Allah or draw the worshiper closer to Him

Chapter Thirty

THE DIVINE
SON OF MAN

"JOHN DOESN'T COUNT."

"I figured you'd say that."

We were back in Webb Center, the same table where David had given me *More Than a Carpenter*. I had spent the weekend studying John's gospel on the internet and praying avidly.

It was not that I was worried. Simply taking sides on these issues meant repeatedly reasserting my commitment to Islam, and I was becoming more devout because of it. Plus, I was convinced that Allah was rewarding my faith with answered prayers and arming me to fight against David's position. I discovered mounds of arguments against the accuracy of John's gospel. Having spent the past few days regrouping, I was prepared to redraw battle lines. Now I was bringing out the big guns.

"So why doesn't it count?" David asked.

"It was the last gospel, written seventy years after Jesus. It looks nothing like the other gospels, which appeared much earlier."

"But we went over this, Nabeel. John's gospel was written by a disciple, or at least in the lifetime of disciples. What it says is trustworthy."

"I wouldn't be so sure, David. Seventy years after Jesus is a decent amount of time. We can't be sure that the disciples were still around that late. But there's a bigger issue here: why does it look so different from the other gospels? Jesus doesn't use a single parable in John, and he talks about himself a lot more frequently than in the **Synoptics**. Plus, there's only one miracle that's actually common to all four gospels.[63] John seems to be telling us about *his* Jesus. A later Jesus. A different Jesus."

> **Synoptics**: A collective term for the gospels of Matthew, Mark, and Luke

"Where did you get this?" David's tone betrayed a hint of fluster. That was truly rare, and I relished the vindication. I wasn't just fighting for my pride, after all. I was fighting for my family and my faith.

"A new search engine I found, 'Google.'"

"No, I meant who are you quoting?" David pressed, his curiosity piqued. "Doesn't sound like a Muslim."

"It was a Christian scholar Shabir quoted in a debate. Bart Ehrman."[64]

A look of understanding crossed David's face. "Bart Ehrman is not a Christian."

"Oh? I thought he was." I smiled, savoring the moment. "He went to seminary."

"Yeah, but later he left the faith."

"I can see why!" I responded, half-jokingly. But only half.

"Okay, back to the deity of Jesus. Did you find nothing in McDowell's book that was convincing?"

"Not outside John's gospel." I was not about to let John off the hook that quickly.

"Alright, how about this. I'll look into John and get back to you. In the meantime, I'll give you another book, and you let me know what you think."

"Sounds good, but you've got to do better than *More Than a Carpenter*, David. Maybe pick something bigger next time?"

David laughed, "You asked for it!"

A couple days later, I was back on the floor of Abba's study, staring at a golden tome. It was called *The New Evidence That Demands a Verdict*, and though this book was also written by McDowell, it was in an entirely different class. It was eight hundred pages of lecture notes that McDowell had collected over his years researching Christian origins.

I was undaunted. My recent victory over David's argument from the gospel of John had given me a newfound confidence. I was more certain than ever that Allah was on my side, that no arguments against Him would prevail, and that the deity of Jesus was an innovation relegated to later Christianity.

If Jesus truly claimed to be God, we could expect his claim to be found in the earliest gospel, not just the last one. I needed to see Jesus' claim to deity found in the gospel of Mark. Without hesitation, I opened straight to the chapter on Jesus' deity and got started.

As if McDowell had presciently read my mind, the very first piece of evidence that he offered was "Jesus' own legal testimony concerning himself" in Mark's gospel. When the high priest asked if he was the Christ, the Son of God, Jesus testified to the Sanhedrin: "I am; and you shall see the Son of Man sitting at the right hand of power, and coming with the clouds of heaven."[65]

Apart from the "I am," I did not find this statement very clear, and I could not immediately see why McDowell would have chosen it as his primary argument. What did Jesus mean by this?

Whatever he meant, one thing was clear. The priests of the Sanhedrin thought he made a statement about his identity that they considered blasphemous, warranting execution. There was only one identity claim that deserved such a harsh penalty: claiming to be God. Claiming to be the Messiah was not enough.[66] But what exactly did Jesus say in his reply to the Sanhedrin that made them think he was claiming to be God?

> If Jesus truly claimed to be God, we could expect his claim to be found in the earliest gospel, not just the last one.

McDowell quoted a New Testament scholar, Craig Blomberg, who explained, "This reply combines allusions to Daniel 7:13 and Psalm 110:1. In this context, 'Son of man' means far more than a simple human being. Jesus is describing himself as the 'one like a son of man, coming with the clouds of heaven' who 'approached the Ancient of Days and was led into his presence' and given authority and power over all humanity, leading to universal worship and everlasting dominion. This claim to be far more than a mere mortal is probably what elicited the verdict of blasphemy from the Jewish high court."[67]

I was perplexed. Was Blomberg saying that the title "Son of Man" was a claim to be God? That was impossible.

I thought back to a **khutba** I heard at a mosque in Washington, D.C., where the imam stood at the head of the prayer hall, proclaiming, "Jesus repeatedly denied being God. He always called himself the Son of Man to drive the point home! He is a human. He never calls himself 'the Son of God.' That is why we know the few times he is called a 'Son of God' by others, it does not mean he is a literal son of God. Jesus is the Son of Man. He is human."

> **Khutba**: A sermon, usually the Muslim Sabbath sermons on Friday

Could it be that the term "Son of Man" actually meant something more?

I had to read Daniel 7 for myself. I grabbed Abba's Bible off the shelf, looked up "Daniel" in the table of contents, and flipped to Daniel 7. There indeed, just as Blomberg had said, was a prophetic vision of one like a Son of Man who was worshiped for all eternity by men of every language. This Son of Man was given authority and sovereign power over an everlasting kingdom.

My mind raced. What could this mean? I recalled that Blomberg said Jesus' response also referred to Psalm 110. Perhaps that could clarify things for me? I looked up Psalm 110 and read the first verse: "The LORD says to my lord, 'Sit at my right hand, until I make your enemies a footstool for your feet.'"

But what did that mean? How does the LORD say something to the lord? Who is God inviting to sit at His right hand?

I took my search online and began looking up as much information as I could about Daniel 7 and Psalm 110. After a few hours, it was clear. Daniel 7 spoke of a Son of Man that shared sovereignty in heaven with God, being worshiped by all men with a reverence due only to God. Psalm 110 spoke of another lord, someone who would sit on God's throne alongside God and serve as His heir.

In Mark 14:62, Jesus claimed to be the divine Son of Man and the sovereign heir of the Father's throne. He was boldly claiming to be God.[68]

But how could this be? Perhaps this portion of Mark, like the gospel of John, did not accurately reflect what Jesus claimed? I fervently searched the internet for a way out, but there was none. Jesus called himself the Son of Man more than eighty times in the four gospels; that he really used the term was undeniable. His position as the one "sitting at the right hand of the power" was deeply embedded in church doctrine, even at the earliest layer.[69] If these were divine claims, Jesus' deity was laced throughout the gospels and earliest church history.

At nightfall, I reluctantly turned off the computer, put McDowell's book away, and just let this new information simmer. I was at an impasse. I could not get myself to admit that the earliest gospel, and in fact every gospel thereafter, was built around the framework of Jesus' deity, but neither could I deny it. On the one hand, the cost was too high, and on the other, the evidence was too strong.

Mercifully, and despite the title of the book, the evidence did not demand a verdict. At least not right away. I did not need to consciously address the incongruity between the evidence and my beliefs. Subconsciously, though, the tension and pressure found an outlet in my life by way of a renewed fervor for Islam. I gained a new zeal for salaat, spent more time studying hadith, and employed Islamic terms more frequently in daily speech.

> Jesus' deity was laced throughout the gospels and earliest church history.

I did whatever it took to avoid the evidence, but I could not escape it forever. And months later, when the tension finally resurfaced, it put my relationship with David to the test.

For much more detail on Jesus' deity in the Gospels, read part 8 of No God but One, *titled "Did Jesus Claim to Be God?"*

Chapter Thirty-One

PAULEMICS AND THE EARLIEST JESUS

RAIN THUNDERED ON THE ROOF of my car. What had been a gentle morning shower a moment before was now a deluge, obscuring the afternoon sun.

It was a new semester, which meant renewed battles with the registrar and the financial aid department. The administrative offices were in Rollins Hall, at the far end of campus, and David had to make the trek. I offered to drive him so he could avoid getting wet, but the rain had since become so fierce that even exiting the car was sure to ruin whatever books and electronics he might have in his backpack. So we sat in my car, waiting for a break in the storm.

Why we picked that moment to talk about the tensest matter between us, I will never know. The storm outside the car was nothing compared to the one brewing inside it.

"So I looked into John's gospel," David started.

"Oh? What did you find?" Even though my problem with John's gospel was moot since I had found a high **Christology** in the Synoptics, I had never admitted this to David.

> **Christology**: An interpretation of Jesus' nature, identity, or role; for example, the Quran has a lower Christology than John, since he is just human in the former yet divine in the latter.

"First, you're right that John looks different from the other gospels, but that's because it comes from a different disciple who had his own perspective. Just like two people telling the same story, they'll tell it differently, but that doesn't mean one of them is wrong."

I decided to engage him, though my heart was not in it. "But John is more than just a little different from the Synoptics."

"Yes, but not so different that it's incompatible." David waited for me to respond, but I had nothing to say, so he continued. "Second, we can't be too sure John was written around 90–100 AD."

"Why's that?"

"The way scholars date John's gospel is somewhat arbitrary. Many of them date it that late because of what it teaches about Jesus. They assume that a high Christology means a later date."

"Doesn't it?" I pushed. "Christians hadn't developed a high Christology by the time the Synoptics were written."

"I think the Christology in the Synoptics is pretty high, but for the sake of argument, let's just say it isn't. You still have a problem. There are writings from before the gospels that prove Christians saw Jesus as God."

David was taking the conversation in a different direction, and he piqued my curiosity. "What writings?"

"The letters of Paul."

By saying this, David had unknowingly lit a short fuse on a hidden powder keg. Muslims are often trained to despise Paul, to see him as the hijacker of early Christianity. From the highest imam in our jamaat all the way down to my father and mother, I had been repeatedly taught that Paul had corrupted Jesus' message, misleading billions into worshiping the mortal Messiah.

"There are writings from before the gospels that prove Christians saw Jesus as God."

Because of what the Quran and hadith teach, Muslims must revere Jesus and the disciples. They were people chosen by Allah to spread His true message, including the fact that Jesus was just a human. But somewhere very early in Christian history, people began to worship Jesus. That was anathema and blasphemy. Muslims are left with no recourse other than to place the blame on an early, influential Christian outside the circle of disciples. Paul is that Christian.

Oblivious, David continued, "The writings of Paul make it clear that Jesus was God to the earliest Christians. Paul started writing in the forties, a decade or so before Mark was written. For example, one of his earliest letters says Jesus 'existed in the form of God' and that he 'emptied himself' to become human.[70] In another of his earliest letters, he divides up characteristics of Yahweh among Jesus and the Father."[71]

"So what?" I said, somewhat annoyed.

"Well, obviously, if the community is already proclaiming that Jesus is God Himself in human flesh, then we can expect a gospel written by that community to contain that belief. We should read the gospels through the contextual lens of the early Christian beliefs, which we can see through Paul's letters."

By this point, I had had enough. I subtly mimicked David in retort.

"Well, obviously, it's not in Mark. Paul must have been the one to invent Jesus' deity. He's the one who corrupted the Christian message."

David was mystified. "What in the world are you talking about?"

I rehashed the arguments against Paul that I had learned in khutbas and religious books. "Jesus told people that he had not come to abolish the law, but to fulfill it.[72] Then Paul came along and said Jesus abolished the law. Jesus told people to worship 'my God and your God,' and then Paul came along and said Jesus was himself God.[73] Paul took the religion taught by Jesus and turned it into a religion about Jesus."

David began reciprocating my agitation. "And why would he invent Jesus' deity? He was a Jew. In fact, he was the top student of Gamaliel, a Jew among Jews. What did he have to gain from inventing the idea that Jesus is God?"

"Isn't it obvious, David? Paul saw a power vacuum. He saw that Jesus was gone and that the disciples were too disorganized to take the reins. He wanted power and authority, and so he fashioned himself a 'disciple,' even though he never so much as met Jesus, and took control of the burgeoning church, promoting his gospel over other gospels that were being taught. Over Jesus' gospel."[74]

David laughed incredulously. "Are you serious? Okay, first off, that still does not explain why a devout Jew would turn Jesus into God. He did not need to do that, even if he was some power-hungry fiend. And second, we know he was not a power-hungry fiend because he was willing to risk his life over and over again for the sake of the gospel."[75] David's voice was getting pressured, his volume rising.

All the same, I cut him off. "Sometimes people can't pull out of their lies, David. Maybe by that time he was in too deep."

"Pull out of his lies? What reason do you have to say Paul is a pathological liar?"

"I told you, he wanted power."

David was now beside himself. "Power?! If all he wanted was power, he could have stayed just where he was. He was the top student of the top rabbi of his time; power was coming his way. He went the total opposite direction, choosing a life of meekness and poverty. The early Christians had Paul and his sacrifices to thank for their survival!"

"Yes, and every Christian will have Paul to thank when they're standing before God, being judged for worshiping a man instead of Him!" The moment the words escaped my lips, I knew I had gone too far. But it was too late, and I was too proud to apologize. I just stared at David, waiting for his response.

David went dead silent. For moments, he did not speak. When he finally did, his words were calm, calculated, and measured, as if each thought was being pressed through layers of filters. "Nabeel, after Jesus, I see Paul as the godliest man of all time. I'm not about to just sit here and listen to you insult him in order to make your theories work. Our friendship is important to me, so I think we should avoid talking about this again." He stopped. "Do you agree?"

"I agree."

"Alright, I'll see you later." With that, David threw open the door and walked out into the storm.

To read an expert contribution on the deity of Jesus Christ by J. Ed Komoszewski, Professor of Biblical and Theological Studies at Northwestern College and co-author of Reinventing Jesus *and* Putting Jesus in His Place, *see page 332.*

Part 6

THE CASE FOR
THE GOSPEL

But what if His majesty is not as important to Him as His children are?

Chapter Thirty-Two

TENSION AND THE TRINITY

OUR ARGUMENT OVER PAUL was not the only time David and I butted heads. Our emotions often got heated as we spoke about our core beliefs. The more important an issue on which we disagreed, the more likely it was that one of us would say something rash. Intense disagreements are bound to lead to intense emotions.

But it didn't matter how rough our relationship got, because we were living life together. Even if we were at our wits' end, vowing in moments of anger to never deal with one another ever again, we would be forced to smooth things out when we ran into each other in forensics practice later that week. Or in class the next day. Or, in the case of our argument about Paul, just twenty minutes later, because David needed a ride.

This is only one of the reasons why a strong friendship is critical. A surface-level relationship might snap under the tension of disagreement, but by living our lives together, we were forced to reconcile.

Of course, beyond mere proximity, we really did love and care for one another. Like true brothers, even after our biggest knockdown, drag-out arguments, we were still brothers. Love covers a multitude of sins.

There was a benefit to our arguments, surprisingly. They showed us where points of tension were hiding beneath the surface, needing to be addressed. One such issue that constantly bubbled to the surface was that of the Trinity. As with the doctrine of Jesus' deity, a strong aversion to the Trinity was woven into my Muslim identity and made for a latent land mine.

The core doctrine of Islam is **Tauheed**. A whole field of Islamic theology is dedicated to this topic, so it is difficult to encapsulate, but essentially Tauheed is the doctrine of God's oneness. This is not merely an affirmation of monotheism but a thoroughgoing cultivation of the concept of God's absolute unity. God's essence, or the very thing that makes Him God, is that He is one: independent, unique, sovereign, set apart, and completely unified. There can be no division within Him whatsoever.

> **Tauheed**: The Islamic doctrine of Allah's absolute unity and self-reliance

Distilling this theology in the context of Muslim-Christian dialogue boils down to this: Tauheed, Islam's most fundamental principle, is antithetical to the Trinity.

Growing up in an ostensibly Christian nation, my Muslim elders galvanized me against the Trinity. I can recall many jumaa khutbas, classes at youth camps, religious education books, and Quran study sessions dedicated to rebutting the Trinity. They all taught the same thing: the Trinity is thinly veiled polytheism.

Roughly, they taught me to see the Trinity like this: Christians want to worship Jesus in addition to God, but they know there is only one God. So they say God is at the same time both three and one, calling Him a Trinity. Even though this makes no sense, Christians insist it is so. When asked to explain the Trinity, they will say it is a mystery and that it needs to be accepted with faith.

> Tauheed, Islam's most fundamental principle, is antithetical to the Trinity.

As a young Muslim in the West, I set out to test this. Whenever I had a discussion about the Trinity with a Christian, the first question I asked was, "Is the Trinity important to you?" When they replied affirmatively, I asked, "How important?" anticipating the response that it would be heretical to deny the Trinity. The third question completed the setup. I would ask, "So, what is the Trinity?" and would receive the rote answer that God is three in one. Then the coup de grâce: "And what does that mean?" I usually got blank stares. Sometimes people would start talking about eggs or water, but no one ever was able to explain what the doctrine of the Trinity actually meant. Three what in one what? And how is that not self-contradictory?

My questions were not abstruse questions on a peripheral topic. They were simple questions of clarification on essential Christian doctrine, yet no Christian I met growing up was able to answer them. That meant every Christian I encountered bolstered what the Quran had taught me about the Trinity: it was a ridiculous doctrine that merited divine retribution.[76]

The elders who taught me to see the Trinity in this light ranged from revered imams to learned leaders to my own parents and grandparents. Everyone I loved and respected taught me to reject the Trinity, and that, combined with the inability of Christians to explain it, makes it easy to see why a repulsion to the Trinity was part and parcel of my Islamic identity. The same is true for almost all practicing Muslims.

A repulsion to the Trinity was part and parcel of my Islamic identity.

David and I had a few conversations about the Trinity, and though he answered with more depth and clarity than many other Christians, my mind had been made up well before I met him that the Trinity was unviable. So we butted heads, and as with the issue of Paul, we decided to table the discussion indefinitely.

It was coincidence that the solution came to me while I was sitting next to him in the unlikeliest of places.

Chapter Thirty-Three

RESONATING
WITH THE TRINITY

IT WAS JULY 2003, the summer after my sophomore year, and big life changes were upon me. I had made the decision to graduate from college a year early, which meant I had to begin contemplating the next phase of life. My decision also meant I had to sit for the August administration of the Medical College Admissions Test, an exam that required organic chemistry, so I sacrificed my summer to grueling doses of o-chem five days a week. Not surprisingly, David took the class with me, which meant I got grueling doses of David five days a week too.

But I was not the only one with big life changes. A while earlier, before boarding a flight to a forensics tournament, David and I had been discussing the resurrection. I made an argument to support the swoon theory, to which David responded, "That weak stuff isn't gonna work on me, man. I come from the trailer park. I got common sense!"

Unbeknownst to us, a new girl on the forensics team had been listening to our debate. She threw her hat into the ring, interjecting, "Oh yeah? Well, I come from single-celled organisms." David and I incredulously turned to her. We barely knew who this girl was, yet she wanted to take us on? One thing David and I agreed on was that blind evolution was statistically impossible. We tackled her arguments together, but she fought back. Over the course of the weekend, we argued with her about truth, relativity, God, evolution, and science. She had spark, and she didn't go down without swinging.

Three days later, Marie was a theist, and David was in love. Two months after that, the two were engaged. By the summer of 2003, David and Marie had been married a year, and we were all eagerly awaiting the arrival of their first child. David and I sat in o-chem on a hair trigger, ready to pick up the phone and race to the hospital. It was a very exciting time.

Despite the need to leave at any moment, and quite despite our incessant note passing and chuckling, we sat front and center in Mrs. Adamski's lecture hall, not more than three feet from her as she taught. I vividly remember the exact location of my seat because it was there that I first opened up to the Trinity, a moment still etched in my mind.

Projected in the front of the room were three large depictions of nitrate in bold black and white. We were studying resonance, the configuration of electrons in certain molecules. The basic concept of resonance is easy enough to understand, even without a background in chemistry. Essentially, the building block of every physical object is an atom, a positively charged nucleus orbited by tiny, negatively charged electrons. Atoms bond to one another by sharing their electrons, forming a molecule. Different arrangements of the electrons in certain molecules are called "resonance structures." Some molecules, like water, have no resonance while others have three resonance structures or more, like the nitrate on the board.

Although the concept was easy enough to grasp, the reality proved to be baffling. Mrs. Adamski concluded her lesson by commenting, "These drawings are just the best way to represent resonance structures on paper, but it's actually much more complicated. Technically, a molecule with resonance is every one of its structures at every point in time, yet no single one of its structures at any point in time."

The rest of the class must have had the same expressions on their faces that I did because Mrs. Adamski repeated herself. "It's all the structures all the time, never just one of them." After another brief pause, she afforded us some reassurance. "But don't worry about that. You're only going to be tested on the structures we can draw," to which the class gave a collective sigh of relief.

But not me. I turned to David, unable to get past what Mrs. Adamski had just said. David subtly shrugged and returned his attention to the professor as she moved to the next topic. It appeared I was the only one still thinking about the bomb she had just dropped.

How could something be many things at once? Many different things? We were not talking about the attributes of something like a steak, which can be hot, juicy, thick, and tender all at once. We were talking about separate spatial and electrical arrangements. What the professor said would be akin to saying that Nabeel is eating said steak in Texas while simultaneously napping in a hammock in the Caribbean. As wonderful as each would be individually, it made no sense to say I might be doing both at once.

I was perplexed, and what made it even worse was that no one around me seemed bothered in the least. I looked around the room, agape at their blind acceptance.

But was it really blind? The professor was teaching rarefied science, describing the subatomic world. At that level, things happen that make no sense to those of us who conceptualize the world at only a human level. Even the apparently simple idea of atoms is baffling when we think about it. It means that the chair I am sitting on is not actually a solid object, innocently supporting my weight. It is almost entirely empty space, occupied only in small part by particles moving at incomprehensible speeds. When we think about it, it seems wrong, but it's just the way things are in our universe. There's no use arguing about it.

I turned my glance away from the other students, concluding they had not blindly accepted a nonsensical concept. They had just realized before I did that there are truths about our universe that do not fit easily into our minds.

My eyes rested on the three separate structures of nitrate on the wall, my mind assembling the pieces. One molecule of nitrate is all three resonance structures all the time and never just one of them. The three are separate but all the same, and they are one. They are three in one.

That's when it clicked: if there are things in this world that can be three in one, even incomprehensibly so, then why cannot God?

And just like that, the Trinity became potentially true in my mind. I looked over at David and decided to say nothing.

Later, I revisited the **doctrine of the Trinity** with a fresh perspective. What do Christians mean when they say God is three in one? Three what in one what? I looked it up in a book called *The Forgotten Trinity* by James White, and it all made more sense after I realized a triune entity was possible.

The doctrine of the Trinity teaches that God is three persons in one being. "**Being**" and "**person**" are not the same thing, which means the Trinity is not a contradiction. To illustrate, consider this: I am one being, a human being. I am also one person, Nabeel Qureshi. So I am one being with one person, a human being who is Nabeel Qureshi. The doctrine of the Trinity teaches that God is one being with three persons: Father, Son, and Spirit.

In the fullness of time, and without any productive discussion with David, I understood the Trinity on my own terms and realized it was a possible model of God's nature. I was not convinced it was the true model, since it contravened Tauheed, but I had to concede it was viable. And when that happened, my thoughts about God became richer.

> **Doctrine of the Trinity**: The belief that God is one in being and three in person
>
> **Being**: The quality or essence that makes something what it is
>
> **Person**: The quality or essence that makes someone who he is

But there was one major Christian doctrine that still hindered me from understanding the gospel. How did Jesus' death pay for my sins? By the time David and I addressed the question, our duo had become a trio.

For much more detail on the explanation of the Trinity in light of Muslim objections, read part 2 of No God but One, *titled "Tawhid or the Trinity: Two Different Gods."*

Chapter Thirty-Four

SALVATION IN THE BALANCE

MY SENIOR YEAR AT ODU WAS ATYPICAL. Apart from the fact that it was actually my third year, it was also my first year living on campus. Up to that point, despite my protestations, Ammi and Abba insisted that living on campus would doom me to depravity. It was not until my senior year that I was able to convince them I simply had too many responsibilities at school to continue commuting.

One of those responsibilities was serving as president of the honors college, and I tapped into that role to choose my dorm room when I finally got my parents' permission to move out of the house. Located in the southwestern wing of Whitehurst Hall on the top floor, my room afforded a grand view over the Elizabeth River, the second best view on campus. The adjacent room had the best view, but I declined it because it had heating problems.

That room was ultimately occupied by someone who quickly became my friend, a Buddhist named Zach. Zach was a philosophy student, soft in speech and methodical in thought, which made him an excellent person to spar with intellectually. A few weeks into the semester, we were already good friends, and I had engaged him in *dawah* more than once.

As fate would have it, Zach attended

Dawah: The practice of inviting people to Islam

some Philosophy Club meetings, where David was the president, and the two had hit it off. So David and I both became good friends with Zach independently of one another. After we learned about our mutual friendships, the three of us began spending time together. We were a motley trio, serving as the butt of more than a few jokes.

On one particular day, when a Muslim, a Christian, and a Buddhist were sitting in a smoothie bar, I brought up the final Christian doctrine that continued to offend my sensibilities: **substitutionary atonement**. It was part of my ongoing efforts at dawah for Zach, which made for a comical scene. Here I was hoping to bring Zach to Islam by indirectly critiquing David, who was evangelizing both of us. Caught in the middle was Zach, who wanted nothing. Literally. His goal as a Buddhist was to attain nothingness.

> **Substitutionary atonement:**
> The doctrine that Jesus is able to take and pay for the sins of man.

"You see, Zach," I pontificated boisterously, pointing my smoothie at him, "Islam is a fair religion. It has none of this nonsense about some random person having to suffer for your sins."

"Now wait just a minute!" David sputtered over his smoothie, trying to interject. I steamrolled over him.

"You wait a minute, I'm not done yet! As I was saying, according to Islam, we will all stand before God, each accountable for our sins. No one will be able to intercede for us. Our spiritual lives are our own responsibilities, and if our good deeds outweigh our sins, we will go to heaven. If our sins outweigh our good deeds, we will go to hell. That's fair and just. See what I'm saying?"

Zach was characteristically stolid. "I do."

"Of course, if God wishes to grant us grace, He may. He is God, after all. But what is completely out of the question is God taking your sins and placing them on an innocent man, as if that man can be punished for your crimes while you get off scot-free. What kind of justice is that?"

David was smiling but looked ready to jump across the table. "You're not representing it fairly."

"It stinks when people aren't fair, doesn't it? Now cool down a bit. Try sipping on that smoothie. I have one more thing to say."

We were all laughing. This was fun, even though the topic was very serious. I wanted to make my most poignant illustration before turning the conversation over to David, who obviously had a lot to say.

"Our national debt right now is, what, seven trillion dollars? Suppose I walked up to President Bush and said 'Hey W., I know our debt is seven trill, but I can pay for it. Here's a dollar, that should cover it.' What do you think Bush would say?"

Zach didn't skip a beat. "He'd say you're an idiot."

"Ex-act-ly!" I exclaimed, accentuating each syllable by jabbing my smoothie at David.

Zach wanted me to spell it out. "What are you trying to say?"

"I'm saying it's bad math. Just like a dollar can't pay for trillions of dollars of debt, Jesus' death on the cross can't pay for everyone's sins. Even if one man could pay for another man's sins, it doesn't add up for just one man to pay for billions of sinners. So not only is Christian **soteriology** unjust, it's bad math. Islam, on the other hand? Simple, easy to understand, totally fair." With that, I returned to drinking my smoothie with a triumphant air of finality.

> **Soteriology**: The doctrine or study of salvation

Zach looked off into the distance, considering. "Well, that makes sense to me, I guess."

David wasn't having any of it. "Are you done?" he asked pointedly, half smiling and clearly amused.

"Nah, I just started drinking it."

"I mean with your rant?"

"The floor is yours." I had once again deployed arguments I had known since childhood in order to build my case against Christianity, and I felt confident in their strength. Smug, even.

"You're inappropriately compartmentalizing Christian doctrines in order to make your case, Nabeel."

I had no idea what he was talking about, so I was unfazed. "Proceed."

"You know full well that Christian doctrine teaches Jesus is God, yet you took that out of your equation when you critiqued the theology. God is not forcing 'some random person' to suffer for our sins. He is paying for our sins Himself.

"God is not forcing 'some random person' to suffer for our sins. He is paying for our sins Himself."

"A better analogy would be a son who has stolen from his father's business. If after wasting the goods, the son returns to the father and sincerely seeks forgiveness, it is within the father's right to forgive him. But not all would be settled yet; the accounts haven't been balanced. Someone has to take the hit for the stolen goods. If the father wants, he has every right to pay for his son's debt from his own account. That's fair."

I was confused. "Who is the son?"

"We are the son, and God is the father. We have incurred a debt against God, and we can't pay Him back. So in His mercy, He pays our sins for us. The wages of our sin is death, and He died on our behalf, balancing the accounts."

I sat silently, sipping my smoothie. Zach chimed in. "Okay, David, I think I get what you're saying. Since our sins are against God, God has the right to forgive us. And if Jesus is God, then Jesus can pay for our sins."

David considered this. "Yeah, I guess you can put it that way."

I wasn't convinced. "But that still doesn't explain how one person can pay for all the sins of mankind."

"Nabeel, you're still forgetting that this isn't just any person. This is God! This was not like paying off trillions of dollars of debt with one dollar. This was paying trillions of dollars of debt with an infinite bank account! God's life is worth more than all the other lives in the universe combined. His death more than paid for all the deaths that the rest of us deserve."

I looked over at Zach to see what he thought, hoping for support. He impassively returned my glance, as if to say, "It's your move." I rallied my thoughts.

"Alright, David, there's another problem. You've been assuming this whole time that if someone sins, then it means they need to die. I'm not buying it."

"It's what the Bible says. Romans 6:23." It always impressed me when David quoted Bible references, but it also irked me. I rarely knew the references to Islamic doctrine, since most of what I learned was from my teachers, who never knew the references themselves. In this instance, his reference to the Bible sharpened our disagreement.

"I honestly don't care if the Bible says it; it makes no sense. What kind of judge is it who punishes the pettiest crime with the same judgment as the most heinous? Think about it. Imagine you were sent to court for jaywalking. The guy before you is found guilty of rape and murder and sentenced to execution. Then you are found guilty of jaywalking and also sentenced to execution. Forget unjust. That judge would be cruel, probably sadistic!"

This argument had real implications for my heart. I knew I was a sinner and that I had rebelled against God's commands at times and chosen my own path over His dictates. But since Muslims believe that salvation is a matter of doing more good deeds than bad, I never really felt anguish over my sins because I believed myself to be on the positive side of the scales. To me, sin was bad, but not that bad.

But if it was true that all sins are so devastating that they lead to hell, what chance did I have? Of course, Allah could show mercy, but the Quran says Allah does not love sinners. What reason would He have to forgive me?

David must have been given some insight because he spoke to the heart of the issue. He shook his head and said solemnly, "Nabeel, you're still seeing Christian doctrines from an Islamic perspective. Christianity teaches that sin is so destructive it shatters souls and destroys worlds. It's like a cancer that slowly consumes everything. That's why this world went from perfection in the garden of Eden to being the sick and depressing place it is today. Do you think God would allow any of that stuff in heaven? Of course He wouldn't. If heaven is going to be a perfect place, by definition there can be no sinners in it. None at all."

> Muslims believe that salvation is a matter of doing more good deeds than bad. To me, sin was bad, but not that bad.

His last words hung in the air, their gravity slowly sinking in.

After a few heavy moments, I spoke. "Then what hope is there for us, David?"

David smiled reassuringly. "Only the grace of God."

"But why would He give me His grace?"

"Because He loves you."

"Why would He love me, a sinner?"

"Because He's your Father."

David's words hit me powerfully. I had heard Christians call God "Father," but it never clicked. Only when trying to figure out why God would give me mercy and grace when I deserved none did the gears start turning.

I couldn't speak. It was all connecting. Would I ever question why Abba loved me? He had loved me since I was born, the day he first spoke the adhan into my ear, not because of anything I did but because he was my father. I never doubted his love and generosity toward me, not because I had somehow earned his favor but because I was his son.

> Was this really how God loved me? Could God be that loving? Could He be that wonderful?

Was this really how God loved me? Could God be that loving? Could He be that wonderful?

It was as if I was meeting my Heavenly Father for the first time. After having just confronted the depravity of my sins, His forgiveness and love was that much sweeter. This God, the God of the gospel, was beautiful. I was spellbound by this message. My heart and my mind were caught in the beginnings of a revolution.

For much more detail explaining the gospel in light of Muslim objections, read part 1 of No God but One, *titled "Sharia or the Gospel: Two Different Solutions."*

Chapter Thirty-Five

ASSESSING THE GOSPEL

THE THREE OF US LEFT the Tropical Smoothie Café, climbed into my car, and started heading back to campus. While driving, I continued to process what I had just grasped. It was as if the last groove of a key had just clicked into place, and my mind was beginning to turn over the message.

David could sense that I was still processing, so he decided to interact with Zach, giving me space, while also affording me the opportunity to interact should I choose to do so. "So, Zach, how do you think the case for Christianity compares with the case for Buddhism?"

Zach had already been with David to one of Mike's Dream Team meetings, so he was used to this kind of questioning. He answered from the back seat, "There isn't really a case for Buddhism. It's a path you can choose to follow. I follow it because of the meditation, but I wouldn't tell anyone else that they should follow it or that it's true in some sense. Christianity is really unique like that. With Christianity, either Jesus died and rose from the grave or he didn't. That's something you can build a case for."

This caught my attention, and I couldn't help but respond. "I think you're right about one thing, Zach. You can build a case for Christianity, but I think you can do the same for Islam."

This was the open door that David wanted. "Alright, Nabeel, time to man up. You said that the case for Christianity rests on three things: that Jesus claimed to be God, that he died on the cross, and that he rose from the dead. We've studied all those issues. On a scale of zero to one hundred, with zero being unfounded and one hundred being the best explanation, how historically likely do you think those claims are?"

This was a moment of truth. Our conversation at the smoothie bar had softened my barriers, and I was not in a defensive posture. I considered his question carefully before responding, "Eighty to eighty-five. It's pretty strong."

I didn't have to turn to the passenger seat to know that David was shocked. "Where do you put Islam?"

All of a sudden, I was in a defensive posture, and the knee-jerk defense of my faith kicked in. "David, it's 100 percent. There's no hole in the Islamic case. Anyone who studies the life of Muhammad honestly will walk away concluding that he was Allah's prophet, and anyone who objectively approaches the Quran will be astounded by its scientific truths and beautiful teachings."

Now, I knew, as did David and Zach, that I had not studied Islam with as much careful scrutiny as I had Christianity. But for me, as for most Muslims, an uncritically reverential and fulsome assessment of Islam was a given. It is as much a part of Islamic culture and heritage as the very languages Muslims speak, and it is absorbed in a very similar way: everyone around us just operates in that paradigm. So my bold response to David was not obstinacy, it was the filter through which I saw the world.

> For me, as for most Muslims, an uncritically reverential and fulsome assessment of Islam was a given.

David did not dwell on my brash response. "Are those your two criteria? Muhammad and the Quran?"

"Yeah, I think so. If I can show with a high degree of probability that Muhammad is a prophet of God, then I can conclude the message he brought is true. Or if I can show that the Quran is a divinely inspired book, then I can conclude that the message it teaches is true."

Although David gave me some grace, Zach did not. He gave an

incredulous laugh and put me on the spot. "Do you seriously think the case for Islam is 100 percent? I mean, come on. Nothing is that strong!"

"I think Islam is, Zach. It's hard to believe, I know. But if you take a look at it, you'll see what I mean."

Zach wouldn't let me off the hook. "If you really think so, then why don't you come to the next Dream Team meeting at Mike's house and make a case?"

"A case for Islam?"

"Well you can start with either Muhammad or the Quran, and we'll go from there. I'm sure Mike won't have any problem with it. We just finished talking about Buddhism, so we're looking for a new topic anyway."

The more I thought about the idea, the more I liked it. I saw it as an opportunity for dawah, and since we weren't planning to argue Christianity, I felt like I would be more in control of the conversation than Abba and I had been when we discussed Jesus' death. "Sure. Let's start with Muhammad next time, and I'll discuss the Quran after that." David checked the calendar and determined that the next Dream Team meeting was two weeks away. Our plans were set, and we were all looking forward to it for our own reasons.

Through it all, I had no idea that I was coming to the end of an era. I had innocently accepted the world that had been built for me by my family and culture, a world in which Islam was unassailable. What lay before me was a critical dismantling of my very foundation.

To read an expert contribution on the Trinity and the gospel by Robert M. Bowman Jr., Director of Research for the Institute for Religious Research in Grand Rapids, Michigan, and author of numerous articles and books, see page 336.

Part 7

THE TRUTH ABOUT MUHAMMAD

·:·

How can I bear witness that Muhammad ﷺ is Your messenger?

Chapter Thirty-Six

MUHAMMAD REVISITED

THE MESSAGE OF ISLAM is intertwined with its messenger. Allegiance to one more than implies allegiance to the other; it is often defined by it. What makes this surprising is that the same is not the case for Allah. Muslims who question Allah are usually tolerated by other Muslims, but questioning Muhammad is grounds for excommunication, or worse.

Even though every Muslim would quickly admit that Muhammad is human, in theory fallible like any other man, they often revere him as flawless. To that end, Islamic theology has accorded him the title *al-Insan al-Kamil*, "the man who has attained perfection."

But far closer to the Muslim heart, Muhammad is the man that embodies Islam, a symbol for the whole of Islamic civilization. Because of hadith and tradition, Muslim religion, culture, heritage, and identity all find their core in the person of Muhammad. That is why Muslims see an attack on his character as equivalent to a personal attack on them and everything they stand for.

That is also why, generally speaking, Muslims cannot dispassionately discuss Muhammad. They bring immense baggage to the table, and the discussion will doubtless be colored by apparently unrelated things, such loyalty to kin or even current affairs between Israel and Palestine.

So no one really grasped the full depth of my motives when I was back in Mike's living room, discussing Muhammad. I was excited, hoping to make a strong case for Muhammad and to glorify Islam by representing him with vigor. The other attendees were there to learn and ready to examine critically what I had to say.

Had they known the effects that their questions would have, they probably would have been gentler. In retrospect, I'm glad they didn't know.

The turnout was more varied than I had expected. Of course, Mike, David, and a few other Christians were there, and Zach was there representing Buddhism, but there were also atheists and agnostics from disparate walks of life: a police detective, an astrophysicist, and a couple school teachers.

After the introductions, I had the floor. I used an easel and a flip chart to make my case for Muhammad, sharing the information that had crafted me from childhood. The result was a description of Islam and Islamic history that Muslims often share with non-Muslims in the West as an attempt to build bridges and perhaps win some converts.

The greatest concern in the post–9/11 West among the average Muslim was to distance himself from a violent image of Islam, and this was particularly true for me as an Ahmadi Muslim. I started off by emphasizing that Islam is a religion of peace and that Muhammad was the most merciful and irenic man in history. I assured everyone that the attacks on the World Trade Center and the Pentagon did not represent Islam, driving the point home by relaying an aphorism I recently had heard from an imam: "The terrorists who hijacked the planes on September 11 also hijacked Islam."

I explained to everyone that the word *Islam* actually comes from the same Arabic root word that means "peace," and the life of Muhammad reflects this. I recounted the story of Muhammad's mercy on the day he conquered Mecca, when he forgave Meccans despite their horrific treatment of Muslims. I also discussed the other battles Muhammad fought, emphasizing that they were all defensive and that Allah had miraculously intervened to give Muhammad His divine stamp of approval.

I then provided arguments along a different vein, like Muhammad's miraculous insights into science. This is a common step among Muslim apologists. I argued that Muhammad knew about subjects like embryology, astronomy, and geology, knowledge he could have attained only if Allah had revealed it to him. Yet again, this showed that Muhammad had Allah's blessing and was a true prophet.

Another common dawah technique among Muslim apologists is to build bridges by referring to the Bible while simultaneously advancing the argument that Islam is the culmination of the Old and New Testament messages. To accomplish this, I pointed to two passages from the Bible, one from the Old Testament and one from the New Testament, as prophecies about Muhammad. The first was Deuteronomy 18:18, which told of a prophet like Moses who would come. I made the case that this had to be Muhammad, since Jesus was not like Moses at all. Referring then to John 16:12–13, I argued that Jesus had pointed forward to a promised counselor or comforter who would come after his own time and lead people to the truth. This man had to be Muhammad, since no major religious figure emerged after Jesus except for Muhammad.

I followed through by arguing that Islam was the final message and that Muhammad came not as one who abolished Judaism and Christianity but one who reinforced and redirected them toward the one, true God. Muhammad's message—the "eye for an eye" justice of Moses combined with the "turn the other cheek" mercy of Jesus—was the heart of Islam, the final message for all mankind. In the course of this last point, I made it clear that Muslims worship the same God as Jews and Christians.

I spoke for about forty-five minutes and felt like I had represented Islam well and made the case for Muhammad's prophethood with zeal.

But then came the questions.

They were innocuous, simple questions of clarification, just like the questions I asked Christians about the Trinity. But for the first time, I was on the receiving end.

Mike started. "Nabeel, I have a question for you. I have heard it said that Islam was spread by the sword, but you're saying Muhammad engaged in only defensive battles. Can you tell me why your position is more accurate?"

This question was common enough, so I quickly responded, "The Quran teaches *la-iqraha fi-deen*."[77] Imams often recited the Arabic for an extra air of authority, so I did the same. "This verse is translated 'there is no compulsion in religion,' and Muhammad followed the Quran so closely he was practically a living version of it. It would make no sense to say that Muhammad spread Islam by the sword when he preached that there is no compulsion in religion."

Whenever I had discussed Islam in the past, people had considered that response adequate, but it turned out that Mike had read a bit about Islam while preparing for his debate with Shabir, and he was prepared to ask a follow-up question. "But Nabeel, there are other verses in the Quran, like 'slay the infidels wherever you find them.'[78] How do we know the verse you quoted takes precedence?"

Fortunately, I had heard this issue explained in a recent khutba, so I had a ready response. "That verse refers to a very specific circumstance, when the polytheists of Mecca had breached a contract with Muslims. It's not a general principle. The general principle is peace."

Then Mike asked his most simple, yet most devastating, question: "How do you know that?"

"I'm sorry?"

"How do you know the historical context of the Quran?"

"From hadith, books that record traditions about Muhammad."

"But how do you know those are trustworthy? Keep in mind, Nabeel, that I'm a historian. These are questions I ask of historical documents, even when critically investigating Christianity. I can rely on the gospels because the four of them were written very soon after Jesus' life, in the community of eyewitnesses. How do we know that the books of hadith are trustworthy? Were they written early? Were they written by eyewitnesses?"

The role reversal was difficult for me. I had never seen anyone question Islamic tradition the way we had always questioned the Bible. This was unheard of. Around the room, the rest of the attendees were leaning forward in their seats, intrigued to see how this line of questioning would progress. I rallied the information I had learned through the course of my life.

"Mike, the eyewitnesses of Muhammad's time passed the stories orally until they were written down. Those who wrote them down were well-respected men who thought critically, making sure that the chain of transmission for each story was strong. That's why we can trust the hadith."

That was the best I had, but Mike wasn't satisfied. "I see what you're saying, but how do we know that, Nabeel? When were they ultimately collected?"

I had never seen anyone question Islamic tradition the way we questioned the Bible. This was unheard of.

Bracing for the deluge of criticism that I knew would come, I responded, "About two hundred to two hundred fifty years after Muhammad."

At one and the same time, everyone in the room leaned back in their seats, as if the issue had been settled. Perhaps it was just a few, but I definitely perceived that the whole room was beginning to turn against my position.

Mike picked up his point and spoke in a soft tone, trying his best not to sound disparaging. "Nabeel, two hundred fifty years is a really long time to wait before writing stories down. Legends grow wildly in that span of time. Villains become much more villainous, heroes become much more heroic, ugly truths are forgotten, and many stories are created entirely out of whole cloth."

I understood what Mike was saying, but he was undervaluing authority in our culture, almost offensively so. What right did Mike have to question the great imams of old, like Imam Bukhari and Imam Muslim? Or was he implying that those who passed on the traditions, great personalities like Hazrat Aisha or Hazrat Ali, were untrustworthy?

Mike was calling the reliability of early Muslims into question, and that is a concept so preposterous to Muslims that it is never even discussed. His questions jarred me on many levels.

"Mike, you don't know the people that you're questioning. These were great men and women with sharp intellects and honest hearts. It is by virtue of their character that the hadith are reliable."

"You're right, Nabeel," David interjected. "Mike doesn't know these people. But what he's saying is that neither do you. The sources are just too late, and we have no reliable way to test the character of the people who passed on the stories."

Mike shook his head, "No, that's not my point, though it is a valid one. What I'm saying is that even if the most honorable, well-meaning people wrote down the traditions, they're still people. Stories grow over time, especially if they are removed from the source by generations. This is especially true for stories that relate to a figure who's important for a culture's identity, like Muhammad was to the early Muslims. We just can't be sure how accurate these stories are."

David and Mike continued interacting with one another, and soon, more and more voices contributed to the conversation, often probing various points I had raised. The Christians in the room seemed more invested in the discussion, especially when challenging the prophecies of Muhammad in the Bible. They argued that I was leaving out important aspects of the verses I quoted, such as the fact that in Deuteronomy the one who would come would be an Israelite, and that the Comforter in John was identified as the Holy Spirit.

On the other hand, the agnostics and Zach were observing more than participating, but they did raise a few questions about Muhammad and science, challenging the idea that embryology or astronomy was unknowable in Muhammad's time. But I was not able to really process their points. I had been so mentally rattled by the initial line of questioning that I was on the defensive and unable to assimilate more of our conversations into my mind.

In fact, I did not change my opinion about anything that night. Only one thing mattered to me, and it mattered tremendously: I had failed to move the mind or heart of a single person toward Islam. All my gusto, preparation, and prayers had not been effective. Far from achieving my objective, I was actually going to walk away with a sense of defeat. Why was I unable to defend Muhammad, a man who needs no defense? Why could I not gain any headway in the conversations?

By the end of the evening, my friends convinced me that I had to study more carefully to learn the truth about Muhammad. What's amazing is that they did this without saying anything specific about

Muhammad's actions or character, let alone anything negative that would force me into a defensive posture.

I decided to study Muhammad from the beginning, with a critical eye toward the question, "How do we know?" We agreed that I would return to another Dream Team meeting for a second discussion about Muhammad before talking about the Quran.

But those talks never happened. What I learned about Muhammad threw more than just a few plans off course.

Chapter Thirty-Seven

THE PICTURE-PERFECT PROPHET

ALMOST EVERYTHING MUSLIMS know about Muhammad comes to them orally, rarely from primary sources. Unlike Christians learning about Jesus from the Bible, the Quran has very little to say about Muhammad. Whether in the East or the West, Muslims usually only hear stories about him. They have no concept of details that might have been accidentally distorted or intentionally altered. It comes as a surprise to most of them, as it did to me, that even the earliest records of Muhammad's life expressly admit that they have intentional alterations.

Muhammad's first biography, *Sirat Rasul Allah* by Ibn Ishaq, comes down to our day only through the transmission of a later biographer, Ibn Hisham. In his introduction, Ibn Hisham explains that he altered the story of Muhammad's life. "Things which it is disgraceful to discuss, matters which would distress certain people, and such reports as [my teacher] told me he could not accept as trustworthy—all these things I have omitted."[79]

> Even the earliest records of Muhammad's life are altered versions of previous stories that were also altered.

This shows that even the earliest records of Muhammad's life are altered versions of previous stories that were also altered.

I do not doubt that Ibn Hisham had noble intentions, but it does not change the fact that he altered Muhammad's story to make it more palatable and to remove the things he considered unbelievable. The same filtration happens with our parents and teachers when they pass on traditions about Muhammad's life.

What young Muslims learn about Muhammad is an airbrushed portrait—this blemish removed and that feature emphasized—that makes him fit a desired image. Through selective quotation, Muhammad becomes the picture-perfect prophet.

The vast body of hadith and sirah literature particularly enables this phenomenon. If a Western Muslim wants to paint a peaceful portrait of Muhammad, all they have to do is quote peaceful hadith and verses of the Quran, to the exclusion of the violent ones. If an Islamic extremist wants to mobilize his followers to acts of terrorism, he will quote the violent references, to the exclusion of the peaceful ones.[80]

This method of selective quotation is pervasive, often egregious. For example, the Quranic verse that I have seen quoted more often than any other to defend a peaceful view of Islam is 5:32. I have seen it cited on CNN, MSNBC, ABC, and innumerable dawah materials to show that the Quran discourages murder. What each of these references omitted was the first line of the verse, which makes it explicit that the prohibition of murder was directed specifically to the Jews; it was not a teaching sent to Muslims. It is the next verse that directly relates to Islam and Muslims: "the penalty for those who wage war against Allah and His Messenger and strive upon earth [to cause] corruption is none but that they be killed or crucified or that their hands and feet be cut off from opposite sides or that they be exiled from the land." Unfortunately, that verse is also ignored in the process of selective quotation.

I did not know any of this until I sought to find the truth myself. I decided to start studying Muhammad's life by getting a better hold of the available information. Once I had a grasp of the material, I would be able to determine how to best approach its historicity.

I asked David to help, and he was more than willing. He had given a speech early in his college career that extolled Muhammad as a great and influential leader, and he was eager to revisit what he had learned with a more critical eye. He promised to get back to me in the near future.

In the meantime, I decided to start by reading all the hadith I could get my hands on. Abba's library had a full copy of Sahih Bukhari, all nine volumes, so I flopped down on my stomach and began there. This is the collection that almost all Muslims consider the most historically authentic, so I expected it to paint the same picture of Muhammad that I had always known.

For the first time in my life, instead of being directed to a hadith, I was reading them with my own eyes, straight from the source. It did not take long for me to realize that the Muhammad I had come to know was a filtered version. Honestly, it took me about thirty seconds.

In the very first volume, the third hadith told the familiar story of Muhammad's first revelation in the Cave of Hira. It included the details I had learned in childhood, but there were more particulars here than I had heard before. Instead of recounting that the angel simply asked Muhammad to recite, Muhammad reports that "the angel caught me forcefully and pressed me so hard that I could not bear it anymore." Each time the angel asked Muhammad to recite, the angel "pressed" Muhammad so hard that he could not bear the pressure. After his encounters with the angel, Muhammad returned to his wife terrified, his "heart beating severely." After this, the angel did not come back for a while and "the divine inspiration paused."

This was not the picture of Muhammad I had come to know. It was raw, far less flattering. Here was an unfiltered, or at least a less-filtered, version of Muhammad. What's more, there was a cross-reference to another hadith in Sahih Bukhari that elaborated even further: 9.111. I retrieved volume nine from Abba's bookcase, found hadith 111, and read through it.

In an instant, the hadith shattered my illusion of familiarity with Muhammad. It said that when he saw Gabriel, his "neck muscles twitched in terror," and when Gabriel had gone for a while, the Prophet became so depressed "that he intended several times to throw himself from the tops of high mountains and every time he went up the top of a mountain in order to throw himself down, Gabriel would appear before him and say, 'O Muhammad! You are indeed Allah's Apostle in truth,' whereupon his heart would become quiet and he would calm down."

I was shocked motionless. Was this Sahih Bukhari really saying Muhammad contemplated suicide?

As if to emphasize, the hadith went on to say that whenever the break in inspiration became long, "he would do as before, but when he used to reach the top of a mountain, Gabriel would appear before him."

> I was shocked. Was Sahih Bukhari really saying Muhammad contemplated suicide?

I stared at the book in disbelief. Far from a noble call to prophethood, Muhammad was violently accosted by a spiritual force that terrified him, driving him to contemplate suicide on multiple occasions. And this was not just any book, this was Sahih Bukhari, the most trustworthy book of hadith.

It was then that I began to realize that I had inherited an airbrushed image of Muhammad.

Of course, the real Muhammad was not a picture. He was a historical man with a real past. That was the Muhammad I resolved to know, and if anywhere, he would be found in the pages of history. But it was as if each effort to regroup and learn more resulted in another bomb being dropped.

Chapter Thirty-Eight

VEILING THE VIOLENCE

AS I CONTINUED READING from volume 1, hadith 3, I found many hadith with teachings I had heard often, including that Muslims should avoid harming others (1.10), feed the poor and greet strangers kindly (1.11), and even follow the golden rule (1.12). No doubt, this was the loving, peaceful Islam I had always known.

But when I arrived at hadith 1.24, my jaw dropped.

In it, Muhammad says, "I have been ordered by Allah to fight against people until they testify that none has the right to be worshipped but Allah and that Muhammad is Allah's Apostle, and offer the prayers perfectly and give the obligatory charity ... then they will save their lives and property from me."

Were my eyes playing tricks on me? Muhammad was saying that he would fight people until they became Muslim or until he killed them and took their property. That was impossible! It ran counter to everything I knew about Muhammad, and it contradicted the Quran's clear statement that "there is no compulsion in religion."

I simply could not believe it, and so I hurriedly moved on to the next hadith. But 1.25 said that the greatest thing a Muslim can do after having faith is to engage in jihad. As if to clarify what kind of jihad, Sahih Bukhari clarifies, "religious fighting."

The mental dissonance was too much to bear. I could not process it, could not think, could not even get myself to move, in fact. From right where I was, flopped on my belly in Abba's library, I called out to my father for help. "Abba, I need you!" Sons do not normally summon their fathers in our culture, but Abba heard my cry and came right away. He was my father after all.

"*Kya baat hai, beyta?*" he asked while briskly approaching me, a note of concern in his voice.

"I don't know what to do with these. Look." I handed Abba the two open books, pointing to the hadiths with Muhammad's contemplation of suicide and his vow to kill or convert non-Muslims. Abba silently considered them for a short while. He tried to mask his surprise, but I could read him too well. That he had to check the cover of the books to make sure this was actually Sahih Bukhari was also a dead giveaway.

All the same, he did not betray any concern when he finally spoke. "Nabeel, there are some things that we do not understand because we are not scholars. Read the scholars' books, and it will all make sense."

"But Abba," I protested, as Abba began searching the bookcases, "if the hadith are the most trustworthy sources, those are what I'd rather read."

Abba found what he was looking for and removed a book from the shelf. "Beyta, it takes years and years to learn all this information well enough to draw appropriate conclusions. It's good that you are starting, but these scholars are farther down the road. They've asked the questions you're asking and have found the answers. It's wise to learn from their efforts instead of reinventing the wheel." He gently but firmly placed the book before me.

I surveyed its green and golden cover. It was written by a man with a Western name, Martin Lings, and its title boldly read, *Muhammad: His Life Based on the Earliest Sources*. It looked like Abba might be right; this was the kind of thing I was looking for, a story of Muhammad's life based on the earliest sources.

I thanked Abba and decided to research the author online before reading the book. I soon learned that Martin Lings was an Englishman who had studied at Oxford, a student and close friend of C. S. Lewis. But despite being steeped in Protestant English tradition, he converted to Sufi Islam.

Lings' conversion and ensuing book sent ripples of jubilation throughout the Islamic world, and he became a household name among learned Muslims. His sirah is renowned for its scholarship and held aloft as an example of Muhammad's irresistible character and truth. For me, this was a reassuring sign that critical Westerners who studied Islam with sincerity would embrace its truth.

With a surge of newfound excitement, I returned to Lings' book and flipped straight to the section about Muhammad's first revelation. My elation was short lived. Here again, I found an incomplete picture. Lings referred to Muhammad's terror, but he made no mention of suicidal thoughts. There was no reference to it at all, not even an explanation for its omission. It was as if Martin Lings did not know, or did not want us to know, that it even existed. I quickly looked for Allah's order to Muhammad to convert or kill non-Muslims, and I could not find that either.

Lings was certainly using the earliest sources to write his biography, but at the end of the day, it was still a filtered biography. It ignored the problematic traditions instead of explaining them. In that sense, this widely acclaimed scholastic account of Muhammad's life was no different from the stories my parents told me. Where was the truth? Why did no one deal with the difficulties in Muhammad's past?

As I read through Lings' book, I came across another section that challenged what I knew about Islam. Titled "The Threshold of War," the chapter seemed to say that it was the Muslims who were the first aggressors against Mecca after Muhammad had migrated to Medina. Muhammad sent eight Muslims to lie in wait for a Meccan trade caravan during the holy month. Even though this was a time of sacred truce for Arabs, the Muslims killed one man, captured two others, and plundered their goods.

Lings made every effort to exculpate the Muslims, but that did nothing to allay my growing concerns. My teachers unrelentingly had asserted that the Muslims were always the innocent ones, the victims at the receiving end of Meccan ridicule and persecution.

That is why they fled to Medina. Could it be that after Muhammad and the Muslims were finally able to live freely and peacefully, they were the ones to draw first blood?

If I had learned anything through my new insights, it was that I did not know the whole story, and modern biographers were not about to tell me the facts if it did not fit their portrait. Was Lings leaving anything out?

For the next few weeks, I began studying these matters on the internet, my online research slowly consuming me. I uncovered reams of information about Muhammad that I had never known. It seemed that each point had been brought under the microscope of anonymous online investigators who were either criticizing or defending Muhammad. The online debates were rank with rhetoric on both sides.

On the one hand, non-Muslims would criticize violent stories about Muhammad, sometimes being gracious in their conclusions but usually defaming our beloved prophet. In response, Muslims would zealously defend Muhammad either by dismissing the stories outright or providing an explanation.

Examples of dismissals are plenty. One such account is when Muhammad ordered a warrior to assassinate a mother of five, Asma bint Marwan. She was breastfeeding a child when she was murdered, her blood splattering on her children. When the assassin told Muhammad he had difficulty with what he had done, Muhammad showed no remorse.[81]

Even though this account is in the earliest biographies about Muhammad, the Muslims online pointed out that it is not in Sahih Bukhari or other trustworthy hadith. Therefore, they just dismissed it outright. As a Muslim who trusted in the limitless compassion of Muhammad, I really wanted to believe that they were right.

But sometimes the Muslims online tried to provide an explanation for a horrific event, and I just could not go along with it. For example, in the aftermath of the Battle of the Trench, Muhammad captured and beheaded over five hundred men and teenage boys from the Jewish tribe of Qurayza. After the Muslims killed the men, they sold the women and children into slavery and distributed their goods among themselves.[82]

Since this account was found in both hadith and sirah, the Muslims online could not argue that it was fabricated. They instead looked to justify Muhammad's actions, usually arguing that the Jews had been treacherous and deserved what they got.

But I could not accept these explanations. The merciful, kind Muhammad that I knew as my prophet would never order men and boys to be beheaded. He was a prophet of mercy and peace. Nor would he sell women and children into slavery. He was a defender of the rights of women and children.

I found one violent story after another about Muhammad. I consciously tried to dismiss each one, just like the Muslims online, but subconsciously, the pressure was building. How many could I dismiss? How was I going to go on like this?

For much more detail on Muhammad's character, read part 9 of No God but One, *titled "Is Muhammad a Prophet of God?"*

Chapter Thirty-Nine

MUHAMMAD RASUL ALLAH?

IN A FEW WEEKS, David got back to me with his studies on Muhammad. To say that he had been thorough would be an understatement.

We had set out to study the question, "Is Muhammad a prophet of God?" Surveying *Sirat Rasul Allah*, Sahih Bukhari, and Sahih Muslim, he found dozens of traditions that he argued stood against Muhammad's prophethood. He compiled them in a binder and handed it to me. He was pursuing the following question: "Would an objective investigator conclude that, based on Muhammad's life and character, he is a prophet of God?"

In his binder, there were a whole host of issues that I had not come across. Some of these bothered him a lot more than they bothered me. For example, Islam commands Muslims to have no more than four wives at a time, yet Muhammad had at least seven at one point. I told him that Allah had given Muhammad special permission in the Quran to have unlimited wives, so it was not really a problem.[83] He responded, "Don't you think that's suspicious? At least a little?" My knee-jerk reaction was to say it was not.

David also took serious issue with Muhammad's marriage to Aisha. According to a handful of hadiths, she was six when Muhammad married her, and he consummated the marriage with her three

years later, when he was fifty-two.[84] David argued that because of
his example young girls all across the Muslim world are forced to
marry at an age far too young for their well-being.[85] But my jamaat
taught that these hadith were inaccurate, too, so I was not bothered
by them either.

One by one, David presented additional traditions that challenged the idea of Muhammad's prophethood, each progressively
more offensive. Muhammad had been poisoned;[86] on his deathbed,
he felt as if the poison were killing him;[87] he had black magic cast on
him;[88] he revealed verses he later admitted had been from Satan;[89] he
tortured people for money;[90] he led an attack on unarmed Jews;[91] he
caused his adopted son to divorce so he could marry his daughter-in-
law Zainab;[92] he told people to drink camel's urine.[93] The list went
on and on.

At first, I tried to respond to the particulars of each tradition, but
with each additional story, it was clear I was not being objective. In
my frustration, I began studying books on hadith methodology by
acclaimed scholars, listening to scholastic lectures, and reading commentary after commentary, trying to determine how to discredit
the traditions that maligned Muhammad's character and defend the
hadith that portrayed the prophet I loved. But there was just no razor
I could use to dissect the two. None except the idea, "Muhammad
must be a prophet, and therefore these stories must be false."

But there were just too many
stories, even from reputable
sources of hadith.

Over time, they reached a critical mass, after which I just denied
the authenticity of each tradition.
It was all I could do; otherwise, I
would be overwhelmed. I began
to understand why the biographers and my teachers had all done the
same thing.

When I realized I was trying to dismiss about a hundred such
stories, I could no longer avoid a hard truth: these stories came from
sources that built the historical foundations of Islam. How much
could I dismiss without causing the foundations to crumble?

> These stories came from
> sources that built the
> historical foundations of
> Islam. How much could I
> dismiss without causing the
> foundations to crumble?

Put another way, I realized that if I kept denying the reliability of the traditions, I had no basis for calling him a prophet in the first place. I could no longer proclaim the shahada, not unless there was something else, something other than history, that could vindicate Muhammad.

There was only one way out of the dilemma: the Quran.

To read an expert contribution on the historical Muhammad by Dr. David Wood (PhD in philosophy, Fordham University), Director of Acts 17 Apologetics and host of Jesus or Muhammad, see page 339.

Part 8

THE HOLINESS
OF THE QURAN

⋯

So much that I thought I knew about the Quran simply is not true.
Is it really Your book?

Chapter-Forty

THE CASE FOR
THE QURAN

IF YOU CAN IMAGINE God's mystery and wisdom, His power, depth, and perfection, His divine mandates and prophecies, all synergistically inhabiting the physical pages of a book, vivifying it with the very essence of God, you will begin to understand how and why Muslims revere the Quran.

It should not be assumed that the Quran is the Islamic analogue of the Bible. It isn't. For Muslims, the Quran is the closest thing to an incarnation of Allah, and it is the very proof they provide to demonstrate the truth of Islam. The best parallel in Christianity is Jesus himself, the Word made flesh, and his resurrection. That is how central the Quran is to Islamic theology.[94]

It was now the foundation of my faith. The historical Muhammad, who once stood as the second pillar of my worldview, now also rested on the Quran for authentication. By the time I began scrutinizing the scripture, I was acutely sensitive to its weight.

> My life as I knew it hinged on the divine inspiration of the Quran.

The truth of Islam, everything Muhammad stood for, and my life as I knew it hinged on the divine inspiration of the Quran.

Just as when I began investigating the life of Muhammad, I was convinced the Quran would stand up to scrutiny. No one in the ummah doubted its divine inspiration. To the contrary, we knew that the Quran was so perfect and miraculous that no one would dare question it, not even secular Westerners. We considered our arguments incontrovertible.

The boldest argument for the divine inspiration of the Quran was its inimitability, primarily its literary excellence. "No one can emulate its eloquence," other Muslims would say alongside me. Our argument stemmed from the Quran itself. When people in Muhammad's day accused him of forging the Quran, the Quran responded multiple times that doubters should try writing something like it.[95] When they tried, even if they had help from men and jinn, they fell short.

> Its inimitability is the only defense the Quran provides for itself, yet here was a book that effectively responded to the challenge.

This is the challenge of the Quran: no one can produce anything that rivals it.

Having read these challenges in the Quran from childhood, and given that my worldview was forged by teachers who continually proclaimed the Quran was preeminent in its beauty, I and most Muslims like me were more than confident that the Quran was truly unmatchable.

Imagine my incredulity when I discovered an answer to the Quran's challenge, *Al-Furqan al-Haqq*. Translated "the true measure of discernment," it is a book that responds to the challenge of the Quran by writing Christian teachings in Quranic style.[96] This book apparently reproduced the Quranic style so effectively that some who recited it aloud in public areas were thanked by Arab Muslims for having recited the Quran itself.

Its inimitability is the only defense the Quran provides for itself, yet here was a book that effectively responded to the challenge. This news was explosive.

I was not the only one to consider *Al-Furqan al-Haqq* dangerous. At least one nation has "for the maintenance of security ..., hereby absolutely prohibit[ed] import of the book ... including any extract there from, any reprint or translation thereof or any document reproducing any matter contained therein."[97]

My faith in the Quran was such that, in my view, it was impossible for its challenge to have been answered. I concluded that the challenge must actually mean something else. I did my best to ignore the difficulty, marshaling additional arguments.

Muslim apologists do not limit themselves to the Quran's own defense of its inspiration. The four other arguments they most commonly appeal to are these: fulfilled prophecies, mathematical patterns, scientific truths, and textual preservation. I set out to examine each of them, not to see whether they were reliable but rather to build my positive case for Islam, to make the truth of Islam as obvious to the objective investigator as it is to the ummah. As it was to me.

The first two arguments fell very quickly. There are no compelling prophecies in the Quran. There are many verses that can be construed as prophecies, but the Quran does not assert that they are in any way predictions of the future. Regardless of details, they certainly were not clear enough for me to build a strong, objective case.

Similarly, I could not accept the argument that mathematical patterns in the Quran were an indication of divine inspiration. Many purported patterns were simply fudged data, and the rest were of the kind that can be found in the Bible, in the works of Edgar Allan Poe, and even in online message boards.

Thankfully, those two arguments had not been a foundational part of my worldview as I was growing up. The final two arguments held powerful sway over my regard for the Quran, however. I believed from childhood that the Quran contained advanced scientific truths that Muhammad could not have known without divine revelation. These scientific truths were enough to prove that God wrote the Quran.

Trumping even the scientific argument, most Muslims have faith in the Quran's perfect preservation. Muslims believe none of it has been changed, not even a dot. Allah promises to guard the Quran in 15:9, and Muslims believe its preservation is a testament to Allah's protection over His message.

The science argument, and especially the perfect preservation of the Quran, formed the keystone of my faith. I set out to scrutinize this keystone, trusting it to bear the weight of the case for the Quran, indeed to provide the entire basis for my faith.

All the while, I did my best not to be bothered by the niggling question, "What will happen if this keystone fails?" I let the question instead drive me to my knees in prayer, asking Allah to make me a vanguard for Islam. I further embraced Islamic culture, embodied the Muslim persona by leading Friday sermons when possible, and taught sessions on aqeedah. By doing so, I did my best to resolve the dissonance by aspiring to the highest of Muslim standards.

The two opposing forces meant that, should the foundation fail, the collapse would be colossal.

Chapter Forty-One

THE QURAN, SCIENCE, AND BUCAILLEISM

DAWAH HAS BEEN A DRIVING FORCE for Muslims since the time of Muhammad, but the twentieth century saw the Islamic ethos of proselytization powered by an unexpected fuel: modern science. Even more surprising, this vogue came at the hands of a secular Frenchman.

Maurice Bucaille, gastroenterologist and personal physician to a king of Saudi Arabia, fertilized a budding field of Islamic apologetics when he wrote his 1976 work, *The Bible, The Quran, and Science*. This seminal work argues that the Bible is rife with scientific errors, while the Quran stands in contradistinction as miraculously precocious and flawless. He concludes that the Quran is so scientifically advanced that it must be the work of God.

"Epochal" only approximates the book's impact on Muslim proselytism. Much like the Martin Lings phenomenon, a Western intellectual siding with Islam after critically scrutinizing evidence served as a war cry for dawah-oriented Muslims. This scenario was all the more gratifying because Bucaille roundly denounced the Bible in the process.

The technique of referring to the Quran for miraculously advanced scientific truths soon became so commonplace that a term for the method was coined: **Bucailleism**.

An example of one such argument involves the subject of human reproduction. Bucaille declares, "The Quranic description of certain stages in the development of the embryo corresponds exactly to what we today know about it, and the Quran does not contain a single statement that is open to criticism from modern science."[98] The implication is obvious: only God knew anything about embryology when the Quran was revealed. Thus, God must be the author of the Quran.

> **Bucailleism**: The technique of referring to the Quran for miraculously advanced scientific truths in order to defend its divine origin

Within a few years of publication, Bucaille's arguments perfused the more apologetically minded Muslim world, which was the world I was born into. His arguments were a staple of our religious discussions, whether eating around the dinner table, visiting with guests, or reading a book written by jamaat leaders. We were swept up in the elegance and erudition of the arguments, and just like most of what I knew as a Muslim, the fulsome and unanimous reception of Bucailleism was a part of our culture.

We were convinced science confirmed the divine origin of the Quran. This was such a widely held point of pride among Muslims that no one tested it.

When I finally did test it, another foundational pillar of my worldview cracked. I pored over Bucaille's arguments as a student of both medicine and religion. I saw many problems with his exegesis, his reasoning, and his scholarship.

> We were convinced science confirmed the divine origin of the Quran. This was a widely held point of pride among Muslims.

Turning back to his assessment of human reproduction, most academicians would consider Bucaille's unreserved praise as too unctuous to be scholarly, at least by Western standards. But quite apart from his fawning adulation, there are scientific problems with the very Quranic verses Bucaille quotes as miraculous, some rather obvious to physicians and others rather obvious to everyone.

For example, 23:13–14 reads, "Then we made him a sperm in a fixed lodging. Then we made the sperm a hanging (thing), then we made the hanging into a chewed (thing), then we made the chewed into bones, then we clothed the bones with flesh, then we developed it into another creation, so blessed be Allah, the best of creators."

To a student of developmental biology, this verse is singularly unimpressive. Even Bucaille begins his assessment by remarking that, at face value, the scientific statements are "totally unacceptable to scientists specializing in this field."[99] However, he explains that the problem is the seventh-century vocabulary the Quran was forced to use. Once we substitute modern scientific vocabulary (such as "uterus" for "lodging"), the problems are more than resolved.[100]

As a Muslim who grew up with somewhat fluid interpretations of the Quran, I conceded Bucaille's point. But as a student of medicine, I realized that no matter how much we substituted the words, one aspect of this verse was simply inaccurate. The verse explains the sequential development of an embryo, but the sequence is incorrect. An embryo does not first become bones to be later clothed with flesh. One layer of an embryo, the mesoderm, differentiates into bone and flesh at the same time.

I investigated responses to this critique. Most argued that it is a pedantic objection, but even as a Muslim, I disagreed. The very point Bucaille was making by referring to this verse is that the sequence of embryonic development is miraculously accurate; but the sequence is incorrect. This was serious, and though Bucaille treated this verse with some depth, he glossed over the difficulty.

That this inaccuracy is found in the clearest section of the verse, the easiest to understand, only compounds the problem. The first part of the verse requires us to substitute appropriate scientific concepts for the incorrect terms captured by the Arabic. So if we have to fix the first half of the statement and ignore the latter half, what is left to be scientifically miraculous?

I then realized that this verse could not defend the inspiration of the Quran. Far from it, we had to assume the inspiration of the Quran to defend this verse.

More obvious problems arose in the Quran as I continued my search, even in the subfield of human reproduction. Verses 86:6–7 state that sperm gushes "from between the backbone and the ribs."

Believing that it was impossible for the Quran to say something so obviously incorrect, I began looking online for answers. Once again, I found a similar procedure to defend the verse: redefine the words and gloss over the difficulties.

And that was the pattern that emerged. Whether proclaiming scientific miracles or defending scientific inaccuracies, the protocol always called for redefining the clear statements of the Quran to say something they did not say and then glossing over any strain.

After I recognized the pattern, it struck me that Bucailleism was very much like studying the life of Muhammad. I could defend my Islamic beliefs if I approached the issue as a partisan Muslim, willing to redefine certain terms and emphasize certain points in favor of my position. But if I tried to build a case as an objective investigator reading the text at face value, there simply was no scientifically miraculous knowledge in the Quran.

At that point, I did not dismiss the possibility of scientific knowledge in the Quran, but I concluded that something far stronger had to anchor a defense of its divine inspiration. With unrelenting confidence, I now turned to the deepest of all my roots: my faith in the perfect preservation of the Quranic text.

Chapter Forty-Two

HADITH AND THE HISTORY OF THE QURAN

AT LEAST TWO POWERFUL FORCES combine to make the perfect textual preservation of the Quran the bastion of Muslim confidence.

On the one hand, much like the other proclamations of Islamic pride, it is a ubiquitous axiom that becomes ingrained in the Muslim psyche. "At no point has anything in the Quran ever been changed. It comes down to us exactly as Muhammad received it from Gabriel." In this, we are told, is a prophecy of the Quran fulfilled: "Surely We have revealed the Reminder [Quran] and We will most surely be its guardian" (15:9).

On the other hand, this belief in perfect textual preservation also forms the very basis for the condemnation of modern Judaism and Christianity. One of the most well-known dawah initiatives in the United States, called "Why Islam?" summarizes the sentiment well: "The Psalms, the Torah, and the Gospel, according to Islam, are no longer in their original state. They have been added to, cannot be traced directly to their prophets, or were simply altered. Only the Quran has been preserved in its original state, exactly as it was revealed to Prophet Muhammad."[101]

Serving as a basis for the rejection of other faiths and the acceptance of Islam, the preservation of the Quran is critical to Islamic apologetics. But it is even more important to Islamic theology. The Quran is the cornerstone of the Islamic worldview, underlies all of sharia, serves as the fulcrum of daily devotions, and provides the source of Islamic identity. In the minds of most Muslims, if the Quran were not perfectly preserved, their world would be in jeopardy. Since that is not the case, they maintain the utmost confidence in their faith.

Thus, the preservation of the Quran undergirds the unparalleled confidence of the modern Muslim zeitgeist. It is not even a remote possibility in most Muslims' minds that the Quran of today might be different from the Quran of Muhammad's day.

But most Muslims have not read the hadith for themselves. Once again, it was the most trustworthy Islamic traditions that subverted my faith.

Volume 6 of Sahih Bukhari, a volume dedicated to the Quran, details the process of Quran's collection in book 61.[102] We find that Muhammad used to dictate the Quran to Muslims orally, not having first written it down. It came to Muslims a few verses at a time, and sometimes Muhammad would relay the same verse differently to different Muslims.

Because of this, people recited the Quran disparately enough even in Muhammad's time that there were heated, accusatory arguments among pious Muslims over what constituted the real Quran. Since Muhammad was still around, he dispelled the arguments by addressing the parties directly, saying, "Both of you are reciting in a correct way, so carry on reciting." He admonished them not to argue over their differences, since "the nations which were before you were destroyed because they differed."

Once again, it was the most trustworthy Islamic traditions that subverted my faith. This time, it was my faith in the Quran.

When Muhammad died, many people no longer felt the need to remain Muslim. Abu Bakr sent Muslims to fight the apostates, ordering them to fulfill their Islamic obligations.[103] Muslim fought former Muslim until many who had known the Quran lost their lives in battle. Abu Bakr was worried that large parts of the Quran would be lost if the battles continued, so he officially ordered the Quran to be collected under the auspices of one Zaid ibn Thabit.

Sahih Bukhari emphasizes that the Muslims easily forgot Quranic verses, and Zaid found the task of collecting the Quran extremely burdensome. He collected the verses from people's memories and from written fragments. On more than one occasion, only a single person was able to testify to some of the Quran's verses. After Zaid finished, the Quran was ultimately given to one of Muhammad's widows to safeguard.

Even though the primary purpose for this collection was that verses not be lost, it was discovered that Zaid had accidentally left a small portion out of the Quran. Moreover, regions of the Muslim world were reciting the Quran incongruously enough that an appeal was made to the Muslim leaders to "save this nation before it differs about the Quran."

Breaking from the preference of Muhammad, who simply told his people not to focus on the differences, the khalifa Uthman ordered that the Quran be standardized. They recalled the previous copy from Muhammad's widow, edited it, copied it, and distributed the copies to each Muslim province.

Then, to settle the disputes over the Quran once and for all, Uthman "ordered that all the other Quranic materials, whether written in fragmentary manuscripts or whole copies, be destroyed by fire."

This was the story of the Quran's collection as found in Sahih Bukhari. Like the life of Muhammad, Sahih Bukhari depicted a raw, much more realistic story than what Muslims generally teach one another. What I had been taught was that Muhammad would dictate the Quran to scribes while Muslims memorized the revelations, and after Muhammad died, many Muslims had the Quran written and memorized. Zaid ibn Thabit was the first to officially write down the Quran, though this was not a difficult task because he had it memorized. His Quran was confirmed by other leading Muslims, who also had the Quran memorized.

That was it. According to widely accepted knowledge, there were no arguments over its contents, no poor memories, no fear of lost passages, no solitary witnesses, no forgotten verses, and certainly no orchestrated destruction of variants. The process of collecting the Quran recorded in Sahih Bukhari was so choppy that it left the door wide open for lost sections of the Quran. In fact, Sahih Bukhari testifies to this.

When Zaid's standardized Quran was distributed, it left out some sections that a man named Ubay ibn Ka'b used to recite.

> The process of collecting the Quran recorded in hadith was so choppy that it left the door wide open for lost sections.

Ubay insisted that, regardless of Zaid's Quran, he would not stop reciting those verses because he had heard them from Muhammad himself.

I was shocked by the testimony of Sahih Bukhari. Why had my teachers not taught me the whole story? What else did I not know?

I turned to other books of hadith for their story. Sahih Muslim, the next most trustworthy source, records more problems. It documents that a whole surah is no longer found in the Quran, and at least one verse went missing around the time of Muhammad's death.[104] Sunan ibn Majah, one of the next most authentic books, clarifies that the verse went missing because the paper on which it was written was eaten by a goat.[105]

As I continued my research, tradition after tradition kept cropping up that challenged the preservation of the Quran. Much like my incredulity when I studied the historical Muhammad, I simply would not assimilate these hadith into my mind, keeping them at bay by accepting the far-fetched explanations of Muslim apologists or by inventing some of my own. What finally pushed me over the edge, though, was when I revisited a hadith from Sahih Bukhari.

According to the hadith, Muhammad named four men as the best teachers of the Quran. The first one was Abdullah ibn Mas'ud, whom Muhammad distinguished as the foremost expert of the Quran. The last one was Ubay ibn Ka'b, whom Sahih Bukhari identifies as the best reciter of the Quran.

These were the men that Muhammad hand selected as the best teachers of the Quran, but as I studied the early sources, I found that they did not agree with the final Quran, which has been passed down as today's version. They did not even agree with each other.

In addition to the previously quoted hadith in which he refused to stop reciting certain verses, Ubay is known to have had 116 chapters in his Quran, two more than Zaid's edition. Ibn Mas'ud had only 111 chapters in his Quran, insisting that the additional chapters in Zaid's Quran and Ubay's Quran were just prayers, not Quranic recitation.[106]

> Multiple recitations of the same verse, missing verses, missing surahs, disputes over the canon, controlled destruction of all variants — how could we defend the Quran as perfectly preserved?

Multiple early Muslims documented the differences between the many Qurans of the early Muslim world. Though it was thought that all of those documents were destroyed, one resurfaced in the early twentieth century.[107] It shows that, in many places, Abdullah ibn Mas'ud and Ubay ibn Ka'b agreed with one another where Zaid ibn Thabit's Quran differed.

I added up all the pieces in my mind: multiple recitations of the same verse, missing verses, missing surahs, disputes over the canon, controlled destruction of all variants. How could we defend the Quran as perfectly preserved?

I researched defenses online and read the most scholarly Islamic books I could find. As usual, attempts were made to dismiss as many of the sources as possible. Even still, after all attempts at logical explanation were made, the Muslim scholars argued for a shocking position: Allah intended the lost sections to be lost, He intended the variants to be destroyed, and He intended Zaid's edition to be the final Quran.

> The doctrine of the Quran's perfect preservation, far from defending the faith, needed to be defended by faith.

So, in truth, the scholars were not arguing that the Quran had remained unchanged. They were arguing that Allah intended all the many changes that came to it. That was a defensive position at best, not one that could bear the weight of the entire Islamic case.

I was forced to conclude that, once again, the early Islamic sources challenged what modern Islam taught me. The doctrine of the Quran's perfect preservation, far from defending the faith, needed to be defended by faith.

With that final investigation, the keystone of my faith crumbled. The entire structure was ungrounded, poised to collapse at the slightest burden.

What came next might as well have been dynamite.

*For much more detail on the inspiration of the
Quran, read part 10 of No God but One,
titled "Is the Quran the Word of God?"*

Chapter Forty-Three

THOSE WHOM THEIR RIGHT HANDS POSSESS

I HAD READ THE WORDS multiple times since childhood, never really stopping to consider what they meant. But David had just added it to his binder, and now I was forced to research it.

"Those whom your right hands possess" was a phrase found in multiple Quran verses. The three references David included were 4:24, 23:6, and 70:30, none of which made much sense at first blush.

> 4:24: "Forbidden for you are women already married, except such as your right hands possess. Allah has enjoined this on you."
>
> 23:6: "(Successful indeed are those believers who guard their private parts) except from their wives or those whom their right hands possess."
>
> 70:30: "(Worshipers guard their private parts) except from their wives and from those whom their right hands possess; such indeed, are not to blame."

I took the verses to Ammi and asked what the phrase meant. She said it referred to the female servants that Muslim men had married, but that didn't fit. In the verses, wives were clearly separate from those whom the right hands possessed. When I pushed back on her interpretation, she deferred to scholars in the jamaat. I left Ammi, agreeing to ask them when the next opportunity would arise.

In the meantime, I knew I had to research this on my own. The scholars had not been comprehensive before, and I had no reason to think they would be now.

Of course, David had given me his interpretation, but I knew it was wrong. It had to be wrong. He was arguing that "those whom the right hands possessed" were slave women, captured by Muslim conquerors. According to him, 23:6 and 70:30 meant Muslim men could have intercourse with slave women that had been captured as spoils of war. Not stopping there, he argued that 4:24 annulled the marriages of captive women so Muslims could have intercourse with them even if their husbands were still alive.

The mere suggestion was outrageous. He was implying that the Quran condoned rape. What else would it be? If a woman is captured in battle, her father, husband, brother, or son probably just died trying to protect her. Would such a woman willingly engage in intercourse with a warrior who had just slaughtered the men she loved?

That was not the Islam I knew, astaghfirullah! My Muhammad was a liberator of slaves and a commander of saints, not a conquering captor leading an army of rapists. Islam would not allow such an atrocity. It could not. Even though I had learned much over the previous few months that challenged everything I knew, this was in a different league entirely. David was accusing Muhammad of being a moral monster, insinuating that Islam was unconscionably cruel.

During the course of our conversations, I lashed out at David, rebuking him for trying to drag my prophet through the mud. This was lower than low. At first, he fought back, pointing to the Islamic traditions, but when he saw that each defense he provided galled me all the more, he pulled back. He left the issue alone, asking me to just consider why I was so offended and what the Quran was really teaching.

It was when I was alone, when I did not have to defend my faith or my prophet, that I was able to be honest with myself and look at the evidence anew.

> The mere suggestion was outrageous. He was implying that the Quran condoned rape, but the Islam I knew would not allow such an atrocity.

Sahih Muslim gave the historical context for the revelation of 4:24. The hadith reads: "At the Battle of Hunain, Allah's Messenger sent an army to Autas and fought with the enemy. Having over-come them and taken them captives, the Companions of Allah's Messenger seemed to refrain from having intercourse with captive women because of their polytheist husbands. Then Allah Most High sent down the verse '(forbidden for you are) women already married, except those whom your right hands possess (Quran 4:24).' "[108]

I read and reread the hadith. There was no question that this hadith corroborated David's argument. In fact, it appeared David had been gentle. The hadith says this verse not only allowed warriors to have intercourse with recently captured women, it emboldened the men to do so when they were hesitant.

I could not believe what I was reading. My world felt as if it was spinning beneath my feet. I immediately did what I had seen sheikhs and imams do: I concluded the hadith must be weak. A single hadith, even if in Sahih Muslim, is easy to dismiss.

But there it was again in Sunan Abu Daud, which actually pro-vided even more detail. The Muslim warriors were hesitant to have sex with the women because their husbands were still alive and in their presence.[109] One classical commentary explained that when 4:24 was revealed, the men proceeded to have sex with the women, despite their husbands' presence.[110]

Sahih Bukhari contains a similar hadith. It also describes Muslim warriors who were hesitant to sexually engage their captive women but for a different reason: the warriors were worried about getting the women pregnant. Muhammad allayed their concerns, telling them that it was Allah's choice whether the women get pregnant or not.[111] Sahih Muslim adds to this hadith, saying that the Mus-lim warriors did not want to get the women pregnant because they planned on selling them.[112]

That was enough. Not only was David right about the meaning of "those whom their right hands possess" but the truth was inescap-able. It was in the Quran, in Sahih Bukhari, in Sahih Muslim, in Sunan Abu Daud, in commentaries; it was everywhere.

How could it be possible? The Quran allowed men to have inter-course with women whose lives had just been destroyed, sometimes in the presence of their captive husbands? Allah and Muhammad both showed no concern for getting the women pregnant or later selling them into slavery? How could it be possible?

What if it were my people who had been conquered by Muslims? What if I fought to protect my family, only to see Abba killed? To see Baji and Ammi ...

That was more than enough. I was done. I could not think about it any longer. It was revolting, and thinking about it would cause me to despise my prophet and my faith.

I would not allow myself to despise them, but I could find no way to excuse them either. So I was done. I was done fighting.

I was finally broken.

To read an expert contribution on the New Testament and the Quran by Dr. Keith Small, a Quranic manuscript consultant to the Bodleian Library at Oxford University and author of Textual Criticism and Quran Manuscripts, *see page 344.*

Part 9

FAITH IN DOUBT

⋮

I don't know who You are anymore,
but I know that You are all that matters.

Chapter Forty-Four

RATIONALITY AND REVELATION

FOR THREE YEARS, we had wrestled with one another intellectually, and what started in the first month of my freshman year finally came to a head the day before graduation. I was giving up.

But not on Islam. Not yet. I was giving up on reason.

We sat in the front seats of my car, having just returned from an award ceremony. Out of a graduating class of thousands, six students were selected to receive ODU's highest recognition, Kaufman Honors, based on grades, leadership, and community service. David and I were two of the six. This award signified the culmination of my college career.

But it sat heedlessly tossed in the back seat.

I didn't care about it. I couldn't get myself to care about much of anything. I had lived my whole life with a vibrant confidence. Islam, my beliefs, my family, my words, and my actions, all converged into one point: me. I had been authentic and transparent, able to speak my mind and live my beliefs freely and fully.

> I was giving up. But not on Islam. Not yet. I was giving up on reason.

But now? Now I was a shell, outwardly steadfast in Islam while inwardly a torrent of confusion. The honor-shame paradigm hindered me from sharing my inner turmoil, rendering me unable to

speak to friends or family about my struggle without further desta-
bilizing my life.

I did not know who God was, I did not know what the world
was, I did not know who I was, and I had no idea what to do. I was
in a maelstrom, flailing for some-
thing to hold on to. I made a final,
desperate effort to lay hold of the
life I had always lived.

"There's no way I can accept
the Christian message, David."

I kept my eyes glued to the steering wheel while David stared at
nothing in particular through the passenger window. He gave me
space to speak.

"The Christian God demands that I proclaim a fact," I continued.
"He demands that I believe Jesus is Lord. But I wasn't there, so I can't
know whether he claimed to be God. I'm Muslim; I've always seen
the world as a Muslim. My perception is colored in such a way that,
even if Jesus were God, I probably wouldn't be able to know it. How
can God hold me eternally accountable for not grasping a finite fact,
one which I have no access to in the first place?"

This was my last-ditch effort to maintain my Islamic faith: denying my ability to arrive at objective truth.

David continued staring into the distance, considering my
words carefully. When he finally spoke, his words cut to the quick.
"Nabeel, you know that's not true. Your parents see dreams, and
God has directed you with supernatural signs in the sky. You know
full well that if you ask Him to reveal the truth to you, He will."

As soon as David spoke, I
knew he was right. It was as if his
words resonated a raw nerve, one
that had only just been aired. If I
truly believed God existed, why
did I not simply ask Him who He
is? Could He not reveal that truth
to me?

It was then that I realized the value of apologetics and what the
arguments had done for me. All my life, barriers had been erected

that kept me from humbly approaching God and asking Him to reveal Himself to me. The arguments and apologetics tore down those barriers, positioning me to make a decision to pursue God or not.

The work of my intellect was done. It had opened the way to His altar, but I had to decide whether I would approach it. If I did, and if I really wanted to know God, I had to cast myself upon His mercy and love, relying completely upon Him and His willingness to reveal Himself to me.

But at what cost?

Chapter Forty-Five

THE COST OF EMBRACING THE CROSS

THE COST FOR A MUSLIM to accept the gospel can be tremendous.

Of course, following Jesus meant that I would immediately be ostracized from my community. For all devout Muslims, it means sacrificing the friendships and social connections that they have built from childhood. It could mean being rejected by one's parents, siblings, spouse, and children.

This becomes exponentially more difficult if the Muslim has no person to turn to after following Jesus, no Christian who has reached out. I know of many Muslim women who recognize their need for Jesus but have nowhere to turn if their husbands abandon them, or worse. They often do not have the financial means to survive the next day, let alone fight for their children in court. They would have to do all this while reeling from an emotionally violent expulsion from their extended families.

What many do not realize—what I did not realize when I was making these decisions—is that these costs are not considered consciously. They form part of the knee-jerk reaction against the gospel. I never said, "I choose to remain Muslim because it would cost my family if I were to follow Jesus." Far from it, I subconsciously found ways and means to go on rejecting the gospel so I would not be faced with what I would have to pay.

But I was not the only one who would have to pay for my decision. If there were traits my family was known for in the Muslim community, they were my parents' joyfulness, our close-knit relationships, and the honor we had garnered by faithfully following Islam. My choice to follow Jesus meant razing all three.

My decision would shame my family with incredible dishonor. Even if I were right about Jesus, could I do such a terrible thing to my family? After everything they had done for me?

It is this kind of familial dishonor that drives many in the Middle East to commit honor killings. Although there is no command in the Quran or hadith to carry out "honor killings," there are commands in the Quran to kill mischief makers,[113] as well as plenty of commands in the hadith to kill apostates.[114]

These kinds of killings are not limited to the Middle East. A few months after graduation, I received a phone call from Mike telling me about an entire family of Middle Eastern Christians who had just been slaughtered in New Jersey for bringing dishonor to Islam. He asked me if I thought I'd be safe were I to accept Jesus. I appreciated his concern, but I told him that was the least of my worries. My family would never do such a thing, and in reality, the killings are not as common as some fear. Besides, in my view, martyrdom would be an honor.

The greatest concern for me, were I to accept Jesus as Lord, was that I might be wrong. What if Jesus is not God? I'd be worshiping a human. That would incur the wrath of Allah, and more than anything else, it would secure my abode in hell.

Shirk: The unforgivable sin in Islam; it is roughly equivalent to idolatry, placing something or someone in the position due to Allah

Of course, that is exactly what the Quran teaches. In Islam, there is only one unforgivable sin, *shirk*, the belief that someone other than Allah is God. Shirk is specifically discussed in the context of Jesus in 5:72. He who believes

Jesus is God, "Allah has forbidden Heaven for him, and his abode will be the Hellfire."

These are the costs Muslims must calculate when considering the gospel: losing the relationships they have built in this life, potentially losing this life itself, and if they are wrong, losing their afterlife in paradise. It is no understatement to say that Muslims often risk everything to embrace the cross.

But then again, it is the cross. There is a reason Jesus said, "Whoever wants to be my disciple must deny themselves and take up their cross and follow me. For whoever wants to save their life will lose it, but whoever loses their life for me and for the gospel will save it" (Mark 8:34–35).

Would it be worth it to pick up my cross and be crucified next to Jesus? If He is not God, then, no. Lose everything I love to worship a false God? A million times over, no!

But if He is God, then, yes. Being forever bonded to my Lord by suffering alongside Him? A million times over, yes!

Now more than ever, the stakes were clear, and I needed to know who He was. Everything hinged on His identity. I began begging Him to reveal Himself. Standing, walking, praying, lying in bed, I implored Him to show me His truth. Because He had supernaturally guided me before, I had full faith that He would guide me once again.

But the interim was agonizing. I traveled from mosque to mosque, asking imams and scholars to help me with my struggles. None came close to vindicating either Muhammad or the Quran, all of them selectively denying traditions that were problematic and cherry-picking traditions that fit their views. They did not help.

Muslims often risk everything to embrace the cross.

While waiting to speak with them, I read book after book from Muslim scholars on hadith methodology, sirah, and Quranic history until my eyes were scorched. Then my eyes would flood with tears during salaat, while I pleaded with God for His mercy.

Chapter Forty-Six

I AM NEAR, SEEK
AND YOU SHALL FIND

I LAY PROSTRATE in a large Muslim prayer hall, broken before God. The edifice of my worldview, all I had ever known, had slowly been dismantled over the past few years. I lay in ruin, petitioning Allah. Tears blurred my sight. The ritual prayers had ended, and now it was time for my heart's prayer.

"Please, God Almighty, tell me who You are! I beseech You and only You. Only You can rescue me. At Your feet, I lay down everything I have learned, and I give my entire life to You. Take away what You will, be it my joy, my friends, my family, or even my life. But let me have You, O God.

"Light the path that I must walk. I don't care how many hurdles are in the way, how many pits I must jump over or climb out of, or how many thorns I must step through. Guide me on the right path. If it is Islam, show me how it is true. If it is Christianity, give me eyes to see. Just show me which path is Yours, dear God, so I can walk it.

"Dear God, I know You can hear me! I know You are there and my words are not falling on deaf ears. Do not withhold Yourself from me. You have guided me with visions before. You have revealed the future to my father in dreams. Please, show me Your truth. Give me a vision again; give me dreams so I can know who You are."

I knew with utmost surety that God heard my cries and held

the key to saving me. He would open the door to His truth at any moment. I knew that the case for Christianity was strong: it had been shown to me that the historical Jesus claimed to be God and then proved it by dying on the cross and rising from the dead. If Allah confirmed to me personally that He was actually the God of the Bible, I would accept Him, Jesus, as my Lord. In anguish, though, I hoped beyond hope that Allah would reveal Himself to be the God of Islam. The cost would be too much to bear otherwise.

> If Allah confirmed to me personally that He was actually the God of the Bible, I would accept Him, Jesus, as my Lord.

Every day, in every prayer, I clung to two verses:

- Surah 2:186 — "When my servants ask about me, I am near. I answer their prayers when they pray to me. So let them hear my call and believe in me, that they may walk in the right way."
- Matthew 7:7–8 — "Ask and it will be given to you; seek and you will find; knock and the door will be opened to you. For everyone who asks receives; the one who seeks finds; and to the one who knocks, the door will be opened."

Because of these verses, I had full faith that God — whether Allah or Jesus, whether the God of the Quran or the God of the Bible — would answer the prayers of my heart. The question was when and whether I could brave the storm until then.

Five months later, He gave me my answer.

Chapter Forty-Seven

A FIELD
OF CROSSES

ON DECEMBER 19, 2004, Abba and I were in Orlando, Florida. I had just finished my first semester of medical school, having once again chosen the school closest to home so I could be with my family. Ammi and Abba saw me diligently studying the whole semester and wanted to reward me, so when Abba needed to go to Florida for a conference during my winter break, he invited me to come with him. I gladly obliged, not only because it was my first opportunity to go to Florida but also because it would be the first time Abba and I would go on a trip by ourselves.

We had a fantastic time traveling to Orlando, cracking jokes and sharing stories. I recounted our antics in the anatomy lab, and he shared humorous accounts of his early years in the navy when he worked as a medic. Except for in the airport security line, when we were under the post–9/11 microscope, we goofed off the whole way to Florida. We were forging a new aspect of our relationship: a father-son friendship.

That night in the hotel room, after Abba and I prayed isha salaat together, we discussed our plans for the next morning while getting into our beds.

"Billoo, you can sleep late tomorrow and then relax in the hotel. I have to go to a meeting first thing in the morning. When I finish in the afternoon, we'll go to Epcot together."

"I've got an idea, Abba. How about I drop you off so I can have the rental car? That way, I can go to Epcot when it opens, and then you can join me there."

"Okay, but you'll need to get up first thing in the morning to drop me off."

"That's not a problem, Abba."

"Challo, beyta. Recite: *Allahuma bismika amutu wa ahya*."[115]

This was the nightly prayer that Abba had me recite whenever he tucked me in from the time I was three years old. Kids will always be kids to their parents.

I recited it and kissed him on the cheek. "I love you, Abba."

"Of course you do; you're my son." That was Abba's way of saying, "I love you too." With that, he turned the lights off.

It was dark in the room, but enough light poured in from around the curtains that I could make out the objects in the room. The day had been filled with laughter and joy, but my mind and heart were in a constant underlying state of perturbation. When the lights went off in Florida, just like every night in Virginia, my mind was immediately flooded with a longing for the truth about God.

As soon as I was sure Abba was fast asleep, I got out from under the comforters and crept to the edge of my bed. The precariousness of my fate manifested itself in my mind. Tearfully, I contended with God, pleading once again that He would reveal Himself. I admitted that, despite all I thought I knew, I actually knew nothing. I needed God to show me the truth. I couldn't do it without His help, and I could not take the uncertainty much longer. It was quite probably the most humble moment of my life, and I begged Him desperately for a dream or a vision.

At that instant, the room went pitch dark. I looked out into the blackness before me. Where there had been a wall just a few feet from my bed, the wall was no longer. What I saw instead was a field with hundreds of crosses. They were glowing, in bright contrast to the darkness around them.

The tears ceased. My body was paralyzed, and time stood still. I panned over the crosses, but they were beyond number. And just as quickly as it had come, the vision was gone. I was back in the hotel room, at the edge of my bed.

In stunned silence, I considered what I had just seen. After a few moments, I looked up toward the heavens and said, "God, that doesn't count!"

One side of my mind was asking, "Did God just reveal Himself to me? Did He finally answer my prayers? I saw a field of crosses. That must mean He wants me to accept the gospel."

But the other side played devil's advocate, arguing, "Nabeel, if you're wrong about this, Allah will send you to hell forever. This could be Satan trying to confuse you because you have been flirting with shirk, the polytheism of Christianity."

And, somewhere in my mind, the more rationalist side of me thought, "Maybe you're just jet lagged and seeing things. Do you really want to make the biggest decision of your life based on one sleepy, emotional moment? Are you ready to give up everything for this?"

I turned toward Abba, who was softly snoring on his side of the room. I finally concluded to myself, "No, I can't give him up just based on this. God will understand. I need more."

I returned to God, shamed but emboldened. I prayed, "God, that doesn't count! I don't know if that was really what I thought it was. I could subconsciously want to become a Christian, and my mind could be deceiving me. So, I'm sorry I asked for a vision. Please give me a dream, and if the dream confirms the vision, I will become Christian."

Perhaps I was subconsciously trying to stall the inevitable, but God would not allow it. He gave me a dream that very night.

To read an expert contribution on belief and doubt by Dr. Gary Habermas, Distinguished Research Professor and chair of the Department of Philosophy and Theology at Liberty University, see page 347.

Part 10

GUIDED BY THE HAND OF GOD

---·:·---

Give me eyes to see. Just show me which path is Yours, dear God, so I can walk it.

Chapter Forty-Eight

DECIPHERING DREAMS

IT WAS STILL DARK when I dropped Abba off at his meeting. There was some time before Epcot opened, so I decided to go back to the hotel and sleep. A few hours later, my eyes shot open, heart pounding.

God had given me a dream. And I had no idea what it meant.

The quality of this dream was unlike any I had ever experienced. Even while in the dream, I had an awareness that this was a message from God. I don't know how; I just knew. But the dream was cryptic, full of symbols I did not understand.

> Even while in the dream, I had an awareness that this was a message from God.

After waking, I remembered the dream with crystal clarity and none of the vague fuzziness that accompanies my other dreams. Though it was emblazoned on my mind, I did not know how long I would remember it, so I wrote everything down, my mind still reeling from this apparent revelation. This is what I wrote that day:

> In the beginning of the dream there was a poisonous snake with red and black bands going around it, separated by thin white stripes. All it did was hiss at people when they stepped into the garden. The people in the garden couldn't see it—it was far away and watching from a perch on a stone pillar. This pillar was

across a chasm. The perch then became my vantage point for the first half of my dream.

In a garden-like area with hills and lush green grass and trees, there was a huge iguana, like a dragon. It would lie still and hide by becoming like a hill—no one who walked on it knew it was an iguana. If they had known, they would be scared, but the iguana liked the fact that no one knew. Then a giant boy came, and this giant boy knew that the iguana was an iguana, and he stepped on it, accusing it of being an iguana. The iguana got angry, so he reared back to bite the giant boy, who had stepped on its tail.

As the iguana was about to bite the boy, the boy had a huge cricket that challenged the iguana to a fight. My vantage point changes now, and I am directly beneath the iguana, looking up at its head. The iguana nodded and accepted the challenge, and as the cricket flew away to go to a fighting place, the iguana turned to me and tried to lunge at me and kill me. The cricket saw that the iguana was lunging at me, so he came back and bit its head off, decapitating it.

All morning, my thoughts were consumed with this dream. What did it mean? What were the symbols, and how did they fit together? I immediately tried fitting the pieces together:

The snake on the stone pillar had to symbolize evil. What else could it be? The garden was the world. That I started seeing the world from the snake's perspective means I must have some hidden evil inside me from the beginning of my world. This strikes me as a Christian concept: original sin. Or perhaps it means that Islam, which was in me from the very beginning, is evil? I'm not sure, but both seem to point to Christianity.

As I looked into the world, what seemed to be a natural part of the landscape was actually another reptile, reminiscent of the snake but so massive that people were walking on it thinking it was a hill. Then a boy came along and challenged it, calling it out for what it actually was. In tandem, these symbols only fit one explanation: the boy was David, calling out the iguana, Islam, as a falsehood. The iguana, Islam, was naturally deceptive and tricked people into thinking it was a natural part of the world.

The boy's cricket had to be Christianity, which challenged the iguana. That the cricket could speak and the iguana could not means that Christianity is able to speak for itself, or in other words, it has a strong case. That the iguana could not speak means it is unable to provide proof for itself. This is confirmed when the cricket challenged the iguana but the iguana tried to kill me instead of rising to the challenge.

When the iguana tried to kill me, the cricket saved me. This strikes me as salvation, which comes from no merit of my own — another Christian concept.

I turned the dream over and over in my head, trying to find meanings that would fit better, but this was the best I could come up with. But it was pro-Christian, so I did not have much confidence in my interpretation. I began to think about ways to get the dream interpreted without revealing my internal struggles.

I decided to survey people for advice. I called David just as I walked into Epcot and saw the iconic sphere, Spaceship Earth.

"Nabeel, the real deal! What's up? How's Florida?"

This was not a moment for small talk. "Not bad. I'm having fun. I've got a question for you. Do Christians get dreams from God?"

David didn't miss a beat. "Why, what did you see?"

"I didn't say I saw anything. Answer the question."

David thought for a moment before answering. "The Bible is full of stories where people get dreams from God. Joseph, for example."

"Joseph the prophet or Joseph the father of Jesus?"

He chuckled. "Both, actually. In the New Testament, Joseph the father of Jesus gets like five dreams, which were clear instructions from God. But I was referring to the Old Testament Joseph, who was able to interpret really symbolic dreams. That's how God rescued him from prison."

The Bible talked about interpreting symbolic dreams? This was exactly what I was seeking. "So how did Joseph interpret the dreams? How do Christians interpret dreams today?"

"He had a gift of interpretation from God. I don't know of any Christians who interpret dreams today, but I don't doubt that if God gave someone a dream that needed to be interpreted, then He would also provide the means to interpret it."

His words triggered a memory in the recesses of my mind. Ammi sometimes referred to a dream interpretation book, written by ancient dream interpreter, Ibn Sirin. Maybe God would guide me through it?

Anxious to call Ammi, I hurried to get off the phone with David. "Alright, thanks man. I'll catch you later."

"Yo, you going to tell me the dream you saw, or what?"

"I didn't say anything about seeing a dream."

"I didn't say you said anything. But are you going to tell me?"

"Yeah, I'll tell you. But let me sit on it for now."

I got off the phone with David and immediately called Ammi. This was going to be tricky. I wanted to share the symbols in my dream without telling her the whole story.

"Hello?"

"Assalaamo alaikum, Ammi."

"Wa alaikum salaam. Are you with Abba?"

"I'm at Epcot. Abba will be meeting me here after work. I can't talk much right now, I want to make the most of my time at the park. But I had a dream last night. Do you have Ibn Sirin's book nearby?"

"It's upstairs. What was your dream?" Ammi's tone took on a note of concern, which I found exasperating. How was it that everyone could see right through me?

"Ammi, it was long and complicated, nothing to worry about. I'll share the details with you when I get home. I just want to know what some symbols mean so I can think about it for now."

"It doesn't work like that, Billoo. You have to share the whole thing for me to interpret it."

"But Ammi, can't you just read me what the book says? I want to interpret it for myself."

"Beyta, the book says a lot. The symbols depend on their context. Challo, tell me the first symbol."

"A snake."

"Astaghfirullah!" she gasped. "What kind of dream is this?!"

"Ammi!"

"Okay, fine. Was the snake in water? Was it sleeping? Was it eating? What did it do?"

"Why does that matter?"

"The book says different things. Just a snake means a deceptive or avowed enemy, but if the snake eats someone or if someone turns into a snake, then it can mean something else."

Her last words caught my attention. Shortly after the snake was introduced into my dream, I started seeing from its vantage point. Was that me turning into the snake? I probed the matter as discreetly as I could.

"Well, it can't be all that different from 'enemy,' right? Like, what does it mean if someone turns into a snake?"

Ammi answered, "It means that person is questioning his religion."

My heart froze. Did she just say what I thought she said?

I probed some more. "Well, the snake was on a pillar. What does that mean?"

Looking it up, she read, "A pillar is the symbol for someone's religion." This was getting to be too much. Was she reading my mind? She continued, "Do you remember what the pillar was made out of?"

"Stone."

She paused for a moment. "This is strange ... not what I would have expected. The book says that a stone pillar means someone's religion or the way they see the world is changing very quickly."

I could not believe what I was hearing. It was as if every symbol spoke exactly to my situation. I was quickly becoming certain that God intended me to interpret the symbols based on this book.

"Okay, Ammi. That's good enough. What about an iguana?"

"What's that?"

"It's a big lizard."

After flipping through some pages and clarifying the symbol, Ammi found this under *monitor lizard*: "It means a cruel, hidden enemy who appears very great and fearsome, but if it is challenged, it will fail because of inability to provide proof."

I was stunned. Could it really say all that? Those were my exact concerns about Islam, which is how I had understood the symbol. Plus, in the dream, the iguana started off hiding through deception, ultimately unable to speak for itself. "What about a boy?"

"What kind of boy? A newborn, a little boy, a teenager?"

"A little boy," I said, hurriedly. I was eager to piece together what God was telling me. "Little boy by age, not size."

"A young boy in a dream is a friend who will help you overcome your enemies. He is the bearer of good news."

Good news? That's exactly what the word *gospel* means! David was my friend who came bearing the gospel. And overcoming my enemies? In the dream, the boy helped me overcome the lizard. My head began reeling.

"Wait," Ammi added. "Was the boy beautiful?"

"Yes, actually. He was quite handsome."

"Then not only will this friend help you overcome your enemies, he will provide you with something you are seeking, something that will give you an abundant life."

By this point, I could hardly speak. "Last one, Ammi. Cricket."

"A cricket bat or a cricket ball?"

"No, not the game. A cricket, like a grasshopper."

Like iguana, the symbol was not in the book, but she found something related under *locust*. "A locust is a warrior." Once again, the interpretation fit the dream perfectly. "Did it cause you harm?"

"No, it caused my enemy harm."

"If it did not cause you harm, then it means a warrior that will bring you joy and happiness. Oh, and here again it says it will help you overcome your enemies. Beyta, I don't know the dream you had, but the symbols are related. I think this dream was from Allah."

"Acha, Ammi. I have written it down. You can tell me your interpretation when I come home. I have to go, Ammi, before the park gets busy!"

"Okay, have fun, beyta. Call me when Abba gets there."

"Acha."

"Or call me if he's taking too long."

"Acha."

"You know what? Just call me."

"Acha, Ammi, I will! I love you, khuda hafiz."

When I hung up the phone, I could hardly believe what had just happened. Every single symbol fit perfectly, all pointing to the interpretation I came up with shortly after seeing the dream. And far from barely fitting, they fit almost too well.

But the devil's advocate started whispering. I began focusing on the two symbols that did not fit with perfection: it was not a monitor lizard, it was an iguana; it was not a locust, it was a cricket. Why would every other symbol have fit perfectly when these only came close?

I began turning the words over in my mind. Cricket. Iguana. Cricket. Iguana. Cr ... I ... Cr ... I ... Christianity. Islam.

No, it was too much. It was all too much. I needed some time to sit on this.

Chapter Forty-Nine

THE NARROW DOOR

I SAT ON THE DREAM for another two months, each day the devil's advocate in my mind growing louder and louder. Could I really hinge my life and eternal destiny on a dream? Just one dream? And that dream so symbolic that I needed Ibn Sirin or Joseph to interpret it for me?

Perhaps I interpreted the dream in favor of Christianity because, subconsciously, I wanted Christianity to be true? Or perhaps I wanted Islam to subconsciously be true, so Shaitan was trying his best to trick me into damnation? Like the vision in the hotel room, the dream was just so ambiguous that I could imagine explaining it in a variety of ways.

In fact, that is what happened. I shared the dream with Ammi, who told me she did not know exactly how all the symbols fit together, but it was a sign from Allah that ought to confirm my confidence in Islam. When I shared the vision and dream with David, he said there was no doubt that the dream pointed me to Christianity.

All these thoughts mixed in my head, and I did not dare ask God for another dream or vision. In my heart, I knew He had given me one of each, but I was too broken to be sure what they meant. The opposing forces, the uncertainty, and the potential costs almost paralyzed me.

Almost.

I remembered what David had said about the Joseph in the New Testament. God had given him "clear instructions" through dreams. That was what I needed. And, surely, if God wanted to guide me, a broken skeptic, He would know that I needed more.

"Three," I said to myself. "Allah likes odd numbers, and the Christian God is triune.[116] Why not ask for three dreams?" So I returned to Allah in prayer with a very specific request.

"Instead of just one dream, please give me three. If they all point to Christianity, then I will become Christian. Please, Lord, show me mercy. Please make the next dream so easy to understand that it requires no interpretation."

On the morning of March 11, 2005, I had a new dream to scrawl onto paper.

> I am standing at the entrance of a narrow doorway that is built into a wall of brick. I am not in the doorway but just in front of it. The doorway is an arch. I would say the doorway is about seven and a half feet tall, with about six and a half feet of its sides being straight up from the ground, and there's a one foot arched part on the top capping it off. The doorway is slightly less than three feet wide and about three or four feet deep, all brick. It leads into a room, where many people are sitting at tables that have fancy and good food on them. I think I remember salads, but I'm not sure. They were not eating, but they were all ready to eat, and they were all looking to my left, as if waiting for a speaker before the banquet. One of the people, at the other side of the door just inside the room, is David Wood. I am unable to walk into the room because David is occupying the other threshold of the doorway. He is sitting at a table and is also looking to my left. I asked him, "I thought we were going to eat together?" And he said, without removing his eyes from the front of the room, "You never responded."

When I woke up from the dream, I immediately had an interpretation: the room was heaven, the feast was a feast in the kingdom of heaven, and it was a wedding feast of sorts. In order to get into the room, I had to respond to David's invitation.

If there was one thing I did not get about the dream, it was the door. It was the most dramatic symbol in the dream, but what did it mean? Why was that the most vivid image? And why was it so narrow?

By this time, Ammi was becoming suspicious of my questions about dreams, and since this one had David in it, there was no way I could ask her what she thought it meant. I called David, though, to see what he thought.

"Nabeel," he responded, "this dream is so clear it doesn't need to be interpreted." His words immediately reminded me of what I had prayed to God a few days earlier. Asking for more, he told me to read Luke 13:22.

Instead of Abba's King James Version, I turned to a study Bible that David had given me the previous year as a gift. I had never even opened it until this point. It was a Zondervan NIV study Bible. When I arrived at the passage, in big, bold letters, the section heading read: "The Narrow Door."

My heart skipped a beat. I had never seen this section of the Bible before. I carefully read it and reread it:

> Then Jesus went through the towns and villages, teaching as he made his way to Jerusalem. Someone asked him, "Lord, are only a few people going to be saved?"
>
> He said to them, *"Make every effort to enter through the narrow door, because many, I tell you, will try to enter and will not be able to. Once the owner of the house gets up and closes the door,* you will *stand outside* knocking and pleading, 'Sir, open the door for us.' ...
>
> "There will be weeping there, and gnashing of teeth, when you see Abraham, Isaac and Jacob and all the prophets in the kingdom of God, but you yourselves thrown out. People will come from east and west and north and south, and *will take their places at the feast in the kingdom of God.*"[117]

I stopped reading and put the Bible down. I was overwhelmed. God had given me a dream that was so clear that I did not need to interpret it. The interpretation had been recorded in the Bible for two thousand years.

The narrow door was the door to salvation. Jesus was telling me to make every effort to enter into it, and I knew from the dream that

I needed to respond to David's invitation in order to enter and take my place in the feast of the kingdom of heaven. If I did not enter, I would be left standing outside, asking to come in.

God had given me a dream that was so clear that I did not need to interpret it. The interpretation had been recorded in the Bible for two thousand years.

That is where I stood, just outside the narrow door of salvation, wondering why I had not been let in. Thankfully, the owner had not yet come to close the door.

There was now no question left. I knew what I had to do. I had to accept the invitation.

Chapter Fifty

A STAIRWAY OUT
OF THE MOSQUE

I HAD ASKED FOR THREE DREAMS, though, and God is unbe-
lievably gracious. In the early hours of April 24, 2005, I received a
third dream.

> I am sitting on the first step of a flight of white stairs in a masjid.
> The stairs go up, and they have ornate posts at the first step, with
> hand railings going up to the left. I am not sure of the material
> of the stairs, though I'm thinking either stone/marble or wood.
> I am facing away from the top of the stairs. I can see myself in
> this dream, and the angle of view is of my right side as I sit on
> the stairs and look forward, where I'm expecting someone to
> speak, possibly at a brown wooden podium, though I'm not sure.
> The room has green carpeting, and people are expected to sit on
> the floor, though I am on the first stair and feel nothing wrong
> with this. I expect people to fill in the section to my left, which
> is also to the left of the stairs. Nothing is going on in the right
> side of the room.
>
> As the room gradually fills up, the imam sits down on the
> floor slightly behind me and to my left. He is wearing white
> and is looking in the same direction as everyone else. Since I
> expected him to be the speaker, and since he is a holy man and
> the imam, I am surprised and confused that he is on the floor
> behind me. Out of respect, I try to get off the stairs and sit

behind him, but I am unable to get off the stairs. I feel as if I'm being held on the stairs by an unknown/unseen force. The force did not seem particularly brusque, nor was it particularly kind. It just held me on the stairs.

The dream ended with a sense of confusion, as I did not understand what I was to do, and I did not understand what everyone was waiting for and didn't know who was going to speak after all.

For me, the dream was clear enough. I was on stairs that led out of the mosque. The Muslims I had always respected now sat behind and below me. Although I wanted to show them respect, I was no longer able to take my place behind them. I was now ahead of them, on the way out of the mosque. God was making sure of it.

What's more, the imam was not actually the person we were all waiting for. We were waiting for someone else, someone of far higher authority. Perhaps someone who was not coming to the mosque after all. This dream, like the second dream, ended by showing me where I was, not what I would ultimately do. I was waiting for the one to come, but this time, I was confused because I was in the wrong place.

Since this dream portrayed a mosque and an imam, I felt comfortable asking Ammi to interpret it. Using Ibn Sirin once more, she said the stairs represented a rise in my status both in this world and the hereafter; my position on the first step meant I was only just beginning my journey; the empty mosque at the beginning meant I was pursuing religious scholarship; the full mosque toward the end meant I was going to be a wise teacher of religious knowledge and an effective counselor; the imam represented all Muslims in the ummah; and that he was wearing white represented their well-meaning hearts.

She could not explain why he was sitting behind me or below me, nor could she explain why he was sitting on a carpet. Seeing a man on a carpet means that man has gone astray and is likely to provide a false report. She concluded that the true meaning of the dream was hidden from her, but it was certainly one that held glad tidings for me.

When I shared the dream with David, his response was much more concise. "Stairs leading out of the mosque? Come on, Nabeel.

Does God need to smack you with a two-by-four before you'll become a Christian?"

He had a point. What was I waiting for now? I had three dreams and a vision. Individually, the last two were clear, and all four were powerful. Cumulatively, there was no question.

I now knew the truth: God was calling me to accept the gospel.

I acknowledged the truth to myself but not to anyone else, not even God. Some might say my behavior at the time was inexplicable, perhaps inexcusable. That might be so. The third dream did not mark the beginning of my walk as a Christian, but it did mark the beginning of a period of mourning, gradually building into what would be the most painful time of my life.

> I had three dreams and a vision. Cumulatively, there was no question.

Chapter Fifty-One

TIME TO MOURN

THROUGH THE SUMMER OF 2005, I continued resisting the gospel. I traveled to more mosques and spoke with more imams, searching for answers but finding none. I even traveled with Abba to mosques in Europe, trying desperately to overturn what I had learned over the past four years, to no avail. All the while, I begged God for more dreams, but He gave me none. I already had exactly what I needed.

But the impending pain was daunting. I knew the cost I was about to pay, but I did not know what it would look like. Would Ammi and Abba hate me? Would they kick me out of the family? Would they die from heartbreak? This last one seemed the most likely to me.

Honestly, I did not know what would happen. All I knew was life was never going to be the same.

At the end of the summer, I was set for the next year of medical school. I planned on moving in with a roommate, so the night before the first day was a sort of farewell from my family. On the one hand, I was moving only twenty-five minutes away, so they did not see it as a big deal. On the other hand, I knew it was going to be one of the last loving and intimate moments we would ever share as a family. I savored each bittersweet laugh, relished each millisecond of every embrace.

> But the impending pain was daunting. I knew the cost I was about to pay.

Ammi and Abba had no clue what I was about to do to them; no clue what I was considering. I was beset with hidden guilt. How could I destroy this family? What was I about to do?

I was barely able to drive to school the next day. My tears overwhelmed me. Forcing myself to leave home, I kept reminding myself how important this day was and that I had to keep it together. The second year of medical school is arguably the most academically difficult year a physician will ever face, and the first day was one of the most important days. I had to compose myself.

But I simply could not. Instead, I began pleading to God out loud. "Ya Allah! O God! Give me time to mourn. More time to mourn the upcoming loss of my family, more time to mourn the life I've always loved."

As I approached the school, I knew I was in no state to go inside. I drove instead to my new apartment, right across the street from school, where Abba and I had moved my belongings just a few days before. At this moment, there were two books that I particularly sought, hoping for God's comfort.

As soon as I entered the apartment, I went straight to the bookcase and retrieved my old Quran and my study Bible. I sat down on the couch and opened the Quran first. I flipped through the pages, looking for verses of comfort, at first carefully reading each page for the subject matter, then more quickly thumbing through the index, and then frantically flipping from page to page, hoping for something, anything, that would comfort me.

There was nothing there for me. It depicted a god of conditional concern, one who would not love me if I did not perform to my utmost in pleasing him, one who seemed to take joy in sending his enemies into the hellfire. It did not speak to the broken nature of man, let alone directly to the broken man in need of God's love. It was a book of laws, written for the seventh century.

Looking for a living word, I put the Quran down and picked up the Bible.

I had never read the Bible for personal guidance before. I did not even know where to start. I figured the New Testament would be a good place, so I opened to the beginning of Matthew. Within minutes, I found these words:

"Blessed are those who mourn, for they shall be comforted."

The words were like a current sent through my dead heart, electrifying it once more. This was what I was looking for. It was as if God had written these words in the Bible two thousand years prior specifically with me in mind.

It was almost too incredible to believe. To a man who had seen the world only through Muslim eyes, the message was overwhelming. "I am blessed for mourning? Why? How? I am imperfect. I do not perform to His standard. Why would He bless me? And for mourning, no less. Why?"

> Looking for a living word, I put the Quran down and picked up the Bible.

I continued reading fervently. "Blessed are those who hunger and thirst for righteousness? Not 'blessed are the righteous' but 'blessed are those who hunger and thirst for righteousness'? I hunger and thirst for righteousness, I do, but I can never attain it. God will bless me anyway? Who is this God who loves me so much, even in my failures?"

Tears flowed from my eyes once more, but now they were tears of joy. I knew that what I held in my hands was life itself. This was truly God's word, and it was as if I was meeting Him for the first time.

I began poring over the Bible, absorbing every word as if it were water for my parched soul, a soul that had never before drunk from the fountain of life. As I read, I perused the study notes at the bottom of the page and cross-references in the margins, not willing to miss a single angle of a single verse. Questions would come into my mind, and within moments, either the text I was reading or its footnote would lead me to the answer. This happened more times than I could count.

I could not put the Bible down. I literally could not. It felt as if my heart would stop beating, perhaps implode, if I put it down. I ended up skipping the whole day of school, but I really had no choice in the matter. The Bible was my lifeline.

Chapter Fifty-Two

THE WORD SPEAKS

OVER THE NEXT FEW DAYS, my heart was filled with a new joy, the joy of meeting God Himself. I thought I had known Him my entire life, but now that I knew who He really was, there was no comparison. Nothing compares to the one true God.

Some might ask why I did not just go ahead and recite the sinner's prayer. The answer is quite simple: I had never heard of the sinner's prayer. All I knew was that I loved the God of the Bible, and so I pursued Him more and more by reading as much as I could.

I read my study Bible relentlessly, living on each word, following every footnote and cross-reference, only coming back to Matthew if there were no more trails to pursue. It took me about a week to read from Matthew 5 to Matthew 10.

Just after midnight one evening, still captivated by this new-found glory, I found these words in Matthew 10:32–33: "Whoever acknowledges me before others, I will also acknowledge before my Father in heaven. But whoever disowns me before others, I will disown before my Father in heaven."

My heart sank. I had not even acknowledged Jesus to Jesus, let alone to others. But to acknowledge Him meant destroying my family. Could He really charge me to do such a thing?

As if the living word of the Bible were in conversation with me, Jesus began responding to my heart, verse by verse. "Do not suppose that I have come to bring peace to the earth. I did not come to bring peace, but a sword. For I have come to turn 'a man against his father, a daughter against her mother, a daughter-in-law against her mother-in-law—a man's enemies will be the members of his own household.' "

But how could this be? How could Jesus turn me against Ammi and Abba? They are such wonderful people. Why would God do such a thing?

Jesus answered in the next verse: "Anyone who loves their father or mother more than me is not worthy of me; anyone who loves their son or daughter more than me is not worthy of me."

It was not that Jesus was turning me against my parents. It was that, if my family stood against God, I had to choose one or the other. God is obviously best, even if that caused me to turn against my family. But how? How could I bear the pain?

He assured me that inconceivable pain and social rejection is part of the Christian walk: "Whoever does not take up their cross and follow me is not worthy of me." To be a Christian means suffering real pain for the sake of God. Not as a Muslim would suffer for God, because Allah so commands him by fiat, but as the heartfelt expression of a grateful child whose God first suffered for him.

"But Lord," I pleaded, "acknowledging my faith in You will mean the end of my life. If I don't die a physical death through emotional torment or at the hands of some misguided Muslim zealot, at least my entire life as I know it will come to an end."

"Nabeel, my child," I felt Him say, "whoever finds their life will lose it, and whoever loses their life for my sake will find it."

I had to give up my life in order to receive His life. This was not some platitude or cliché. The gospel was calling me to die.

Burdened by these words, I lay awake deep into that night. But far from resisting rest, sleep was ashamed to fall upon me. I had denied God long enough. On August 24, 2005, at three o'clock in the morning, I placed my forehead on the foot of my bed and prayed.

"I submit. I submit that Jesus Christ is Lord of heaven and earth. He came to this world to die for my sins, proving His lordship by rising from the dead. I am a sinner, and I need Him for redemption. Christ, I accept You into my life."

The difficult night that had not granted me peace was quickly fading away as sleep washed over me. I had finally proclaimed the truth of the gospel. I was finally a believer.

Although I believed, I did not yet know the power of the gospel. To teach me that, God was going to break me completely.

Chapter Fifty-Three

FINDING JESUS

I WAS A CRUMPLED HEAP ON THE GROUND, trembling before God. Two weeks after accepting my Lord, I tried to plead with Him, while wailing and stammering through quivering lips.

"Why, God ...?" But I could not formulate my words. The shaking was uncontrollable.

The night before, I had looked into Abba's eyes as they welled with tears. Those eyes that had so tenderly cared for me since the day he whispered the adhan into my ears. The eyes that softly closed in prayer every night as he invoked the protection of God. The eyes that would turn back lovingly as he went off to sea, serving his nation and his family. To be the cause of the only tears I had ever seen those eyes shed, I could not bear it.

"Why, God ...?"

Though Abba did not say much, what he did say has haunted me ever since. The man who stood tallest in my life, my archetype of strength, my father, spoke these words through palpable pain: "Nabeel, this day, I feel as if my backbone has been ripped out from inside me." The words tore through me. It felt like patricide. I had not given up just my life to follow Jesus, I was killing my father.

He has never stood as tall since that day. I extinguished his pride.

"Why, God ...?"

Ammi had even fewer words than Abba, but her eyes said more. "You are my only son. You came from my womb. Since you were born, I have called you my *jaan kay tuqray*, a physical piece of my life and heart. I cradled you, sang to you, taught you the ways of God. Every day since you came into this world, I have loved you with all of me in a way I have loved no one else.

"Why have you betrayed me, Billoo?"

Her eyes seared my soul and remain branded in my memory. They were the final image I saw before Abba ushered Ammi out of my apartment and to the hospital across the street. None of us were sure she would make it through the night.

She survived, but her eyes have never been as bright since that day. I extinguished their light.

Decimated before God, eyes pouring, nose and mouth unable to withhold the grief, I was finally able to sputter my question through tears and mucus: "Why, God, did You not kill me the moment I believed? Why did You leave me here? Why did You leave me to hurt my family more deeply than they've ever been hurt? They never deserved this! I've destroyed it all! Nothing is left!

"Why didn't You kill me?" I pleaded with God, full of despair because it was too late. "It would have been better if You had killed me the moment I believed so my family would never have had to taste betrayal. This is far worse for them than my death would have been. At least our love would have lived on. At least our family would have always been one.

"Why, God?"

At that moment, the most agonizing moment of my life, something happened that was beyond my theology and imagination. As if God picked up a megaphone and spoke through my conscience, I heard these words resonate through my very being:

"Because this is not about you."

I froze with my mouth agape. The tears, the sobs, the shaking—everything stopped. I was rooted to the ground, as if electricity had just shot through me and paralyzed me. For about ten minutes, I sat, unable to move, unable to close my mouth even.

He was rebooting me.

When I was able to move, I felt no sorrow, none whatsoever. It was as if my prayers of anguish and self-pity had been words uttered in a previous life. Rising from the ground and walking out of the apartment, I gazed at everything intently—the trees, the sky, even the stairs I stood upon.

Yet again, I was seeing the potential of the world in a new light. I had been wearing colored glasses my entire life, and they had been taken off. Everything looked different, and I wanted to examine it all more carefully.

Then I saw something that I had seen countless times before: a man walking down the sidewalk toward the medical school.

But that was not all I saw. Though I had no idea who this man was, I knew he had a dramatic story, replete with personal struggles, broken relationships, and splintered self-worth. Taught by the world that he was an outcome of blind evolution, he subconsciously valued himself as exactly that: a byproduct of random chance, with no purpose, no hope, no meaning except what pleasures he could extract out of the day. Chasing these pleasures resulted in guilt and pain, which caused him to chase more pleasures, which led to more guilt and more pain. Burying it all just beneath the surface, he went about his day with no clue how to break the cycle, how to find true hope.

What I saw was a man who needed to know that God could rescue him, that God had rescued him. This man needed to know about God and His power.

Did he know?

Did he know that God loved him from the foundations of the earth? With a power far exceeding the immensity of the cosmos, He turned all His attention to creating that man and declared, "You are My child. I love you."

Did he know that God made him exactly how He wanted, knowing each hair on his head and each second of his life? God knew full well that the hands He gave to this man would be used to sin against Him, that the feet He gave to this man would be used to walk away from Him. Yet, instead of withholding these gifts, He gave him the most precious gift of all: His own Son.

Did he know that God entered into this world for him, to suffer in his stead? Received with slaps and fists by the very people He came to save, He was scourged until His skin fell off in ribbons, only to be pierced through both arms and feet, nailed naked on wood for all to ridicule. He scraped His skinless back on splintered wood with each rasping breath, His last breath finishing the task of rescuing us, of securing our eternity with Him.

Did he know?

Of course not. We have to tell him.

While I was wallowing in self-pity, focused on myself, there was a whole world with literally billions of people who had no idea who God is, how amazing He is, and the wonders He has done for us. They are the ones who are really suffering. They don't know His hope, His peace, and His love that transcends all understanding. They don't know the message of the gospel.

After loving us with the most humble life and the most horrific death, Jesus told us, "As I have loved you, go and love one another." How could I consider myself a follower of Jesus if I was not willing to live as He lived? To die as He died? To love the unloved and give hope to the hopeless?

This is not about me. It is about Him and His love for His children.

Now I knew what it meant to follow God. It meant walking boldly by His Spirit of grace and love, in the firm confidence of everlasting life given through the Son, with the eternal purpose of proclaiming and glorifying the Father.

Now I had found Jesus.

*To read an expert contribution on dreams and visions
by Josh McDowell, an internationally recognized evangelist,
and author or co-author of more than 130 books, see page 351.*

EPILOGUE

AUGUST 24, 2015

The sun is drifting below the horizon, leaving the last vestige of an English drizzle hanging in the air. My first summer at Oxford has passed as a hazy dream, mostly on account of my three-week-old daughter, who is snoring softly at my right. Today is exactly ten years after I bent my knee to Jesus.

In the first publication of this book, I did not write much in the epilogue because I saw *Seeking Allah, Finding Jesus* primarily as a tool for teaching and only secondarily for sharing my story. I tied up the loose ends and left it at that. But many readers felt the epilogue was too short and asked for more details about what happened within my family after my conversion, how I entered into ministry, and even how I met my wife. I was honored that people wanted to know more, even though I found it surprising they were interested. I hope you will find valuable insights in the further experiences and lessons I share here.

HOW I TOLD DAVID

It was early on a Wednesday that I acknowledged Christ as my Lord, but I did not tell anyone until that Sunday, when I asked David if I could go with him and Marie to their church. My request didn't surprise David, as I had already gone with them to church the week prior. It was the weekend before my conversion that David had poked and prodded me all day to accept Christ. Given my behavior, I can't blame him.

It must have been a comical scene. David and Marie were leading a Bible study for a few teenagers on the Sermon on the Mount, and I was super excited to join because I had been immersed in those very chapters of Matthew. When they finished teaching, the youth started asking questions, but before David and Marie could answer, I interjected with answers of my own. I had become so steeped in my study Bible that I even provided commentary and cross-references to other books of the Bible. I remember David saying afterward, "Nabeel, accept Christ already! You're acting so much like a Christian that you're even trying to lead Bible studies!"

So the following Sunday, when I asked to come to church again, David did not think much of it. We were joined at church by Zach, who had become a Christian just a few months prior and was looking for a church home.

It felt very strange to be in a church for the first time as a believer, and as easy as it should have been, I had no idea how to tell anyone that I had decided to follow Jesus. It felt like too weighty a matter to mention casually, but I also did not want to cause a scene. Plus, what would I say? That I had "become a Christian"? Those words were still too alien for my lips to utter.

The perfect opportunity presented itself after the service. The four of us and a handful of church members decided to go to lunch at a Chinese buffet not far from David's house, and just before beginning the meal, David asked if anyone would like to pray over the food.

I enthusiastically volunteered, to which David responded, "Really? A bunch of Christians gathered for a meal and the Muslim is the one offering to pray?" Marie smacked him on the arm, and everyone bowed their heads.

I honestly do not remember what I prayed, but I remember closing my prayer, "In the name of the Father, the Son, and the Holy Spirit." Everyone at the table raised their heads, stunned. David blurted, "Dude, you even pray like a Christian now! When are you going to become a Christian?"

Catching on more quickly, Marie grabbed his arm and exclaimed, "David, don't you get it? He *has* accepted Christ!"

David turned to me as if this couldn't possibly be true, and when I nodded, he was speechless. The rest of the people at the table rejoiced and embraced me, until David was able to muster some words. "You finally become a Christian, and you choose the Happy Buffet? We could have gone anywhere today; I'd have paid for a Brazilian steakhouse, even!"

HOW AMMI AND ABBA FOUND OUT

After rejoicing and embracing, we all returned to our food. David asked me when I wanted to get baptized, and I replied that I was ready to be baptized immediately. My urgency was not for any theological reason, but because I wanted to be baptized by David, and he was about to move to New York City. He had decided to go to Fordham University to get his PhD in philosophy of religion, and he was leaving in just a few days.

But David wasn't ready to baptize me. His tone turning serious, he explained to me that baptism is a public proclamation of faith, and that I had to tell my parents about my conversion before he would baptize me. He knew me well, and what he assumed was true: I would hesitate to tell my parents about my decision to follow Jesus, perhaps indefinitely.

We began to argue with one another, like so many times before, until I decided to end the conversation. "David, you *are* going to baptize me before moving to New York, and I am *not* going to tell my parents."

"Fine," retorted David with finality. "Then I'm going to pray for your parents to find out without your telling them."

Apparently, God was listening.

A few days later, ostensibly on account of a miscommunication, Ammi and Abba came to my apartment when I was not there. Normally, I would not have left my apartment without locking the front door, I would not have left my room without locking the bedroom door (on account of roommates), I would not have left my computer without putting up the password screen, and I would not have left my instant messenger open while away. That day, I somehow had missed all four steps. When Ammi and Abba knocked, no one answered. They let themselves in and looked around to find me.

What they found instead was a message on my computer from a Christian acquaintance congratulating me for my upcoming baptism.

When I returned home, I was shocked to see them in my living room, and the looks on their faces told me everything they could not say themselves.

ADVICE TO NEW BELIEVERS FROM MUSLIM BACKGROUNDS

It is one of the greatest regrets of my life that I was not the one to break the news to my parents. I really did owe it to them. If there is anything I could change from those days, it would be that moment. In the ten years since, I have ministered around the world and have met hundreds who have left Islam for Jesus. When these believers from Muslim backgrounds come to me for counsel, the first question I ask is whether they have informed their family of their decision. I do not want anyone to make the same mistake that I did.

I now realize this is a common problem. The honor-shame paradigm, combined with the cost of following Jesus, paralyzes many former Muslims into secrecy and deception. I have even met an immigrant in America who has been a Christian for more than two decades and still has not told his parents that he left Islam.

My counsel to all such new brothers and sisters in the faith is that they walk in the light and hide nothing. Jesus intends for us to walk openly and freely, whereas secrecy and deception are the domain of the devil. This is particularly important for Muslims from honor-shame contexts, as they are prone to hide difficult matters. It is only after we are unfettered by fear that we can live boldly, as true Christians. Yes, it is painful and potentially dangerous, but that is where the Holy Spirit meets us and shapes us into the image of Jesus, our suffering Lord.

My advice is actually more controversial than it might sound at first. Shortly after entering the world of ministry to Muslims, I learned that many missionaries tell new believers from Muslim backgrounds *not* to inform their families they have converted. They suggest that new believers maintain their relationships with their Muslim circles rather than proclaim the divine Lordship of Jesus. These ministers often spread the gospel among Muslims while omitting the teaching that Jesus is God. This practice is so widespread that it has become a common approach among missionaries, called the Insider Movement.

I have a great love for Christian brothers and sisters who dedicate their lives to reaching Muslims, but I find this approach so horribly misguided that I resolutely condemn it as blasphemy. A gospel devoid of Jesus' deity is no gospel at all. The good news is that God Himself loves us enough to enter into the world and suffer for us, that despite humanity's inability to save itself, God saved us. He did not send someone else to do His dirty work. He rescued us Himself. No one else could do it. That is the beauty of the gospel; it is all about God and what He has done out of His love for us. A gospel without the deity of Christ is an eviscerated gospel.

Thus, I advise insider missionaries and reluctant former Muslims that we must embrace Jesus' teaching: Following Him often means dividing our families and potentially being killed for our faith (Matt. 10:32–39). Anguish and suffering are not just risks of following Jesus, they are means of following Jesus. If Jesus was denounced by His family (Mark 3:31) and did not run from His execution (Mark 10:33), how are we His followers if we avoid following His example?

The expectation of Christian suffering is exactly why we have Scriptures like Philippians 4:6–7, Luke 18:1–8, and Matthew 6:25–34, and in my first year as a Christian, I immersed myself in those verses for comfort. The greatest lesson I learned in that time is that suffering binds us closer to Jesus and opens us to the tangible presence of the Holy Spirit, the Comforter, more than anything else. Perhaps that is why one of our first acts after becoming Christians is baptism, symbolizing our willingness to die to this world. Although many Christians see it as a symbolic death, none should assume the symbol is meaningless. To follow Jesus is to die that we might live.

MY FIRST DAYS AS A CHRISTIAN

On a bittersweet Sunday, David baptized me in a backyard pool and then left for New York City. That was also the last Sunday his church ever met, as the pastor of the church felt his time in Virginia had come to an end. Zach and I were left to figure out what it meant to follow Jesus without guidance and without a church. We connected with two other young men from the church who had just committed their lives to Christ, and the four of us decided to pursue Jesus together. Between us we had less than a year's experience following Jesus. All we knew was that we wanted to be like Christ. That's when we found a book titled *So, You Want to Be Like Christ?*

Written by Chuck Swindoll, the book was exactly what we needed. It focused on spiritual discipline, living according to the manner of Jesus. Every Wednesday, the four of us gathered to implement what we were reading and pore over the Scriptures, sometimes until 4:00 a.m., eschewing other responsibilities in our zeal for God and His truth. We prayed together, fasted together, memorized Scripture together, confessed our sins to one another, and otherwise pursued the Lord with everything we had as a fourfold cord. During that time, we experienced miracles, prophecies, visions, and even an exorcism. I have little doubt this passionate pursuit of Jesus is what laid the foundation for my Christian convictions in the decade since.

Unfortunately, this golden period in my early walk with Christ ended after about seven months. We joined a church, and our Wednesday night meetings became less frequent. After finishing the Bible, I started paying more attention to school and less to Scripture. The supernatural occurrences mostly ceased as I immersed myself in the world around me once more.

My parents, after recovering from the initial shock, made two matters very clear: they felt utterly betrayed, yet they loved me regardless. For the most part, they saw me as an innocent victim, blaming David for "brainwashing" me. In their eyes, David was evil incarnate. Even though I insisted that I had chosen Jesus for myself after years of careful consideration, they simply could not believe my words, thinking me to be out of my mind and under David's control. For months emotions raged, harsh words were said, and arguments flared, but Ammi and Abba did not ostracize me. On the one hand this was a blessing because I remained a part of my family. On the other hand it was extremely painful because I had to weather emotional storms constantly, listening to Ammi scold me for hours on end. She cried every time I saw her for almost two years, often while painfully indicting my Christian faith for destroying our family.

In order to "unbrainwash" me, they insisted that I meet with imams and leaders of our sect. Some imams traveled hundreds of miles to our home to speak with me; other times we went hundreds of miles to meet with them. They often demanded to know what great fault I had found with Islam that I would run to Christianity as a crutch, and some even began to drill me with the same apologetics questions I had used against David for years. Through it all, a common theme in their perspective was, "How could anyone leave Islam for Christianity? It is simply not possible." I find that many Muslims have the same reaction to my story even today, the ones who do not know me assuming I must have converted for some personal gain. One taxi cab driver even said to me in a thick Egyptian accent, "It is not possible; you were bought! How much did they pay you?" ("They," upon asking, turned out to be the CIA.)

On the opposite end of the spectrum, many Christians ask me why devout Muslims are not immediately convinced by my arguments for Christianity. I have to remind them that the lens through which many such Muslims see the world simply does not allow it. Their prevailing understanding is that "Islam is obviously true; Christianity is obviously false," and any input they receive is filtered accordingly. The difference between an Islamic perspective and a Christian perspective is tremendous, and switching between the two requires massive mental tectonic shifts. A single conversation is not going to move all the pieces into place. For these reasons, the imams simply could not believe my answers and at times could not even understand what I was saying.

Ammi and Abba could not understand either. After they saw me rebutting the imams' questions, they wondered how I had become so disobedient and whether I had developed some kind of mental disorder. Ammi began sending me to a psychiatrist, insistent that something must be wrong with my brain. Ammi alerted the psychiatrist that I believed I could speak with God and that I believed He would, at times, speak back. But despite Ammi and Abba's protestations, the psychiatrist never diagnosed me with any illness, instead suggesting family counseling. At this, Ammi and Abba developed a rather bitter taste for Western psychiatry and dropped the matter.

HOW I MET AND MARRIED MY BRIDE

Time passed agonizingly slowly in those days, and I yearned for Christian community. There was a period of time when I would stop at

Christian bookstores just so I could be in the presence of other believers, even though they never spoke to me. I decided to start attending multiple churches throughout the week, one of which was a church that focused on ministering to university students. They were planning to go to a conference called Passion, a four-day gathering in Atlanta of more than twenty thousand Christian university students from around the country with world-class speakers and worship music. There was no way I was going to miss that! And I'm really glad I didn't, because it was there I met the woman who was to become my bride.

Michelle was in her third year at the Coast Guard Academy in Connecticut, and I was introduced to her by a mutual friend, a classmate of hers who had transferred to the academy from Old Dominion University. I wish I could say I was smitten and it was love at first sight, but honestly, I did not take too much notice of her at the time. I was there to worship God, and I was preoccupied with other matters. But Michelle was intrigued by my story and what God was doing in my life, so she asked if we could stay in touch.

At the end of the four days, Michelle went back to Connecticut and I went back to Virginia. We continued our conversations via email and instant messenger. Through written correspondence I began to discover Michelle's heart and mind. She is the most sincere, self-sacrificial, loyal, honest, servant-hearted person I have ever met. It did not take me long to realize that this woman was a rare gem, a unique daughter of God whom I would be a fool not to pursue. But that meant fighting more battles.

When I met her parents, they were very kind and hospitable, but it was clear they had reservations about a former Muslim man pursuing their daughter. Of course, it didn't help that Michelle was only twenty-one years old and I had no income or social support. So when I asked for her hand in marriage, they refused. Twice. Thankfully, the third time was a charm.

I still had to convince Ammi and Abba. Ammi simply refused to entertain the notion that I would marry a Western woman. She would say, "Nabeel, if you've become a Christian, why can't you marry a Pakistani Christian woman? At least she will know our culture!" I responded that it was too late for that, as I had sought God's guidance and felt confirmed that Michelle was a perfect match for me.

Abba, on the other hand, began to soften somewhat to my decisions. On one occasion, when Ammi had left the room in tears and frustration, Abba said to me, "Nabeel, if Michelle is going to be my daughter-in-law, I want to meet her." And he did meet her, the week before our wedding, when Michelle finally moved to the same state as me in preparation for our union. Realizing that the wedding would move on regardless, Ammi met Michelle as well.

FAMILY FALLOUT

Yet they refused to bless our marriage, and they refused to come to our wedding. Aside from four dear cousins and an uncle, no one from my family came. The entire ordeal was agonizing for me, and just thinking about it still elicits pain. I acknowledge, though, that the same was true for my parents, especially Ammi. She had many hopes and dreams for me, her only son, and on account of my Christian convictions, I had chipped away at them, first by leaving Islam and then by marrying a non-Muslim, even a Western girl.

Throughout these changing family dynamics, my sister, Baji, simply attempted to keep the peace. She had known that my conversion was coming, because I had confided in her the week I received my first dream in December of 2004. But she was always far more concerned with family unity than my religious views. This makes sense because her view of Islam had taken on a Western tint, and she thought it quite possible that Allah would want me to follow Him through the path of Christianity.

Regardless, Baji was most worried about the repercussions of my decision on the family, not about my soul or salvation. As I continued to follow my Christian convictions, Baji continued to grow concerned that there would be a falling out of our family, and her advice to me was consistently, "Just do or say whatever you can to make things better." She was afraid we were coming to the last straw.

And we were. In 2009, upon graduating from medical school, I decided to enter into full-time ministry instead of practicing medicine. When I told my parents my decision, they could not understand. I remember Ammi saying, "Nabeel, you became a Christian, fine. You married Michelle, fine. But now you are leaving medicine?

This is the only thing I have left, the only thing I can be proud of! Will you not obey me in anything?"

I tried to tell her I was called to ministry, but the idea of a calling simply made no sense to her. She kept saying, "No, there are Christian doctors; I know you can be a doctor if you want. There's no need for you to talk publicly about Christianity and Islam." At that point, she concluded that I was making all these decisions in rebellion, simply to hurt her and Abba. They finally decided to cut off all communication with me.

MY CALLING INTO MINISTRY

Even though I had that discussion with my parents in 2009, my decision to leave medicine was in the works since at least 2006. The pastor of my church knew that I had become a Christian after studying the Bible and the historical Jesus with David, so he asked us to preach a series of sermons together responding to *The Da Vinci Code*, which had just been released in theaters. On May 21, when David returned to Virginia Beach for his summer break, we tag-teamed our first sermon. At the end, two atheists came forward to accept Christ. Other churches started asking us to speak to their congregations, and our call to ministry became evident.

Before continuing, I must say that believers from Muslim backgrounds are thrust into ministry far too soon and far too often. Their Christian friends are excited that they have become believers, so they are asked to share their testimonies at church. The testimonies often sound exotic and powerful, and word spreads quickly. Soon, new believers from Muslim backgrounds are speaking and teaching without having had any time to grow in Christ, without deep roots or spiritual transformation. That is what happened to me; I had not been a Christian for even a year before I was teaching at churches, debating imams, and sharing my testimony before hundreds. I advise strongly against that, suggesting on average two years of discipleship and growth before pursuing ministry. I made some huge mistakes as a young minister because I lacked the grace and wisdom that comes only from spending time with Christ and His Word. Although I have seen a handful of new believers stumble on account of this trajectory, the Lord graciously preserved me through my many shortfalls.

David and I named our ministry Anastasis Apologetics, a Greek reference to our central message, Jesus' resurrection. Ultimately, after realizing that Anastasis Apologetics was a mouthful and rather hard to spell, we changed our ministry title to Acts 17 Apologetics. By the time I was graduating from medical school, I had ministered to thousands of people at dozens of venues, and I knew I was built to be a teacher and an evangelist, not a doctor. I decided to use my medical training for foreign missions, but my vocation was ministry.

David and I ministered together until, because of a convoluted series of events over the course of two years, Acts 17 became mostly focused on free speech, sharia, and Islam. As important as these matters were, I did not want to focus my ministry on Islam. My heart was with the beauty, love, and power of the triune God, and I wanted to focus on proclaiming the good news of the gospel and its historical truth. The work of Acts 17 was important, but it did not require both David and me. Encouraging him to continue, I departed from Acts 17 in June of 2011 and started Creed 2:6 ministries, but C2:6 was not meant to exist for long.

In September of 2011, I received a call from Ravi Zacharias International Ministries, a global organization of evangelists and thinkers. One of their speakers had to pull out of an event at the last second, and they were desperately looking for someone to fill in for him. None of their other speakers were available, and all the associates they usually worked with were busy as well. In a last-ditch effort, they asked their associates if they knew anyone at all who could fill in, and two of them mentioned my name.

By this most tenuous of encounters, I began my relationship with RZIM. In December of that year, Michelle and I met with the founder of the organization, Dr. Ravi Zacharias, and he asked us if I would be willing to join the team. We responded affirmatively, without hesitation.

Being a part of the speaking team at RZIM has been a dream come true, because it not only has given me a platform to fulfill my calling but also has given me a Christian family to share life with. I'm daily surrounded by amazing thinkers from various walks of life who are passionate for the cause of Christ, and they have become like brothers and sisters to me. For the first time in perhaps my entire life, I feel like I belong.

THE PRESENT

After about a year of being cut off from my family, Abba called me out of the blue. There was a family emergency, and he wanted us to stand united. Michelle and I immediately drove up to be with them, and from that time until 2014, our relationship resumed but continued to be very rocky. Although we talked fairly regularly, we did not function like a family.

But something changed in 2014, and though I'm not certain why, I have a pretty good idea. When this book came out, I started receiving emails and letters from all around the world from people I had never met but who had committed to pray for my family. God must be hearing these prayers, because that is the only explanation I can find for the sudden, dramatic improvement in our family relationships. Ammi no longer cries all the time, only shedding occasional tears. Abba and I have adult conversations that do not constantly get dragged into religious disputes. We have fun talking and sharing stories. We are finally beginning to function like a family again. In fact, they are arriving here in England tomorrow to visit their new granddaughter, Ayah. I cannot wait to show them our life here in England, and I have tons of questions to ask them about how to do this whole parenting thing. They are great parents, after all.

I will be eternally thankful for all of you who have prayed, and continue to pray, for my family.

The reason I am in England is because I remain passionate about the matters that led me to leave Islam and accept Jesus. I first built a base of theological knowledge shortly after becoming a Christian by studying at Biola University, and then I critically studied Christianity and Islam at Duke University, under Christian and Muslim professors. I am currently pursuing a doctorate in New Testament studies at Oxford, and I hope to equip truth-seekers and the church with solid reasons to have confidence in the Christian faith.

David and I are still good friends, but he and Marie now have four sons in New York who keep them very busy, so I see them less often. That said, Michelle and I plan to host them this fall, and they will have the chance to meet our beautiful Ayah. I will keep a sharp eye on their sons when the introductions are made.

It is also worth mentioning that Ayah is, at the moment, lying on a cloth given to us by Betsy, the Christian girl who sought to share the gospel with me in high school. Betsy connected with me after hearing of my conversion, and our families have met together a few times since to discuss what the Lord has been doing in our lives. I thank the Lord for her and the hundreds of people who reached out to me or prayed for me against all the odds, especially when it seemed fruitless.

REACHING MUSLIMS

Two final matters remain. First, some Christians who read my story thought it dubious that God would reach Muslims through visions and dreams today, believing that this would clash with the authority and sufficiency of Scripture. I certainly believe in the authority and sufficiency of Scripture, but I also believe God is a gracious God who is able to do immeasurably more than we can ask or imagine, and He is reaching Muslims in ways that might surprise those who are not on the mission field. That said, in every story I personally know involving Muslims who received visions or dreams, God led those Muslims either directly to the Bible or to Christians who elucidated the teachings of the Bible. In my story, the vision and dreams ultimately led me to the book of Matthew, and it was in the pages of Scripture that I encountered the living God.

Second, I have met a few people who, after reading this story, thought they needed to know all the answers about Islam before connecting with Muslims. That is certainly not the case. David barely knew anything about Islam when we started talking. What people need before befriending Muslims is not advanced knowledge of Islam but a willingness to discover what is important to their Muslim friends and the desire to invest the time to learn and discuss those matters as the relationship progresses. When it comes to a basic knowledge of Christianity, though, it is important for people to be able to articulately explain what they believe and why. That, at least, is what 1 Peter 3:15 tells Christians to do.

A CLOSING APPEAL

In closing, I wish to appeal to those who are considering following Jesus, especially those who will sacrifice much. I will honestly say that my first year as a Christian was extremely difficult, without a doubt the most painful period of my life. Each and every day was a struggle, and I experienced depths of anguish I did not know possible.

But I will also honestly say, looking back ten years later, that it was the most powerful and important time of my life. It shaped me, molded me, changed me into a disciple of Jesus. The Holy Spirit was my Comforter, His Word was my sustenance, and I would not give up that time for anything. The suffering is what made me into a true follower of Jesus. My life now, including my walk with God and my relationship with my wife, is blissful, far more wonderful than I ever could have imagined when I was a Muslim.

All suffering is worth it to follow Jesus. He is that amazing.

AFTERWORD

Mark Mittelberg

The path of the righteous is like the morning sun,
shining ever brighter till the full light of day.

—PROVERBS 4:18

I GLANCED OUT THE WINDOW as my early morning flight began descending into uncharacteristically sunny Houston. It had been only a couple of weeks since Hurricane Harvey deluged the region, but what I saw was mostly beauty, including intensely green yards, parks, and wooded areas. *I guess fifty or sixty inches of rain over a few days will liven up any landscape,* I mused.

Then something jolted me from my sleepy introspection. My eye caught a series of bright flashes emanating from a plot of ground far below. What could be causing this strobelike effect? I stretched to look down just in time to see that the sun was intermittently reflecting off the many granite gravestones in a cemetery.

What a poignant picture, I thought. The reason for my trip was to visit Nabeel Qureshi, one of my closest friends, as he clung to life in the palliative care unit of a Houston hospital. Nabeel had been fighting stage 4 stomach cancer for a little over a year, and it seemed clear that his battle was nearly done.

298

Like those polished headstones, this unusually gifted young man brightly reflected a light that was not his own. Ever since I first met Nabeel, just over a decade earlier, his life had shown a love and passion that seemed . . . well, supernatural. He truly did, as Paul put it in 2 Corinthians 3:18 (NLT), "reflect the Lord's glory," the one true God who "makes us more and more like him as we are changed into his glorious image."

You have learned much about Nabeel by reading his powerful story. Allow me to highlight here six things he deeply cared about.

First, Nabeel loved *knowledge and truth*. In fact, he went to school for almost his entire life! Besides his undergraduate degree, Nabeel earned an MD degree, and when he became a Christian while in the middle of getting his MD, he decided to pause and get an MA in Christian apologetics from Biola University. Then after he had finished both of those programs, he earned another MA, this one in religion from Duke University. Soon after that he went to Oxford to work on a PhD, and he had progressed through another MA degree before finding out he had cancer. So by the time Nabeel turned thirty-three, he had earned four advanced degrees from four prestigious universities.

Proverbs 1:7 says "fools despise wisdom and instruction," but Nabeel loved both, even when they challenged his long-held beliefs. Like any of us, he didn't enjoy finding out he was wrong, but he was not willing to blindly perpetuate hand-me-down ideas. He had to know that what he believed, what he built his life on, was based on reality, not speculation or tradition.

On a more personal level, Nabeel referred to me as one of his mentors, and in spite of his brilliant intellect and extensive education, I always found him to have a humble and teachable spirit. He was *hungry* for godly wisdom and instruction, and he often came looking for it.

Second, Nabeel loved *God*. Initially that meant following Allah wholeheartedly. But his love for truth led him to dig deeper. When he found the true God—when he found Jesus—he was immediately committed to loving and serving Him with all of his heart, soul, mind, and strength (as Jesus instructed in Mark 12:30).

I never saw Nabeel waver in his love for God. He prioritized

God above all else, including his family, his career, and his future. We sometimes discussed how he was living out the words of Jesus in Matthew 19:29: "And everyone who has left houses or brothers or sisters or father or mother or wife or children or fields for my sake will receive a hundred times as much and will inherit eternal life." Nabeel understood the cost of following Jesus, yet he followed Him faithfully anyway.

Third, Nabeel loved his *family*. It absolutely broke his heart to think of his beloved father and mother finding out that he had left Islam to follow Jesus. You have read about the pain this caused for him, and for them. But I can assure you that all the way to the end of his life, nothing was more important to Nabeel than helping them, along with his treasured sister and other relatives and friends, to come to know the true Savior, and we often prayed together to that end.

I should add that after landing in Houston the morning I went to the hospital where Nabeel was receiving palliative care, he introduced me to his father, mother, and sister. They are wonderful and loving people who have a real passion for their Muslim faith. Yet I believe, as Nabeel did, that they need the grace and forgiveness available only through Christ.

Nabeel also loved his wife and daughter, deeply. I believe his greatest sadness in facing death was not that he would lose his own life but rather that his precious wife, Michelle, would lose her husband and that his sweet little daughter, Ayah, would lose her daddy. I think it was more for them than for himself that he so earnestly prayed for divine healing or successful medical intervention.

Fourth, Nabeel loved his *friends*. This book is in large part the story of an extraordinary friendship. Yes, Nabeel and David sparred with each other (that never ended; Nabeel dedicated *No God But One* "to David Wood, a great friend and total doofus"), and at times they got frustrated with each other. But they walked together throughout life, and that will continue into eternity.

I was introduced to Nabeel by our mutual friend Michael Licona, whom you read about in this book. Our backgrounds couldn't have been more different, but Nabeel and I hit it off immediately as friends. We had similar musical tastes, enjoyed great meals together, loved God, and were both passionate about knowing and spreading the truths of Christianity. I was so confident about the sincerity of Nabeel's faith that I wrote about it way back in my 2008 book, now titled *Confident Faith: Building a Firm Foundation for Your Beliefs.*

In addition, Nabeel's quick wit, fun sense of humor, love of laughter, and mischievous personality all combined to make him a delight to be with.

Fifth, Nabeel loved *ministry.* How much did he love ministry? Enough to walk away from what undoubtedly would have been a successful career in medicine, and in spite of years of hard work getting his MD, with hefty school loans to show for it. It was a difficult decision that a few of us were privileged to walk through with him. Ultimately, he was adamant that he wanted to commit his best years to serving God and reaching people. Looking back, how happy I am that he invested his limited time so well.

Nabeel started off in an apologetics ministry with David Wood called Acts 17. Then he went solo with Creed 2:6, but soon after was hired by Ravi Zacharias to become a speaker for Ravi Zacharias International Ministries (RZIM). This opened many doors for Nabeel, and God used him in greater and greater ways around the world. If you had the privilege of seeing Nabeel speak, you know he came *alive* when he stood in front of a group of any size, proclaiming the truth of the gospel.

In addition, Nabeel enjoyed mentoring younger Christians, as he did frequently, including when he would stay in our home and build into the lives of my own kids, Emma Jean and Matthew. Nabeel's influence was part of what led Matthew to study at Oxford University with Ravi Zacharias's Oxford Centre for Christian Apologetics (OCCA) and to serve as a fellow with that organization.

In addition to writing *Seeking Allah, Finding Jesus*, Nabeel wrote *Answering Jihad: A Better Way Forward*, and finally *No God but One: Allah or Jesus? A Former Muslim Investigates the Evidence for Islam and Christianity.* Two of his books became *New York Times* bestsellers. Nabeel also recorded dozens of online videos in which he talked about his life and taught about Islam and Christianity.

Sixth, Nabeel loved *good food.* I can't end without mentioning Nabeel's love for great cuisine. It was a key component of many of his relationships. I have great memories of meals with Nabeel at a dodgy

Japanese restaurant near the heart of Washington, DC; at a wonderful bistro in Carmel-by-the-Sea, California; at a sushi restaurant in Denver, Colorado (though I prefer my sushi *grilled*, thank you); and at my home, where he, my kids, and I would devour my wife Heidi's Louisiana-style prime rib roasts. I should add that Nabeel had his own recipe for broiling steaks, and one time he almost ignited our kitchen in the process of preparing them for us!

As you have probably guessed, my journey to Houston that day was the final visit I had with Nabeel. He died just five days later, full of faith and hope in the Savior who had redeemed him.

It is with both joy and sadness that I remember my friend. Joy for the life he lived, the great memories, and the impact of his highly effective ministry. Sadness because he left us too soon, though I know I'll see him again in heaven. You will see Nabeel there as well, if you put your trust in the Savior he loved and served.

We can learn much from Nabeel's example. In a video he recorded on April 13, 2017—several months before he died—he prayed, "Lord, please help me be a good son, a good husband, a good father, a good friend, and a good minister. Lord, when this is all done, people are going to remember how much we loved them and nothing else. And so Lord, I pray that I might be a reflection of You, God, and of Your love for Your children."

If we follow the one who declared in John 8:12, "I am the light of the world," then we too, like Nabeel, can be, like the beams of light reflecting from the granite headstones that morning, a bright reflection of His light and love to people all around us.

> Wherever the Spirit of the Lord is, there is freedom. So all of us who have had that veil removed can see and reflect the glory of the Lord. And the Lord—who is the Spirit—makes us more and more like him as we are changed into his glorious image.
>
> —2 Corinthians 3:17–18 NLT

A WIFE'S REFLECTIONS

Michelle Qureshi

I STOOD ROOTED TO THE SPOT at the Coast Guard base in Portsmouth, Virginia, where I was lodged for the summer. I was completing an internship before my senior year at the Coast Guard Academy, and I had come to the picnic area at the conclusion of a workday to pray and read Scripture. Little did I expect God would meet me there in the most profound way I had ever experienced. Once released from my stunned silence, I raced back to the barracks and pulled out my journal.

30 May 2007
I have just had an encounter with God.
I heard a voice inside me say, "My child."
I turned to face the sun and said, "Yes, Lord."
God told me to sit on a nearby bench, and as I looked toward the west, the sun glowed brilliantly between a grove of trees, perfectly nestled within their branches.
"I am the way, the truth, and the life."
The words burst forth boldly and without question from the blinding rays of the sun.
I said to the Lord, "I am unable to gaze upon Your beauty, for it is too much for me."
"I know," He said with a voice of understanding.

I began then to think of Nabeel, something I first passed off as a distraction from my Lord.

"Nabeel will give you a ring."

My heart jumped, and I put up a defense to keep it in check, for I feared my own longings were interfering with the message from my Lord.

But the words seemed stronger than mere desires of the flesh.

Words came yet again to my mind, saying, "I want you with Nabeel."

I pleaded with God, asking Him for guidance and a clear sign that the voice was truly His own.

The Lord was gracious to me, and He led me to close my eyes.

He gave me a vision.

I pictured myself in the Qureshi household; the prominent figure was Nabeel's mom.

I was speaking Urdu and wore traditional clothing, paying all respects I could in their culture. Yet tension was in the home.

"Is this what I must do?" I asked.

The answer was yes.

I had been dating Nabeel Qureshi long-distance for a mere four months at the time. But on that day, God spoke clearly to me, making known His intentions regarding our relationship. Despite the revelation of continuing hurt in his family relationships, I was unreservedly committed—my heart was smitten, and my spirit trusted my Lord's desires. Eight months later, we were engaged.

On September 16, 2017, after nine years of marriage, Nabeel was welcomed home to heaven for eternity.

God knew full well from the beginning what He asked of me.

My relationship with Nabeel began with an intense burden for the Qureshi family. During our initial meeting in Atlanta at the 2007 Passion conference, Nabeel shared with me a link to the first written version of his testimony, an article on Answering Islam's website titled "Crossing Over." Tears streamed down my face as I read, contemplating the anguish of strained family ties as well as the incredible character of a man so in love with Jesus that he willingly sacrificed everything he once held dear.

Despite the pain in the relationship with his parents, Nabeel was not to be swayed from his dedication to do the ministry to which he was called, a pursuit which yet again cost him. During our engagement, Nabeel warned me to fasten my seatbelt because it was going to be a rollercoaster ride of a marriage. As a naive twenty-one-year-old from a protected, conservative Christian, homeschooled background, I responded with innocent enthusiasm, having no idea what was in store for us.

My military service obligation, which spanned the first five years of our marriage, coupled with Nabeel's educational and ministerial objectives resulted in significant time apart. We experienced eight two-month separations, one year-long period of living in different states, and countless one- to two-week timeframes without seeing each other. These became so common they began to feel normal. The separations, on top of moving eight times in nine years, prevented the development of deep-rooted community, yielding seasons of loneliness and the necessity to wrestle through many challenges in isolation.

But while the cost of obedience to the Lord can be high, it will always result in fruitfulness. In my obedience to marry Nabeel, which was happily in line with my desires, I found myself becoming beautifully refined: my faith deepened as exposure to Christian apologetics taught me to ask myself why I believed what I believed, my stringent military training and hardline personality loosened up in response to Nabeel's carefree manner, and my tendency to be a homebody was challenged in a healthy way by Nabeel's adventurous spirit.

Similarly, Nabeel's obedience to his call to ministry saw many lives changed: his speaking engagements encouraged Christians and non-Christians alike to further investigate their beliefs, his teachings on Islam brought well-rounded clarity, and his writings transformed countless people around the globe. The summer of 2016 found Nabeel at the pinnacle of his career, a sought-after speaker of Ravi Zacharias International Ministries, a *New York Times* bestselling author with a third book about to release, and a mere two years away from fulfilling his lifelong dream of obtaining a PhD through Oxford University.

Then on August 24, 2016, the cancer diagnosis struck. But not just any cancer: stage 4 stomach cancer, with a 4 percent chance of survival.

Ministry and schooling screeched to a halt. All plans for the future hung in the balance as we began the year-long battle for Nabeel's life. Wrenched both from our community in Oxford and the house we had just built in Atlanta, we and our then one-year-old daughter, Ayah, relocated to Houston to seek medical care at MD Anderson. To further compound our season of upheaval, the baby we were expecting miscarried within the first two months of our move. We were beyond distraught.

Yet through the adversity, God drew us closer to Himself and taught us what it really means to trust with all of our hearts. Apart from any effort of our own, Nabeel and I suddenly found ourselves in an amazingly dedicated community of believers. These incredible people challenged our worldview, exhibiting great expectations of a great God, and delighting in Jesus with their whole being. They were undaunted by the gravity of our situation and showed us that we too could obtain the joy, peace, and strength that come from tapping into the power of the Holy Spirit.

As the treatments progressed and Nabeel's condition worsened, I came to realize that, apart from Jesus, I really can't do anything. But I also realized that I really can do all things through Christ who strengthens me. When I finally submitted to the fact that a sovereign, good, and trustworthy God was the one in control, not me, I was set free from the hold that fear and anxiety had on me. God was for me, so, regardless of my circumstances, what could be against me?

Despite Nabeel's spending the great majority of his remaining weeks hospitalized and in a state of decline, I stood strong upon the Rock that cannot be shaken. During his last few days in palliative care, I was reminded that at the end of the day, I can only rely on the Word of God. No message of intended inspiration or encouragement can ever compare to the hope and confidence provided by the one infallible Truth.

In the months following Nabeel's burial, I realized anew, with startling clarity, that this life is not purely physical, nor is it arbitrary. The spiritual realm is very real, and God's perfect plan for our lives is full to the brim and overflowing with purpose. He is all about far exceeding our expectations.

Nabeel was a God-fearing man, fully dedicated to the Great

Commission. I am convinced that his death will lead to a more glorious end than we would have seen if he were still alive. What a privilege to have been chosen to lift high his message for the season I was called to be his wife. I look forward to what the Lord has in store for the seasons to come.

REMEMBERING NABEEL

A Conversation between David Wood and Nabeel Qureshi

The following conversation was recorded in Atlanta, Georgia, during the Evangelical Theological Society's annual meeting in November 2015. Nabeel and David got together to reminisce about their friendship, Nabeel's conversion, and what they'd learned about ministering to Muslims.

Nabeel Qureshi: When was the first time we met? I remember being on the forensics team with you at Old Dominion University, but I don't recall the very first time we met.

David Wood: You came to the meetings, and it didn't take long to figure out you were a Muslim. I was thinking, "Cool, maybe he's not here by coincidence."

Nabeel Qureshi: You had had a Muslim friend before, though, right?

David Wood: That didn't work out well. It was right after I'd become a Christian. I didn't know a lot, either factually or characterwise, about being a Christian. I had a good friend who was an imam, and he was my weightlifting partner. You're probably thinking I've never been in a gym in my life, but this was a long time ago. We'd be lifting weights and arguing, and it was just a mess. We would get very vocal, very quickly. So we were friends for six months or so, then it didn't work out. When I met you, I thought, "I need to make sure I don't dial it up to a ten very quickly like I did with my other friend."

Nabeel Qureshi: Do you remember the first time we had a discussion on religion?

David Wood: You started it. We were in a hotel room on a trip, and I was reading my Bible, praying, "God, my last conversations with a Muslim did not work out very well. If you want me to talk to this guy, let him start it." That's when you said, "So are you a hardcore Christian?"

Nabeel Qureshi: That evening we started talking about how the Bible was passed down. As a Muslim I was very confident I knew a lot about the Bible, even though now in retrospect I know I didn't. How did you perceive my knowledge of the Bible? My attacks against the Bible, how did they strike you?

David Wood: I'd talked to Muslims before. I knew that they are very confident, because they hear certain things all their lives. It was just, "This guy really believes this, and it's totally wrong; I hope he eventually sees that." I didn't know then we were going to be friends for years.

Nabeel Qureshi: Coming into that conversation, I was convinced Christians didn't know what they were talking about. I thought if Christians had any education, they would've known the Bible was corrupted. I thought Christians were polytheists. All I had to do was tell people Christianity was false, and they would realize they were wrong.

We had a conversation that night, and I recall for the first time thinking, "Here's a Christian who knows what he's talking about." So even though I saw myself as sparring with you, I had respect for you, because you had a backbone, you actually had some knowledge about your faith, you didn't believe it blindly. Shortly after that point, I thought, "We're the same sort of person. He's Christian, I'm Muslim, but we have the same values; we have the same conviction in our faith."

David Wood: I was thinking some of the same things. In

college people can become totally relativistic, and it's hard to have a conversation. You were telling me, "Islam is proven by history, it's proven by science, it's proven by logic, and any evidence you can find is all in favor of Islam." I was thinking, "I can deal with that. We can go through the evidence and see where it points."

Nabeel Qureshi: There was a specific moment I recall thinking, "Now we're brothers." Someone was trying to argue against you, and they were clearly in the wrong. Do you remember this?

David Wood: I remember it very well. My whole life I've usually been the biggest guy around, so people don't stick up for me. A girl was blaming me for something, really yelling at me, and it was after she had talked to a bunch people about me. Then you, who didn't even know me well, said, "I think if you're going to say something about someone, you should go to that person first." It was cool that you stood up for me.

Nabeel Qureshi: After that point, I felt like we were brothers. We started signing up for classes together. The most catastrophic was evolutionary biology.

David Wood: We would have had a problem anyway, just because you love to talk so much, but—

Nabeel Qureshi: Wait, you do too; come on.

David Wood: I know, but the professor had crazy hair, and you couldn't stop talking about it. I couldn't even take notes.

Nabeel Qureshi: She was an atheist, right?

David Wood: Rabid.

Nabeel Qureshi: She would come against theism with hard-core attacks in the middle of class. I would kind of vent by making fun of her hair. I would talk about—

David Wood: The evolution of her hair.

Nabeel Qureshi: Talk about the kingdom, class, phylum, genus, species of her hair. I had to drop out of that class.

David Wood: You didn't drop out of genetics. That was really bad. We could be sitting there talking for half of the fifty minutes, and I didn't hear one word the professor said, but then he would ask, "Any questions?" You would turn, your hand would shoot up, and you would start asking a question about what he was talking about. I was impressed.

Nabeel Qureshi: You've got to make the professor think you're paying attention.

David Wood: I got the highest grade in the class, though.

Nabeel Qureshi: Did you beat me? Are you sure? Something tells me I had a higher grade, but we'll let you remember it the way you remember it. Can you recall the time we met Marie? It was the evening of a forensics trip.

David Wood: We were arguing about the resurrection. We explained to her what we were arguing about, and she said, "You're both right." We both, all of a sudden, were united.

Nabeel Qureshi: Because I was saying, "Look, he did not rise from the dead." You were saying, "He is risen from the dead."

David Wood: Those are the only two possibilities. One is right; the other wrong. What she meant was all religious views had the same status.

Nabeel Qureshi: But neither Christians nor Muslims believe that.

David Wood: That's the point. We were united that, no, we can't both be right.

Nabeel Qureshi: We argued with her for the rest of the plane ride. Later that night at the hotel, you said, "I'm going to marry her."

David Wood: And I did.

Nabeel Qureshi: You did. A year later you did.

David Wood: You and I became better and better friends. Somewhere between two and three years later, I noticed you didn't have the same sort of confidence in arguments you used to use. So I asked a question I had asked years earlier: "Why are you a Muslim?" You terrified me when you said, "God knows our faculties are limited. We can't get to the ultimate truth of things. So I'm just going to remain a Muslim."

Nabeel Qureshi: The ironic thing was as I was losing confidence in my ability to know Islam is true, I was acting more and more Muslim. I started leading the Muslim youth group in our city. I was covering up the cognitive dissonance, because it's a shameful thing to doubt Islam. I've seen it quite a bit. Now I have people say to me, "I was trying to reach out to my Muslim friend with the gospel, but they've just become more and more Muslim." I actually think it's a good sign. I think it shows that they're losing confidence in their faith.

At the end of that conversation, you told me, "Nabeel, hasn't your father had prophetic dreams? Haven't you? Don't you think God is willing to tell you the truth if you seek him?" I remember it was a powerful moment, because we were graduating from college, I was going to medical school, but I just felt broken. You said, "You need to pray; you need to ask God."

David Wood: I was thinking that's all I could do at that point. If you no longer trust your ability to get to the truth, all I can do is pray and hope God does something.

Nabeel Qureshi: That's actually a good thing, right? When someone has gotten to a place where they're not relying on themselves.

David Wood: I regard that as the point of apologetics now.

Nabeel Qureshi: Exactly. I did start asking God. It took many months; I remember shedding tears. I would say, "God, I'm absolutely, one hundred percent convinced You're there; why aren't You answering this prayer?" It hurt. But in retrospect, I know God was tenderizing my heart. Then I had a dream one night, a very symbolic dream. I knew it was from God the moment I woke up. I called you and said, "David, do Christians believe God can give people dreams?"

David Wood: I remember talking about Joseph, saying yes, in the Bible God gives people dreams.

Nabeel Qureshi: I didn't want to tell you what I had seen in the dream because I had a feeling deep down that God was pointing me to Christianity, and I didn't want you to be right. Instead, I called my mom, and she started trying to interpret the symbols in my dream using an Islamic dream book. As she was interpreting the symbols, one after another after another, it was very clear God was telling me Christianity would save me and Islam would be the death of me.

Nabeel Qureshi: Later, when I told you the dream, you said—

David Wood: "Does God need to whack you with a baseball bat? What's it going to take?"

Nabeel Qureshi: My response was, "Look, it's a symbolic dream; I can't wager my eternal destiny, my family, everything I have, on a dream." We had discussed the death and resurrection of Jesus for years, and we had talked about Muhammad and the Quran for years. I had reasons my confidence in Islam was shaken. But I wanted something more clear. So I asked God for a second dream. It didn't come for a few more months. But when the second dream came, I remember calling you first thing in the morning when I woke up.

David Wood: When you have a dream that inserts you into a Bible parable you hadn't read before, I took that seriously.

Nabeel Qureshi: Yes, in the dream I was standing at a narrow door, watching a feast, knowing there were Christians inside, because you were there. But I was not allowed in; I had to respond to an invitation you'd issued me in order to enter the feast, which I knew was in heaven. People ask, "How did you know?" I just knew in the dream that the room was heaven.

When I called, you said the Gospel of Luke has this passage in it, Luke 13:22.

David Wood: The narrow door.

Nabeel Qureshi: I remember in my dream the narrow door was the most powerful symbol.

David Wood: So you converted right after that, right?

Nabeel Qureshi: No, I asked for a third dream. My reason was because in Islam, Allah prefers odd numbers, and in Christianity God is a trinity. The third dream came pretty quickly. It was a dream of me on a set of stairs leaving the mosque, and I could not get off those stairs. No matter how much I wanted to fall in line behind the imam, who I loved and trusted, I couldn't get off the stairs.

David Wood: By this time it was even funny. When you asked how I would interpret the first dream, it was possible to come up with all kinds of interpretations, but there's only one that fits you on a stairway leaving a mosque and you can't get off the stairway. So you became a Christian then, right?

Nabeel Qureshi: I was wrestling with what I was going to have to do and asking God for comfort and guidance.

David Wood: That was rough. When I became a Christian, I could have told my family that I had become a Buddhist; it wouldn't have made a difference to my grandmother. My family didn't care as long as I wasn't doing bad things. But your family was the closest family I'd ever seen. So I'm thinking, "I've been telling this guy he needs to believe in Jesus, but his life is going to be destroyed in a lot of ways. This could be devastating for my best friend."

Nabeel Qureshi: It was very difficult. How did my family strike you when you first got to know them?

David Wood: When people post on Facebook about Muslims being evil or they're all terrorists, the first thing that pops into my head is your family. I was at your house so much; I know there are really good Muslim families. So that was the situation. You're my best friend. I want you to become a Christian. I want you to know Jesus. At the same time I understand what that's going to do to your mom, what that's going to do to your dad.

Nabeel Qureshi: I have had Christians say, "I don't think you should become a Christian based on dreams," but that's not how I became a Christian. First the apologetics tore down the barrier between me and God. I got to a point where I needed to rely on God. Then it was dreams and visions, which I trusted as a Muslim, that opened my heart to see God answering my prayer. But the final step was reading Scripture. I remember reading through Matthew, asking God to comfort me, to give me peace.

David Wood: Is this when you were coming to our Sunday school?

Nabeel Qureshi: It was right before. When I looked through the Quran to ask Allah for comfort, there was nothing. It was all conditional; if you repent, Allah will respond, or if you do this, God will do that. That's not what I needed. I needed a God who just loves me and wants to comfort me. I turned to the Bible and came to Matthew 5 where it says, "Blessed are those who mourn, for they shall be comforted." The next verse says, "Blessed are those who hunger and thirst for righteousness, for they shall be satisfied." Not those who perform righteousness, not those who are righteous. In that moment I fell in love with the Bible. The next Sunday, I went to church with you.

David Wood: My wife and I taught Sunday school, and it was just hilarious that you would come and start pointing things out to the kids there.

Nabeel Qureshi: I, as a Muslim, was teaching Christian kids how to do exegesis on the Bible. After that, you pulled me aside and said, "Nabeel, you're trying to teach Bible studies; when are you going to become a Christian?"

David Wood: Just think about it, right? You were living like a Christian, yet you were a Muslim.

Nabeel Qureshi: I didn't convert that day either. It wasn't until the next week I actually committed my life to Christ. It was on a Wednesday, but I didn't tell you until Sunday. Do you remember?

David Wood: We ended up going to a Chinese restaurant after church. Someone asked, "Who's going to say grace?" You said, "I'll say it." And I was thinking, "I have a Muslim praying over my food now," and—

Nabeel Qureshi: You didn't think that internally. You said it out loud.

David Wood: Right! Then you concluded your prayer with the words, "I pray this in the name of the Father and the Son and the Holy Spirit." Everyone else at the table got it. I didn't. I was thinking, "My goodness, now he's even praying like a Christian."

Nabeel Qureshi: You actually said, "What's wrong with you? Why don't you become a Christian already?" Marie, your wife, grabbed you and said, "Don't you get it, David? He did." You looked at me like, "No." And I just nodded.

A question: Is it easy for the lighthearted to minister to Muslims?

David Wood: No, you will be criticized if you start reaching out to Muslims.

Nabeel Qureshi: You need to have thick skin.

David Wood: You have to be in it for the long haul. I had Christians tell me I was wasting my time, because you and I were spending years going through everything. Some told me, "You could be talking to so many atheists right now; you're a former atheist. You're spending all this time with the same guy, going back and forth arguing about things." At the same time, if God put us together, who was I to say it's time to stop now?

A part of why it took so long is the barriers that Muslims face, right? When a Muslim hears the Good News, he's thinking, "This will send me to hell." It doesn't come across as good news. Also, you are fortunate that you managed to still have a relationship with your parents. I know Muslims who say, "The last time I saw my parents is when I told them I became a Christian."

Nabeel Qureshi: With Muslims, you need to have a long-term relationship, not just during evangelism but after the person has accepted the Lord. They need someone to turn to. They need someone for discipleship. They need a new community, a Christian community to come around them.

In our friendship, was it always sunshine and roses?

David Wood: No, there were very heated discussions. But that's good; you can have an argument with a good friend, whereas if you had an argument with someone who's not your friend, you might not talk to that person again.

Nabeel Qureshi: Did you have all the answers before we became friends?

David Wood: No, you would claim something, and I would go look it up. That's how I started studying Muslim sources.

Nabeel Qureshi: So you don't have to know everything to

minister to Muslims, but you need to at least have confidence in your own Christian faith. You need to be able to present why you trust the Bible. Do you believe Jesus is risen? Why? Do you believe he's God? Can you articulate the Trinity? Also, it's helpful to know a little bit about Islam, but no Muslim fits perfectly the Islamic mold. Everyone has slight differences.

David Wood: There are different kinds of Muslims, some who are attracted to the love in Christianity. Others, it's like they listen only if you speak aggressively. They respect it more if you stand your ground.

Nabeel Qureshi: To summarize how to minister to Muslims, I think we can encapsulate it with Mark 12: "Love the Lord your God with all your heart, soul, mind, and strength, and love your neighbor as yourself." As we love people, like you did with me, I became your friend. We lived life together. You loved God with all your heart, soul, mind, and strength while you also loved me. I got to see that.

The danger is when people only love their neighbors but don't proclaim the gospel, or on the flip side, they proclaim the gospel but don't love their neighbors. You need to do both, in tandem. That's my final piece of advice for people who minister to Muslims.

This is a spiritual struggle. We need to remember we are agents of God. He has called us, He has equipped us, and we're asking the Holy Spirit to do the work fearlessly. The largest group of religious believers apart from Christians in the world today are Muslims. We need to be prepared to reach out to them and rely on God to do that through us.

Thanks, David, for sticking it through with me. I really appreciate our brotherhood.

APPENDIX 1:
EXPERT CONTRIBUTIONS

GROWING UP MUSLIM IN AMERICA

ABDU MURRAY

Contributing to Part 1: "Called to Prayer"

Abdu Murray is a lawyer, apologist, and former Shia Muslim. Author of two published books on Islam and other major worldviews, he is currently president of Embrace the Truth International.

IN THE SALTY-WHITE LANDSCAPE of the Detroit suburb of my youth, my family was a dash of pepper. We stood out because, at that time, we were exotic—one of the few Muslim families in the area. And I took Islam seriously so that I could stand out even more because that would cause my friends to ask questions about my faith. That, in turn, would lead to opportunities to share what I considered to be the beauty and truth of Islam with the low-hanging fruit of the many non-Muslim, mostly Christian, individuals around me.

I was like many Muslims I knew. Even as a youth, I loved talking about God and my Islamic faith. I was puzzled that the non-Muslims around me found it so uncomfortable to talk about matters of religion. *Don't these Christians really believe their traditions? If their message is true, why are they so afraid to talk about it?* The answer, I told myself, is that Christians know deep down that their religion is silly. They only need to be shown the truth of Islam to see the true path.

Muslims get that kind of confidence from religious training received during their childhood and teen years. Most are students at the informal academy of the American Muslim home. Our parents, uncles, and older relatives sit us down and teach us Muslim apologetics: the defense of the Muslim worldview. The Quran is the word of God, we are taught, because Muhammad was illiterate and could not have come up with such beautiful, profound language on his own. From this informal training, we come to believe that the Quran is proven to be miraculous because it contains scientific information and facts that have only recently been discovered. And we are told, time and time again, that the Quran we have today is exactly the same as was delivered to Muhammad, with no changes whatsoever in fourteen hundred years. Islam provides the best way to live a moral and just life. And on the teachings go. Those kinds of discussions are steady fare at a Muslim family's dinner table.

But we also have a steady diet of polemics. From a young age, I was told that although Christians may mean well and may even sincerely follow their faith, their faith is fatally flawed. Their sacred texts were once the unadulterated word of God, but they fell into hopeless corruption. And Christians had invented logically ridiculous doctrines, like the divinity of Jesus and the Trinity. The Quran was revealed to Muhammad in seventh-century Arabia to undo the harm caused by the biblical corruption and blasphemous teachings of Christianity. Muhammad's mission was to restore true religion. And it was my goal as a good Muslim to continue that mission.

But equipping young people to spread what is believed to be the truth is not the sole motivation for this informal training. Muslims of earlier generations fear that the negative aspects of American culture could be a powerful, corrupting influence on successive generations. They fear their children will succumb to temptation and order their meals from the menu of illicit drug use, drunkenness, and wanton sexual promiscuity that they believe is characteristic of American life. But if young Muslims remain convicted of their Islamic beliefs, they will be better equipped to resist the temptations. As bad as these lifestyle pitfalls are, they pale in comparison to the ultimate dishonor of abandoning Islam, especially if it means becoming a Christian. Islam is not just a set of religious beliefs. It is an all-encompassing identity. It is inconceivable to change that identity, even for those who barely practice their Islamic faith. To do so is like suicide. It kills the identity of the convert and leaves the rest of the family in a state of shameful mourning.

A healthy diet of apologetics and polemics, spiced with cultural pride, it is believed, can help prevent that disaster. And young Muslims are convinced by their families that being a Muslim means to affirm Muhammad's prophethood and the Quran's divine origin while at the same time resisting the very idea of becoming anything else, especially a Christian.

Most Christians have a hard time imagining what it is like to live with the tension of blending in with American society while maintaining a Muslim identity. And so most don't understand the difficulty Muslims have in even considering that the gospel might be true. I thank God that there are those precious (and all too few) Christians who exhibit Jesus' love and caring in their actions and who thoughtfully proclaim the beauty and truth of the gospel in their words. God uses them to carefully navigate the waters of spiritual discussion without running aground (well, as little as possible).

Like so many Muslims who eventually give their lives to Christ, it took me quite some time to embrace the truth, though that truth is worth embracing, despite the tremendous price I paid. I knew that fully embracing the person and work of Jesus Christ would cost me the very identity that had been forged for me at the dinner tables of the Muslim community. Until I was able to see that Christ is worth the cost, I was not willing to pay it. But eventually, I understood what the famed Jim Eliot, who lost his life in service of the gospel, meant when he wrote, "He is no fool who gives what he cannot keep to gain what he cannot lose."[118] Eliot rephrased Paul's words that "for his sake I have suffered the loss of all things and count them as rubbish, in order that I may gain Christ" (Phil. 3:8 ESV). Yet the price that Jesus paid for us dwarfs whatever price we might pay to follow Him. C. S. Lewis wrote that God's love for us "is quite relentless in its determination that we shall be cured of [our] sins, at whatever cost to us, at whatever cost to Him."[119] Following such a God is worth sacrificing our identities so that we can be given a new one that looks more and more like Jesus.

Since giving my life to Jesus, the table set before me is quite different. Before, I gobbled up superficial answers that left my stomach gnawing and my throat parched. But in Christ, my hunger is fed by the Bread of Life and my thirst is slaked by the Living Water who satisfies eternally.

EAST MEETS WEST

MARK MITTELBERG

Contributing to Part 2:
"An Ambassador for Islam"

Mark Mittelberg is bestselling author and primary creator of the course Becoming a Contagious Christian, *which has trained 1.5 million people worldwide and has been translated into more than twenty languages. He served as evangelism director with the Willow Creek Association for more than a decade.*

"IT IS IMPORTANT for you to know that Allah is the one and only God, and that Muhammad, peace be upon him, was his true prophet. God is not divided, and He does not have a son. And Jesus, peace be upon him, was not the Son of God. He was a true prophet, like Muhammad, and we are to honor him, but we must never worship him. We worship Allah and Allah alone."

These bold words, spoken by the imam—a man dressed in white who stood in front of our group and was clearly in charge of the mosque that day—were communicated in a manner that delivered more than just theological content. They were conveyed with an authority that made clear that the message was something we were expected to accept, rather than test.

It was not that the imam wasn't willing to entertain a few questions. Rather, he apparently saw this as a chance to challenge the thinking of an entire group of Christians at one time. So after a short period of teaching, he opened the floor to whatever issues we wanted to raise. But even then, he responded with an emphatic tone, one that relayed his belief that he had the truth and we were there to learn it.

This assuredness was borne out when I finally raised my own question. I asked the imam why he and other Muslims denied that Jesus is the Son of God, that He died on the cross, and that He rose from the dead three days later. As politely as I knew how, I explained that I, and the others from my church who were visiting the mosque that day, believed these things on the basis of the testimonies of Jesus' own disciples. They were the ones who walked and talked with Him for three years and who heard Him make repeated claims to be the Son of God. They saw Him die on the cross and met, talked with, and even ate with Him after His resurrection. And they were the ones who made sure it was all written down in the New Testament gospels.

"What I'm curious about," I said, concluding my question, "is whether you have any historical or logical reasons why we should accept your Muslim point of view over and against what we understand to be the actual historical record?"

The imam looked at me intently and then declared resolutely, "I choose to believe the prophet!" With that, our time for questions was over.

East meets West, indeed! I walked away that day with a fresh awareness that we do not all approach questions about truth in the same way. In fact, years later, I wrote about what I believe is a characteristically Eastern versus a characteristically Western approach to gaining knowledge.[120]

In the East, and for Islam in particular, what is accepted as true is generally what the authorities tell you — and you are expected to embrace what they teach. That is why I call this approach the Authoritarian Faith Path. In fact, the original meaning of the Arabic word *Islam* is "submission." It seems fair to say that the prevailing tenor of the Muslim faith is one of submitting to — not questioning — what the religion teaches.

This squares with my friend Nabeel Qureshi's assessment in this part 2 of his book: "People from Eastern Islamic cultures generally assess truth through lines of authority, not individual reasoning. Of course, individuals do engage in critical reasoning in the East, but on average it is relatively less valued and far less prevalent than in the West. Leaders have done the critical reasoning, and leaders know best."

As Nabeel indicates, this contrasts sharply with the more typical approach in the West, which I refer to as the Evidential Faith Path.

This approach decides what should be accepted as true based not on the word of authorities but rather on logic and experience, including experiences recorded in trustworthy historical records like the ones I cited in my interactions with the imam.

Of course, both sides can have their pitfalls. Westerners in the evidential mindset often need to be reminded to be lovers of truth (2 Thess. 2:10) who are willing to rigorously apply reason and the study of evidence, and then follow them wherever they lead. Too often, people in Western culture fall into an approach that limits possible causes to naturalistic ones, and they won't even consider supernatural causes. This prejudices the outcome and, in fact, makes scientific and historical inquiry atheistic by definition. But if we can help people reopen their minds to the full gamut of possible explanations, then I'm confident that logic and evidence (along with the inner workings of the Holy Spirit) will lead them back not only to a belief in God but also to the Christian faith.[121]

Easterners who embrace an authoritarian mindset need to be reminded that religious authorities are not all created equal; some are worth following, and some are not. If the credentials of the leaders are not scrutinized and their messages not weighed, how can one know which should be followed? The Bible encourages us to "test everything; hold fast what is good" (1 Thess. 5:21 ESV) and warns, "do not believe every spirit, but test the spirits to see whether they are from God, for many false prophets have gone out into the world" (1 John 4:1 ESV).

The question is, Will Easterners have the courage and tenacity to apply the needed tests? This can be challenging because, as Nabeel reminds us, "When authority is derived from position rather than reason, the act of questioning leadership is dangerous because it has the potential to upset the system. Dissension is reprimanded and obedience is rewarded."

Thankfully, more and more Muslims are willing to face the inherent dangers and discomforts in order to seek not only the truth but ultimately the one who said He is the truth (John 14:6). Nabeel is an inspiring example, one I trust many others will emulate.

THE NEW TESTAMENT

DANIEL B. WALLACE

Contributing to Part 3: "Testing the New Testament"

Dr. Daniel B. Wallace is a professor of New Testament studies at Dallas Theological Seminary. He is the senior New Testament editor of the NET Bible and a consultant on four other Bible translations. His book on biblical Greek grammar, Greek Grammar beyond the Basics: Exegetical Syntax of the New Testament, *is the standard textbook in the English-speaking world and has been translated into multiple other languages.*

IN MY SECOND YEAR of college, I transferred to Biola University, a small Christian liberal arts school in Southern California. I went there to study the Bible. I had the good fortune of studying Greek from a bona fide textual scholar, Dr. Harry Sturz. Several weeks into the first semester, on a hot Friday afternoon, Dr. Sturz briefly informed us that not all the manuscripts of the New Testament said the same thing. "In fact, there are hundreds of thousands of textual differences among the manuscripts," Dr. Sturz calmly stated at the end of the hour. Then, without further explanation, he dismissed the class.

I went home that afternoon, bewildered and confused. *How can I have any assurance that what we have today is the word of God? How do I know the Bible hasn't been corrupted beyond all recognition?* I had committed my life to Christ a few years earlier. Now I wanted to know if I had given my life to a myth.

Thus began my lifelong investigation into the reliability of the text of the New Testament. Dr. Sturz wanted his students to own their convictions and to study the evidence for themselves. This is why he sometimes threw his charges into existential crises of faith. I've been studying the New Testament for more than forty years, largely inspired by his model. And I've come to realize that while the great number of variants is only part of the story, it is an important part that attests to the vitality of the gospel.

In my spiritual and academic journeys, I have learned that it is imperative for Christians to pursue truth at all costs. And what I have learned about textual variants and their impact on the Christian faith over more than forty years of examining both published Greek New Testaments and hundreds of individual manuscripts has strengthened my faith in ways I never had thought possible.

In this brief essay, I will lay out three important facts about textual variants and their impact on the Christian faith.

THE NUMBER OF VARIANTS

The best estimate today is that among New Testament manuscripts there are about four hundred thousand textual differences. The reason for this astounding number, however, is the even more astounding number of manuscripts. There is absolutely nothing in the ancient Greco-Roman world that compares to the New Testament in terms of the number of manuscript copies or their dates. The average Greco-Roman author has fewer than twenty copies of his writings still in existence. Usually, there are far fewer. The New Testament boasts more than fifty-eight hundred copies in Greek alone. But the New Testament was translated into various languages early on—languages such as Latin, Syriac, Coptic, Georgian, Gothic, Armenian, and Arabic. Altogether, there are more than twenty thousand manuscripts of the New Testament. To be sure, some of these are small scraps of papyrus, and most are not complete New Testaments. Nevertheless, the average-size manuscript is more than four hundred fifty pages long.

If all the manuscripts were destroyed in the blink of an eye, we would still not be left without a witness. That's because church fathers, from the late first century to the thirteenth century, quoted from the New Testament in homilies, commentaries, and theological treatises. And they did not have the gift of brevity. More than a million quotations of the New Testament by the church fathers have been collected so far. Virtually the entire New Testament could be reproduced many times over just from the quotations of these fathers.

What about the dates of the manuscripts? It is often claimed that there are very few manuscripts of the New Testament written in the first millennium. That is true—*relatively* speaking. Only 15 percent of all New Testament manuscripts were produced before the year 1000. But that is still more than eight hundred manuscripts—more than forty times the amount of manuscripts from the average classical author in more than two thousand years of copying! The average classical author has zero manuscripts extant today produced within half a millennium of the composition of his writings. The New Testament has at least two hundred fifty manuscripts—in Greek alone—produced within five hundred years after the composition of the New Testament. Within three hundred years, the first complete New Testament—codex Sinaiticus—was produced, along with more than one hundred other manuscripts that have survived till today. And some of the manuscripts, though fragmentary, were produced within mere decades of the completion of the New Testament.

The very fact that Christians were more concerned with getting the message out than with crossing their t's and dotting their i's is testimony to the vibrancy of the Christian faith. But did this passion for the gospel end up *changing* the message?

THE NATURE OF VARIANTS

More than 70 percent of all textual variants are mere spelling differences that affect nothing. And several more involve inner-Greek syntax that can't even be translated into English (or most other languages). Then there are variants that involve synonyms, such as between "Jesus" and "Christ." The meaning is the same; no theological issues are at stake. And there are variants that, though meaningful, are not viable. That is, because of the poor pedigree of the manuscripts they are found in (usually few or very late manuscripts), no plausible case can be given for them reflecting the wording of the original. Remarkably, less than 1 percent of all textual variants are both meaningful and viable.

An example of a meaningful and viable variant is "616" (instead of "666") for the number of the beast in Revelation 13:18. But even though meaningful and viable, this variant is not significant enough to affect the essential teachings of the Christian faith.

Far and away the two longest passages that are textually doubtful are Mark 16:9–20 and John 7:53–8:11. These involve a dozen verses each. The next largest textual variants are only two verses long. Only about two dozen variants are between one and two verses long. The consensus of New Testament scholars is that these verses were added to the New Testament later, since they are not found in the earliest and best manuscripts and they do not fit with the authors' known syntax, vocabulary, or style. No doctrines are impacted by these variants. To be sure, they may involve favorite verses for many people, but they do not in the slightest jeopardize a cardinal tenet of the Christian faith.

CHRISTIAN BELIEFS AFFECTED BY TEXTUAL VARIANTS

The fundamental question that these textual variants raise is whether the Christian faith has been fundamentally altered from what the authors of the New Testament originally wrote. Does the resurrection of Jesus depend on textually suspect passages? Is the divinity of Christ found only in verses that are dubious? Such questions obviously should be of profound concern for anyone seeking the truth about Christianity. I wish to conclude this essay by quoting the authority that many Muslims and atheists appeal to regarding textual corruption in the New Testament.

In the appendix to Bart Ehrman's *Misquoting Jesus*, there is a dialogue between the editors of the book and the author:

"Why do you believe these core tenets of Christian orthodoxy to be in jeopardy based on the scribal errors you discovered in the biblical manuscripts?"

Ehrman's response is illuminating: "Essential Christian beliefs are not affected by textual variants in the manuscript tradition of the New Testament."

Even this skeptic, a bona fide New Testament scholar, had to concede that no cardinal doctrine of the Christian faith is jeopardized by textual variants. Many atheists and Muslims who have followed in Ehrman's path have exaggerated his claims way out of proportion to what he actually stated.

The textual history of the New Testament is robust and fascinating. When the dust has settled, we can be assured that what we have today, in all essentials, and even in the overwhelming majority of particulars, is what they wrote then.

My friend Nabeel Qureshi has discovered this same truth for himself. Ever since I met him, shortly after his conversion, I have seen in him an earnestness for truth, an acuteness of intellect, and a heart for God that I have witnessed in only one or two others. I applaud him for his enthusiasm, his zeal to pursue truth at all costs and to know Christ deeply, and his courage in the face of growing opposition from family and friends. I pray that his book, his spiritual autobiography, will be used by the Spirit of God to reach many people for Christ.

DEFINING MOMENTS

MICHAEL LICONA

Contributing to Part 4: "Coming to the Crux"

Michael Licona is associate professor of theology at Houston Baptist University and author of the groundbreaking work The Resurrection of Jesus: A New Historiographical Approach. *He has publically debated many leading agnostic and Muslim scholars and spoken at more than fifty university campuses worldwide.*

THERE ARE TIMES when each of us must make a decision that reveals our character and determines the course our life will take. This is called a "defining moment." Caesar decided to cross the Rubicon, knowing his action would result in a civil war with Rome. Dietrich Bonhoeffer decided to involve himself with a plot to kill Hitler, knowing his actions were morally justified but also that the plan could cost him his life.

In the garden of Gethsemane, Jesus wrestled with His impending torture and brutal execution. He had to decide whether to retreat or face the ordeal. Anyone in similar circumstances would want to leave, and Jesus indicated that was His desire. But He also recognized that His very purpose in this world was to endure such an ordeal. So He decided to face the ordeal (Mark 14:32–15:39; John 18:1–19:30). This was a defining moment in Jesus' life, and it altered the cosmic order.

When I first met Nabeel, neither he nor I realized each of us would soon experience defining moments in our lives. The journeys on which each of us were about to embark were quite similar. At the starting line, both of us were raised in families that took seriously their religious beliefs. From a very early age, both of us had possessed a desire to know God and please Him. Both of us were committed to following truth, no matter where it led. Both of us sincerely believed we were already following the truth and the other was not.

My journey started in 2003 when I began my doctoral research. I began with the objective of proving Jesus' resurrection from a different angle: to show Jesus had risen from the dead, using the standard tools of historical investigation. I began by reading literature on the philosophy of history and the historical method. It wasn't long before I was confronted with the challenge of my personal biases. I wanted Jesus' resurrection to be proven fact. But the literature was informing me that my objective could severely hinder the integrity of my investigation. Of course, skeptics are faced with a similar challenge: they want Jesus' resurrection to be disproved. If left unchecked, our biases will so guide our historical investigations that we will almost always arrive at the conclusion we seek.

After about a year of study, the motivation behind my doctoral research changed. Instead of seeking to prove Jesus' resurrection, I was now consumed with discovering what an investigation of the matter would reveal if I were to place my bias on the shelf as best as I could. I engaged in numerous public debates with prominent skeptical scholars on the question, "Did Jesus rise from the dead?" Prior to each debate, I asked God to reveal truth to me. "If I'm on the wrong track, please show me my error. Humiliate me if needed. Just break through any part of my conditioning that's prohibiting me from seeing truth. I just want to follow You, Lord, even if You're not who I think You are."

Because most of my debate opponents were prominent scholars who are well-informed, I knew there was no room for laziness on my part. I was forced to become well-acquainted with the data and how each opponent would account for it. In a debate, I could not merely reply that their arguments did not convince me. I had to provide reasons—good reasons—for why their arguments were ineffective. Therefore, debates forced me to think through virtually every element of the matter of Jesus' resurrection. My journey was a difficult one, in which I often agonized over keeping a check on my bias. After five and a half years, my journey ended with my concluding that Jesus' resurrection from the dead accounts for the historical data in a manner far superior to any competing hypothesis.[122] My decision to seek and follow truth no matter where it led and my decision to engage in persistent efforts to manage my biases as best as I possibly could during my investigation were defining moments in my life. I remain a follower of Jesus not because I was raised that way but because the historical evidence strongly suggests that His resurrection from the dead was an event that occurred in history.

Nabeel entered his journey with confidence that the evidence would confirm his Islamic faith. His journey was intense and, as far as I could tell, was honest and open-minded. Nabeel unreservedly wanted Islam to be true. It was the way he had been raised, and he was proud to be a Muslim. He also deeply loved his parents and did not want to cause them grief or bring them disgrace from their Islamic community, difficulties that would surely follow if Nabeel left the faith they had taught him and become a follower of Jesus. This is a matter that non-Muslim Westerners rarely consider, since this type of disgrace is not common in our culture. However, like I am, Nabeel is more interested in discovering and finding truth, even when doing so may lead to undesirable consequences. But when we consider that there is a very good chance that our decision about Jesus will determine our eternal destiny, should anything other than a serious pursuit of truth satisfy us? Nabeel's journey may have taken less time than my own, but it was no less agonizing for him. When Nabeel discovered that the strong evidence for Jesus' divinity—His personal claims to being God's heavenly Son, His death by crucifixion, and His resurrection from the dead—was able to withstand the toughest critical scrutiny by Islamic and skeptical scholars alike, he decided to be led by the truth and became a follower of Jesus. This was, indeed, a defining moment for Nabeel.

THE DEITY OF JESUS CHRIST

J. ED KOMOSZEWSKI

Contributing to Section 5:
"Jesus: Mortal Messiah or Divine Son of God?"

J. Ed Komoszewski has served as a professor of biblical and theological studies at Northwestern College and as the director of research for Josh McDowell Ministry. He is coauthor of two influential books: Reinventing Jesus *and* Putting Jesus in His Place, *both focused on the identity and deity of Jesus.*

TENSIONS RISE when the name Jesus is dropped. It has always been this way. In Jesus' own day, the Jewish authorities were just as suspicious of His divine claims as Nabeel had been as a pious Muslim struggling to come to terms with the provocative rabbi from Galilee in modern times. "Who do you think you are?" they demanded upon realizing that Jesus claimed to be greater than Abraham (John 8:53). The scribes and Pharisees were repeatedly confronted with Jesus' claims straight from His mouth, so they couldn't simply dismiss those claims as later corruptions (as Islam had taught Nabeel to do). Quite tellingly, their own explanation—reported in all four gospels—was that Jesus was controlled by a demon (Matt. 9:34; 12:24; Mark 3:22; Luke 11:15; John 7:20; 8:48).

Islam does not stoop so low. In fact, it honors Jesus as highly as its theology allows it to honor any human being. Islam regards Him as a great prophet, second in importance only to Muhammad. It agrees with the New Testament that Jesus (unlike Muhammad) was conceived and born of a virgin. It also teaches that Jesus ascended bodily to paradise or heaven without even dying (again, unlike Muhammad). Although this teaching disagrees with the New Testament, it expresses a noble view of Jesus from a Muslim perspective.

Of course, Christians agree that Jesus was both a human being and a great prophet, but we understand Him to be far more than that. Regrettably, we sometimes give the impression that belief in Jesus as God incarnate derives solely from the gospel of John. And this opens the door to the "John doesn't count" argument that Nabeel used to get around the testimony of the fourth gospel. In actuality, as Nabeel soon discovered, other parts of the New Testament tout an equally high view of Jesus Christ. The following examples only scratch the surface.

The apostle Paul wrote his epistles or letters between the years 49 and 65. Since Jesus died in 30 or 33, this means his epistles were all written within about twenty to thirty-five years after Jesus' death. They are generally recognized as the earliest Christian writings. Remarkably enough, Paul twice called Jesus "God" (Rom. 9:5; Titus 2:13). But his favorite title for Jesus was "LORD," the designation used by Jews in the first century when speaking or writing in reference to the Hebrew divine name *YHWH* ("Yahweh" or "Jehovah"). For example, where the Old Testament referred to "the day of the LORD" (day of Yahweh, e.g., Joel 2:31), Paul referred to "the day of the Lord Jesus" (1 Cor. 5:5; 2 Cor. 1:14; etc.). Where the Old Testament spoke of "calling on the name of the LORD" (the name of Yahweh, e.g., Joel 2:32), Paul spoke of calling "on the name of the Lord Jesus Christ" (1 Cor. 1:2; see also Rom. 10:12–14). Where the Old Testament made the foundation of Israel's faith the confession that there is "one LORD" who alone is God (Deut. 6:4), Paul affirms that Jesus is the "one Lord" through whom all things were made (1 Cor. 8:6; see also Eph. 4:5). Where the Old Testament states that every knee will bow and every tongue swear allegiance to the LORD (Isa. 45:23), Paul says that every knee will bow and every tongue confess that Jesus Christ is Lord (Phil. 2:10–11). These examples make clear that Paul—just like John—viewed Jesus as far more than a prophet.

But if John "doesn't count," then perhaps Paul doesn't count either. Nabeel describes some of the polemical arguments he was taught as a Muslim to call Paul's teaching into question. The problem with this approach, of course, is that soon no early Christian source will count. Yet Jesus is called God not only in John (1:1, 18; 20:28) and Paul (Rom. 9:5; Titus 2:13) but also in Acts (20:28), Hebrews (1:8), and 2 Peter (1:1). He is revered as the LORD (Yahweh) not only in Paul but also in Acts (1:24; 2:21, 36) and 1 Peter (2:3; 3:13–16). Both Hebrews (1:6) and Revelation (5:12–13) teach that the angels in heaven worship Jesus Christ. The belief that Jesus is infinitely exalted permeates New Testament writings.

Consider the gospel of Mark, which most scholars think was the first gospel to be written. Mark begins his gospel by quoting Isaiah 40:3: "Make ready the way of the Lord, make His paths straight" (Mark 1:3 NASB). Yet "the Lord" whose way is made ready is the Lord Jesus, whom John the Baptist said was so far above him that John was not even worthy to perform the menial slave's task of loosening his sandal (Mark 1:7–8). Throughout the gospel of Mark, Jesus speaks and acts in ways that are simply far too exalted even if He were a great prophet. When Jesus healed people, cast out demons, or performed other miracles, He did so not by asking God in prayer to do these things; rather, He spoke the word, and it happened (1:25–27, 41, etc.). He forgave a man's sins, which the scribes recognized was the sole prerogative of God (2:5–7). He claimed to be the Lord of the Sabbath, transcending the laws of its observance (2:28). When He was on the Sea of Galilee with His disciples and a violent storm threatened to pull their ship down, Jesus told the storm to "be still," and it did (4:39). When He was questioned by the high priest, Jesus said that He would sit at the right hand of the Power in heaven (14:62). In other words, He was going to rule from the throne of God alongside the Father.

What about Matthew, usually considered the most Jewish of the four gospels? Matthew's gospel has all of the same elements we have seen in Mark's and includes additional testimonies to the deity of Christ. Matthew's narrative begins by describing Jesus as "God with us" (Matt. 1:23) and climaxes with the resurrected Jesus promising His disciples, "I am with you always, even to the end of the age" (28:20 NASB). In other words, Jesus embodies the divine presence; He is God in the flesh. Another statement along the same lines appears about halfway through the gospel, when Jesus tells His disciples, "Where two or three have gathered together in My name, I am there in their midst" (18:20 NASB). No mere prophet, no matter how great, would or could make such a claim. When the disciples saw the risen Jesus, they worshiped Him, and He claimed to have all authority in both heaven and earth (28:17–18). Clearly, Matthew also viewed Jesus as nothing less than full deity.

All of the principal authors of the New Testament writings—Matthew, Mark, Luke, John, Paul, Peter, and the unnamed author of Hebrews—attest to the divine claims, nature, and prerogatives of Jesus. These men wrote from thirty to sixty years after Jesus' death; all of them except Luke were Jewish men who spent part of their lives in Judea and Galilee. They all either knew Jesus personally or knew people who had known Jesus personally. By contrast, Muhammad did not know Jesus and did not know anyone who had ever seen Jesus. He lived five hundred years later in a different culture and in a different country (Arabia), and it is on the basis of his teaching alone that Islam regards Jesus as a great prophet but not divine. From a strictly historical perspective, the multiple testimonies of the first-century New Testament authors must take precedence with regard to understanding who and what Jesus claimed to be. Nabeel eventually gave the New Testament writings their proper place. And Jesus eternally took His rightful place, as God, on the throne of Nabeel's heart.

THE TRINITY AND THE GOSPEL

ROBERT M. BOWMAN JR.

Contributing to Part 6: "The Case for the Gospel"

Robert M. Bowman Jr. is the director of research for the Institute for Religious Research based in Grand Rapids, Michigan. Rob has taught apologetics, biblical studies, and new religious movements at Biola University and Cornerstone University and is the author of sixty articles and thirteen books, including Why You Should Believe in the Trinity *and* The Word-Faith Controversy.

NABEEL WAS A MUSLIM when he struggled with and even fought against the Christian doctrines of the Trinity and of salvation by the death of Jesus Christ. But it isn't just Muslims and people of other non-Christian backgrounds who have difficulty coming to terms with these beliefs. I myself, though coming from a Christian background, went through a period of intense doubt and searching during my college years regarding these and other Christian teachings. Like many others, I was especially troubled by the doctrine of the Trinity. Not only was it difficult to understand but it was unclear whether the Bible even supported it. I once had discussions with a Sunday school teacher who tried to defend the Trinity by insisting that Jesus is God the Father. I knew that wasn't what the Trinity means.

As I studied the Bible and wrestled with these issues, I came to understand that in a real sense the doctrine was not a human creation, even though its verbal formulations in the creeds were composed by fallible men. Frankly, the Trinity is not the sort of doctrine people invent. When people create doctrines, they generally try to come up with an elegantly simple idea that others can get behind. In doing so, they typically come up with an idea that you can find in a variety of religions throughout history. On the one hand, that is why there are various religions teaching that everything is divine or has divinity in it, why quite a few teach that there are many gods with some greater than others, and why several assert that God is a solitary person who stays outside the universe looking in at us. On the other hand, a God who exists eternally in three distinct persons, one who assumed human nature while still remaining God—this complex, challenging set of ideas is unique among all the religions of the world. You cannot find it outside of historic Christianity.

So where did this doctrine originate? Christians believe that God is triune—that He exists as one God in three persons—because Jesus revealed God in that way. Jesus taught us, foremost, about our heavenly Father. The Lord's Prayer, the most famous of all prayers, begins, "Our Father, who art in heaven." Christians think of God as their Father because Jesus taught us to think of Him that way. At the same time, we see in the gospels that Jesus claimed to be God's "Son" in a way that showed Him to be absolutely unique. For example, when Jewish teachers challenged Jesus for working on the Sabbath (by healing a paralyzed man), Jesus explained that the Father worked on the Sabbath, and as His Son, so did He (John 5:17). In some way, then, Jesus is uniquely the Son of God, but He graciously invites us to "share" in His close, familial relationship with the Father, to become God's "children." Jesus also promised that after His return to heaven, He would send someone else in His place to be with His disciples forever (John 14:16–17; 15:26–27). This someone else was the Holy Spirit (John 14:26). The Holy Spirit is identified in the Bible as God (Acts 5:3–4) but is someone distinct from the Father and the Son, as these and many other texts of the Bible reveal. So Jesus reveals the Trinity to us by revealing (1) the Father as the one who sent Jesus and who invites us to be His children, (2) Jesus Himself as the unique Son of the Father, and (3) the Holy Spirit as a divine person sent from the Father and the Son after Jesus returned to heaven.

The key to understanding this, for me, was to answer the question, Who is Jesus? If Jesus really is the Son who came from the Father, died and rose again for our salvation, ascended into heaven, and then sent the Holy Spirit to live within His people, then something along the lines of the doctrine of the Trinity is true. The more I studied the Bible, the more ways it revealed Jesus to be the eternal, divine Son of God come in the flesh (what Christians call the incarnation). Once

I got past crude caricatures of the Trinity and weak objections to its possible existence, I began recognizing its truth throughout Scripture.

I also came to appreciate how closely the doctrine of the Trinity is linked to the gospel of salvation. The gospel or "good news" is the message of God's victory over the devil and over human rebellion, corruption, and death. It isn't about what I do for God; it's about what He has done and is doing for me. Jesus isn't a character sent by the Creator to tell us to straighten up and fly right; Jesus is the Creator who walked among us in humility to experience our fragility and to rescue us from our hopeless human condition.

His paying the debt for our sins is just one part of how He saves us. Jesus did not pay the penalty for our misdeeds so we can continue disobeying God with abandon; rather, in dying on the cross, Jesus not only canceled our spiritual debt but also cured our spiritual disease. When we put our trust in Christ, He forgives our sins and also begins the work of changing us from the inside to become holy and loving like Him, and like God our Father. Jesus does this through the Holy Spirit, whom He sent. Salvation by grace does not mean we stay impure sinners forever. Rather, it means that God forgives all our sins and does for us what we cannot do for ourselves by paying the penalty for our sins and working to eliminate sin from our lives. He does this in two stages: while we are mortal, the Holy Spirit changes our hearts so that we begin to live in a way that is more pleasing to God, even though we still commit sin; and then in the resurrection at the end of history, we will be made morally and spiritually perfect beings.

Thus, all three persons of the Trinity are involved in our salvation. The Father calls us into a relationship with Him through the Son, whom He sent; the Son creates that relationship by dying to break down the barrier of rebellion that has separated us from the Father; and the Holy Spirit works within us to trust in the Son and to worship the Father according to the truth of the gospel. When we are brought into the Christian faith, this is why we are baptized "in the name of the Father and of the Son and of the Holy Spirit" (Matt. 28:19). It means that we are acknowledging the three persons as the one God who has mercifully rescued us from our sin and given us the gift of eternal life.

THE HISTORICAL MUHAMMAD

DAVID WOOD

Contributing to Part 7:
"The Truth about Muhammad"

*David Wood is the director of Acts 17 Apologetics, a ministry ded-
icated to examining the core claims of atheism, Christianity, and
Islam. He is host of the satellite television show* Jesus or Muhammad, *which is regularly broadcast throughout North America and
the Middle East. He has debated more than two dozen Muslims and
atheists and earned his PhD in philosophy from Fordham University.*

ACCORDING TO THE QURAN, Muhammad is the ideal model of
conduct for Muslims (33:21), and true believers are not allowed to question his decisions (33:36). So it is not surprising that when Nabeel and
I began discussing the character and teachings of Muhammad, things
occasionally got heated. Arguing with a Muslim about his prophet's
relationship with a nine-year-old girl is hardly a path to harmony.

That's where friendship is useful. Even if Nabeel and I got angry
during our discussions, we eventually calmed down, and we always
understood that we had each other's best interests at heart. Nabeel
was criticizing Christianity not because he hated Christians but
because he was convinced that Christianity was false and that his
best friend was missing out on something important. Likewise, I
wasn't complaining about Muhammad because of the 9/11 attacks
but because I wanted my best friend to know Jesus.

When Muslims and non-Muslims attempt to evaluate the life of
Muhammad, we are confronted with a difficulty. On the one hand,
Islam's historical sources are far removed from the events they report,
giving rise to a fair amount of skepticism concerning their reliability.
On the other hand, if we take the Muslim sources seriously, a highly
unflattering (and sometimes disturbing) portrait of Muhammad

emerges. Hence, whether we doubt Islam's sources or trust them, we never find the impeccable figure preached by Muslims.

To see the difficulty in more detail, consider a sketch of what Nabeel and I discovered when we examined the Muslim sources.

A HISTORICAL PROBLEM

Islam's earliest source is the Quran. Yet the Quran is not biographical in nature. Rather, it is claimed to be Allah's eternal word, revealed to Muhammad through the angel Gabriel. As such, the Quran gives us very little direct information about Muhammad and mentions him by name only four times. To interpret passages of the Quran in the light of Muhammad's life, we must turn to non-Quranic texts.

Our earliest detailed biographical source for Muhammad is Ibn Ishaq's *Sirat Rasul Allah*, which was written more than a century after Muhammad's death. Most Muslim scholars today, however, are convinced that Ibn Ishaq's historical methodology was defective, which forces them to turn to even later works for information about their prophet. Islam's most trusted collections of narrations about Muhammad (*Sahih Bukhari*, *Sahih Muslim*, and *Sunan Abu Daud*) were written approximately *two centuries* (or more) after the events they report.

Two centuries is ample time for embellishment and fabrication, especially when competing political and theological factions were vying for power. Indeed, the most important reason for compiling stories about Muhammad was because so many false or contradictory stories were being manufactured. Modern quests for early Islamic historical data have uncovered almost nothing, and the general movement among scholars of Islamic studies over the past century has been toward greater skepticism.

A BRIEF HISTORY OF MUHAMMAD

Assuming we treat the Muslim sources as at least somewhat reliable, we can piece together an outline of Muhammad's life. He was born around AD 570 in Mecca (in present day Saudi Arabia). While still young, Muhammad began work in the Meccan caravan trade, which put him in contact with diverse religious traditions. At twenty-five years old, he married a wealthy widow named Khadija, who was fifteen years his senior. Like many others from his tribe, Muhammad developed the habit of retreating to a cave on Mount Hira for prayer and reflection.

When Muhammad was forty years old, he had a mystical experience in this cave, and he emerged reciting five verses of what would eventually become the Quran (96:1–5). He soon began preaching Islam to friends and family, and later to the public. Due to his increasingly inflammatory condemnation of the Meccan polytheists, Muhammad and his followers were persecuted. After his wife Khadija and his uncle Abu Talib (who had been protecting him) died, Muhammad fled Mecca.

In Medina, having formed alliances with several non-Muslim groups, Muhammad began robbing the Meccan caravans. These attacks eventually led to a series of battles with Mecca. However, as war booty poured in, so did new converts, and the ever-expanding Muslim army allowed Muhammad to subdue not only Mecca but the rest of Arabia as well. Muhammad died in 632 following a prolonged sickness, which he attributed to being poisoned by a Jewish woman.

MUHAMMAD AND VIOLENCE

One of the most unsettling aspects of Muhammad's life concerns his use of violence to achieve his goals. Modern Muslims often claim that Muhammad killed only in self-defense, but history shows that he ordered his followers to murder people for writing poems that were critical of him. Apostates fared no better, for Muhammad commanded, "Whoever changes his religion, kill him" (Sunan An-Nasa'i 5.37.4069).

Although Muhammad promoted peace and tolerance when Muslims were in the minority, his revelations suddenly changed when his followers outnumbered his enemies. Consider three verses from the last major chapter of the Quran to be revealed:

1. "Fight those who believe not in Allah nor the Last Day, nor hold that forbidden which hath been forbidden by Allah and His Messenger, nor acknowledge the Religion of Truth, from among the People of the Book, until they pay the *Jizyah* with willing submission, and feel themselves subdued" (9:29 Ali).

2. "O Prophet! strive hard against the unbelievers and the hypocrites and be unyielding to them ..." (9:73 Shakir).

3. "O you who believe! fight those of the unbelievers who are near to you and let them find in you hardness ..." (9:123 Shakir).

Notice that the main criterion for fighting people in these verses is simply that they do not believe in Islam. Muhammad's final marching orders to his followers, then, consisted largely of commands to violently subjugate non-Muslims.

MUHAMMAD AND WOMEN

No less troubling is Muhammad's example regarding women. While the Quran allows Muslims to marry a maximum of four wives (4:3), Muhammad had at least nine wives at one time (after he received a special revelation that gave him the right to ignore the four-wife limit). One of Muhammad's wives (a girl named Aisha) was only nine years old when the marriage was consummated. Zainab, another wife, was originally married to his adopted son Zaid. However, because Muhammad became attracted to Zainab, Zaid divorced her so that Muhammad could marry her.

On at least one occasion, Muhammad physically struck his wife Aisha for lying. This was in accordance with the Quran's command to physically discipline rebellious wives: "Men are in charge of women, because Allah hath made the one of them to excel the other, and because they spend of their property (for the support of women). So good women are the obedient, guarding in secret that which Allah hath guarded. As for those from whom ye fear rebellion, admonish them and banish them to beds apart, and scourge them" (4:34 Pickthall).

Muhammad had a concubine named Mary, who was a Coptic Christian, and he allowed his followers to possess an unlimited number of sex slaves (see Quran 23:5–6; 70:22–30). Early Muslims were even permitted to engage in a form of prostitution (called *mutah*), according to which a Muslim could pay a woman for sex, marry her for a short time (perhaps a few hours), and then divorce her when finished.

SPIRITUAL CONCERNS

While Muhammad's teachings about violence and women call into question his status as the perfect role model, certain spiritual problems in his life raise concerns about his prophethood. For instance, Muhammad's first impression of the revelations he received was that they were demonic. As a result, he became suicidal and tried to hurl himself off a cliff. Muhammad's wife Khadija and her cousin Waraqah—people who were not with him in the cave and had no idea what he experienced—eventually persuaded him that he was not possessed and that, instead, he was a prophet of God.

Even more startling is that, according to our earliest Muslim sources, Muhammad once delivered a revelation from the devil (the infamous "Satanic Verses"). When Muhammad was initially reciting chapter 53 of the Quran (so the story goes), Satan tricked him into promoting polytheism. Later, Muhammad was supposedly informed by the angel Gabriel that all prophets occasionally fall for this ruse.

Multiple Muslim sources also report that Muhammad was the victim of black magic. According to these accounts, a Jewish magician stole Muhammad's hairbrush and used one of the hairs to cast a spell on him. The spell lasted about a year, and it affected Muhammad's memory and gave him delusional thoughts.

ASSESSMENT

Given the questionable reliability of the Muslim sources and their unflattering portrayal of Muhammad, how can modern Muslims hope to defend the Islamic view of their prophet? For many months, Nabeel took the most common route: He sifted through the texts and drew attention to every favorable story about Muhammad, while reinterpreting or dismissing most unfavorable stories. Yet he eventually realized that such a method could be used to make *any* historical figure appear trustworthy. After pondering the evidence more carefully (and resisting the Muslim tendency to automatically defend Muhammad from criticism), Nabeel was left with a dilemma: either we know next to nothing about Muhammad, or we know that he is not what Muslims claim him to be.

THE NEW TESTAMENT AND THE QURAN

KEITH SMALL

Contributing to Part 8: "The Holiness of the Quran"

Rev. Dr. Keith Small is a Quranic manuscript consultant to the Bodleian Library at Oxford University. He is also a visiting lecturer and an associate research fellow at the London School of Theology and teaches internationally concerning the history of the texts of the Quran and the New Testament. He is the author of Textual Criticism and Quran Manuscripts.

ANY RELIGION in our day must make its case amid the competing claims of secularism and other faiths. Nabeel has poignantly shared one double claim he was raised to passionately believe but then came to question—the conviction that the Quran had been preserved perfectly, whereas other books of scripture had not, and that this supported the Quran's divine credentials.

If this was just an academic question or just a case of overblown religious rhetoric, perhaps it would not carry so much weight. But as Nabeel shares from his own experience, this was a primary question forming his religious foundation. It was a question informing not only his identity as a Muslim but also his perspective on forgiveness of sin, his view of his personal religious obligations to God, and his hope for salvation and eternity. The inviolability of the Quran is truly an eternal life and death issue to Muslims around the world.

Too often, emotions and issues of personal, community, and religious honor eclipse issues of truth. In these situations academic studies can provide dispassionate information for evaluation by individuals on all sides of the issue.

How do we decide which books tell the truth? One test is to see which one squares best with available historical testimony. The claim

344

about the Quran's perfect transmission and the Bible's corruption is significant and goes to the foundation of one's view of Jesus. Muslims claim that one indication of the divine authority of their faith is that their scripture has been kept perfectly, while the New Testament has been corrupted, and that as a result, their view of Jesus is more accurate. This is an enormously significant historical claim that can be tested.

During the last three hundred years, the New Testament has undergone rigorous textual research, studies of how well the text has been transmitted from the earliest available Greek manuscripts through today. The Quran has never undergone such a systematic examination of the earliest manuscripts against the entire Quranic tradition, though this is now starting to be undertaken.

Results from these textual studies are extremely important. First, studies have demonstrated that the transmission of the New Testament books from their original forms until now has happened faithfully without calling into question any cardinal doctrine of the Christian faith. Studies of corrections in these manuscripts have also demonstrated that no one has changed the text to make it support a political or theological agenda—a hollow accusation often made, for example, against Constantine and the Council of Nicaea in the early 300s.

Initial results from the study of Quranic manuscripts confirm, through Islamic historical sources (similar to what Nabeel cites from the hadith), that in Islam's first century there was an official project to establish a precise written text of the Quran. Corrections in the earliest available manuscripts indicate a concern with establishing a precise text. There also existed in Islam's early decades the political, social, and religious conditions necessary to perform such a task and to ensure the widespread adoption of this official text in the growing Islamic empire. Instead of the Quran's text being preserved perfectly from the time of Muhammad, it was shaped after his lifetime into a document that would command political and religious unity under the established and growing political power of the time.

Such historical conditions, however, were never in place for a similar project to occur with the New Testament. Skeptics who assert a conspiracy to change the text of the New Testament, whether reputable scholars or authors of popular fiction, attempt to construct their arguments largely from silence and force controversial assumptions onto very minor textual changes—like claiming a small isolated rivulet is the main river while ignoring the broad, strong, mainstream of the existing textual tradition.

New Testament manuscript evidence provides strong support that the gospels deliver the best historical information concerning Jesus, and recent studies are confirming how Jesus both fits into and challenges the context and ideas of first-century Palestine. Similar studies of the Quran are demonstrating that the Jesus it portrays is more a figure of the theological controversies of the sixth and seventh centuries than a figure of the first century.

The issue of corruption versus perfection of the text is important because Muslims use the matter to justify the authority of their faith over other world faiths like Christianity. In another way, though, this claim to perfect transmission of the Quran is actually a bit of a rhetorical sideshow. The more significant divergence of Islam and Christianity has always been and will continue to be between the teachings of the Quran and the New Testament, and between their historical testimonies about Jesus.

That the New Testament is historically reliable provides not only a solid basis for personal faith in Christianity but also the strong basis for offering to people of any background, religious or nonreligious, the message of the gospel—that they can have their sins forgiven, that they can be freed from lives of futility and shameful habits, that they can actually know God personally and find His purpose for their lives, and that they can have the assurance of an eternity of justice and joy in His inexpressible presence, all through what His Son Jesus accomplished in the crucifixion and resurrection. If Christian scriptures were not grounded in history, all we would have to offer would be our personal opinions.

BELIEF AND DOUBT

GARY HABERMAS

Contributing to Part 9: "Faith in Doubt"

Dr. Gary Habermas is Distinguished Research Professor and chair of the Department of Philosophy at Liberty University. His chief areas of research are related to Jesus' resurrection, though he also has published frequently on the subject of religious doubt. He has authored, coauthored, or edited thirty-six books and written more than one hundred articles and reviews for journals and other publications.

TWO RELIGIOUS DOUBTERS experienced tormenting questions. One began his search as a Christian, the other did not. They came from quite diverse educational, religious, and ethnic perspectives. In both cases, their doubt was resolved after years of research and study. Both concentrated on many of the same academic issues. And the same God met them both.

Recently, Christians have grown more vocal about expressing their religious doubts, and so have unbelievers. If done in the right context, why not? Similar responses are certainly found in scripture. Humans seem always to have doubted and questioned even their deepest beliefs. Why so? Presumably because we do not know everything; we are limited and restricted in our knowledge. Further, these perennial religious issues concern us, often deeply. And from a theological angle, we are sinners. Complicating the issues, these conditions sometimes militate against our desire for personal peace.

I met Nabeel Qureshi during one of my family's yearly visits to Virginia Beach to stay with our close friends, Mike and Debbie Licona. Nabeel had joined a group of searchers who met regularly at Mike's house to discuss scientific, philosophical, and theological issues. There, I met a former rather militant atheist, philosophy student David Wood. Another attendee from the same university, likewise majoring in philosophy, was an agnostic Buddhist named Zach.

Then there was Nabeel, an ardent Muslim believer. Without question, Nabeel was very intelligent and always thoughtful, inquisitive, and exceptionally polite. He defended his faith, and no one minded a bit. Everyone spoke freely.

When Mike debated Muslim scholar Shabir Ally at another local university, Nabeel and I sat together. We later evaluated the dialogue, along with David and Mike. That was the evening when Nabeel made his amazing comment that the only thing that Christian apologetics had over Muslim apologetics was the evidence for Jesus' resurrection. I remarked to Mike later that such a conclusion could be precisely the sort that might continue to impress Nabeel.

Then there was the meeting at Mike's house that both Nabeel and his father attended. Once again, the give-and-take of conversation was fairly and politely granted. Mike even asked Nabeel's father to open the meeting in prayer.

Later, when I heard that Nabeel traveled overseas to ask imams the questions that still bothered him, I was again amazed. Here was a young scholar who was unafraid to ask the tough questions. Eventually, his doubts were a key component in fulfilling his quest.

Although I had been raised in a Christian home, I went through more than ten years of doubt that often grew quite intense. My personal study centered on the resurrection of Jesus, because of my conclusion that, if it had occurred, it could bear the weight of the Christian message. However, after several years, I reached an impasse in my studies and had determined that it could not be shown that this event happened.

Returning to the same subject a little later while writing my PhD dissertation, I was able to work through the stalemate that had bogged me down earlier, only to find that my doubts failed to subside. Little did I know that I still had years of struggle left.

Having concluded long before that addressing the factual component of doubt was the key to my struggles, I had grown convinced that there were several key evidential avenues both for theism in general, as well as for Christianity in particular. But why did my doubts remain, often more strongly than ever before?

Soon afterward, I learned what I dearly wished someone had explained to me much earlier—that there is commonly an emotional element to doubt, although at the time this was seldom recognized in the research. Not only is this emotional element the dominant species of such uncertainty, but it is usually far more painful and often more stubborn than factual elements.

One thing was entirely clear: I simply had to do something to overcome the suffering that hounded me every hour of the day. How could I be sure the Christian hope was grounded, when factual evidence alone was insufficient to do the job?

At this point, I stumbled on research in the area of psychological assurance and related issues that has since changed my life. Falling under the general rubric of the "cognitive" or "cognitive-behavioral method," the central idea is that what we tell ourselves, think, and do will determine how we feel, as well as our subsequent actions. Further, the most painful things in life are not generally what *occurs* to us but what we think and articulate to ourselves *about* those occurrences. Thus, it is not so much the events in our lives but rather how we download and respond to them that determines whether we are able to adjust and live peacefully, with minimal pain and stress.

I learned that the heart of the cognitive method revolves around picking out the false statements that we believe, think, or say to ourselves and then arguing against them. Believers must dispute thoughts like, "Though I've done everything Scripture tells me to do, I still may not be a Christian." Or, "Maybe I'll get to heaven and Jesus will tell me that He never knew me." Even something as simple as, "*What if* Christianity is untrue?" when the evidence shows otherwise can cause very painful repercussions.

Therefore, I had to learn to argue directly against these notions, and the more forcefully the better. I began to work through every aspect of the gospel message (like the deity, death, and resurrection of Jesus Christ) and then ask myself if I believed or had trusted the Lord in light of that (Rom. 10:9–10). If I responded, "I'm not sure," then I needed to press the point with the precise data. "You know you did that, dozens of times as a matter of fact." Or, "You know you believe that, because when someone objected the other day, you were ready with your defense of its truth." When others wondered if they had shown any "fruit" in their lives after salvation, I encouraged them to list items that could be reviewed. Asking a very good friend what they see in us is very helpful too.

Dozens of biblical texts also teach us to stop worrying and being "downcast" by changing what we say to ourselves. Instead, we are to replace these thoughts with meditation on God's truth, His promises, worship, or prayer.[123] Other passages tell us to avoid irresponsible or careless words, anxiety, envy, and other emotions that lead to anguish. Instead, we are to teach uplifting truths to ourselves and to each other, producing healing and peace.[124]

One key passage that occupied much of my thinking was Philippians 4:6–9, where Paul exhorts believers to control their anxiety (v. 6), which often contributes heavily to emotional doubt. I knew that curbing my anxiety would provide a huge advantage in treating my emotional doubt.

Paul issued a four-step remedy. He commanded prayer to God regarding our needs. Peter offers additional details to his anxious readers, telling them to cast their worries on God (1 Peter 5:7).

Paul states that thanksgiving (Phil. 4:6) and praise (Phil. 4:8) should be given as well. Testimony shows that these practices, during anxiety or periods of being downcast, are often fantastically liberating actions that lessen our anxieties and fears.

In perhaps the strongest "cognitive" passage in Scripture, Paul instructs his readers to exchange their anxiety for God-honoring truths. His readers should meditate steadily, deeply, and single-mindedly on God's truths, employing these concepts (Phil. 4:8) instead of the ruminations that led to anxiety in the first place.

Last, Paul adds a behavioral component—practicing the actions that he had just listed (Phil. 4:9). This does not mean that these four steps must be duplicated every time; other texts encourage the same steps, either by themselves or along with different practices.

Many popular writings explain how to implement this process in more detail, but I have long preferred the bestseller *Telling Yourself the Truth* by William Backus and Marie Chapian.[125] Although often very painful, the effects of emotional doubt may be eliminated or at least severely reduced.[126] The remedy is the habitual and forceful application of techniques that correct our mistaken thinking and behavior.

DREAMS AND VISIONS

JOSH MCDOWELL

Contributing to Part 10:
"Guided by the Hand of God"

Josh McDowell has been an internationally recognized evangelist and apologist for more than fifty years, having addressed more than twenty-five million people and given more than twenty-six thousand talks in 125 countries. He is author of several dozen books that share the essentials of the Christian faith in everyday language. He has written or coauthored more than 130 books, including More Than a Carpenter, *which has sold more than fifteen million copies in eighty-five languages.*

MANY WESTERNERS find it hard to understand that God is using dreams and visions in a powerful way to reveal Himself to Muslims. In Isaiah 65:1, it says, "I revealed myself to those who did not ask for me, I was found by those who did not seek me."

Joel proclaimed, "Your old men shall dream dreams, and your young men shall see visions" (Joel 2:28 ESV). As in the days of Joel, when God wanted to teach Israel "I am the LORD your God and there is none else" (Joel 2:27 ESV), He used dreams and visions.

I believe He is demonstrating the same thing to the Muslim people today. In God's infinite wisdom and passion, He reveals Himself to people in different ways that are culturally relevant so they can understand who He is, receive Him, and follow Him.

In many Muslim cultures, dreams and visions play a strong role in people's lives. Muslims rarely have access to the scriptures or interactions with Christian missionaries, yet God is as passionate about having a relationship with Muslims as He is about having a relationship with you and me (Exod. 34:14 NLT).

The phenomenon of God's revealing Himself through dreams and visions is not limited to any one people, language, or country. People experience revelatory dreams from Indonesia to Saudi Arabia and beyond. It's not just limited to the Arab world. In Persian and Turkish-speaking countries and throughout Africa and Asia, many cultures place a high premium on such dreams.

Dreams and visions do not convert people; the gospel does. These seekers begin a personal or spiritual journey to find the Truth. As was the case for Nabeel, the dreams lead them to the scriptures and to believers who can share Jesus with them. It is the gospel through the Holy Spirit that converts people.

Mission Frontiers magazine reported that out of six hundred Muslim converts, more than 25 percent were affected spiritually through dreams.[127] One missionary in Africa reports that "42 percent of the new believers came to Christ through visions, dreams, angelic appearances and hearing God's voice."[128]

No two dreams are exactly the same, but in my experience, many say that in their dreams Jesus is standing with His arms outstretched and says either, "Why are you resisting the Truth?" or "Seek the Truth." I have found that the normal Muslim response is, "What is the truth?" or "Show me the truth."

This is why we get so many response letters asking, "Why has it taken you so long to get me the truth?"

One missionary shares this story:

> I met a man from Baluchistan, which is a region in Pakistan. I met him in a Bible college where I was to give a devotional, and he turned out to be there because Jesus appeared to him, literally at his death bed, healed him, and told him to go to Karachi, study the Word, then return to Baluchistan to spread the gospel.[129]

Another missionary says:

> An Iranian student with whom I had worked here in Paris disappeared from circulation, because of great pressure from his older brother who was a practicing Muslim. Six months later, he returned, beaming a big smile on his face, and told me the great news that now he is very sure that the Bible is true. As we sat together and talked, he told me how hard his brother had beat him many times, and forced him to keep Ramadan. But one night, as he had been struggling with the question, "Which is true, the Bible or the Koran?" he had

a dream in which he saw Jesus, and he asked Jesus all the questions he had, and he remembers how satisfied he was with the answers. He could only remember the last question he'd asked, which, amazingly, was a strange one for us, but not for a Muslim. He asked Jesus, "Now that I am your follower, what shall I eat?" I was pleased to hear that Jesus had said to him, "Eat my Word." I turned to the book of Jeremiah, and I showed him the passage where Jeremiah said, "I found your Word and I ate it." Well, he jumped with excitement and told me, "Jesus must be right."[130]

The following are credible stories of the impact of dreams:

In one African Muslim country, a young man violently tore up a Bible tract and threatened the life of the Every Home for Christ worker going door-to-door with the literature, Dick Eastman of Colorado Springs—based EHFC told NIRR. The next afternoon as the worker sat in his home, he was shocked to see the man knock at his door. "I must have another booklet," the Muslim told him. He explained that the previous night two hands awakened him, and when he turned on the light and asked who was there, a voice said, "You have torn up the truth." The voice instructed him to acquire another booklet, directing him to the EHFC worker's home, the young man said. There, the Muslim read the booklet and became a believer. He has since been expelled from his wealthy family, lives with EHFC's Africa director, and is preparing for ministry to Muslims.[131]

In another incident, several EHFC workers were distributing literature in a marketplace. A man who received a booklet gasped and said he had a vision of the person pictured on the cover in his dream the night before, Eastman said. In the dream, the man was in a deep pit when a rope was thrown to him and two strong hands pulled him up. Upon climbing out, he looked into the face of the man who helped him: Jesus. The workers explained the meaning of the dream and the man was converted on the spot. Later, three other people recounted the same dream and two of them became Christians, Eastman said. God is preparing Muslims, and Christian workers follow through, he said.[132]

In Kawuri, Nigeria, a Christian was beaten nearly to death by his tribe for leaving Islam, according to Open Doors with Brother Andrew. As the man lay close to death, he asked God to forgive his attackers, unaware that they were listening in the next room. That night, two Islamic priests who participated in the beating had visions. One said Jesus showed him his three greatest and most private sins. The next day, the two mullahs repented and led eighty followers to a church, the Santa Ana, Calif.—based group said.[133]

Karima, a Muslim, dreamed she was in a car when it crashed. She was knocked out, but when she opened her eyes (in her dream), she saw that Jesus was the driver. "Come to Me," He told her, "I am with you. I love you." That experience led her to seek out a Christian church, where she responded to the gospel.[134]

Omar had been locked up and tortured for years in a jail cell in a nation ruled by a dictator. One night a messenger visited him in a dream, telling him he would be set free. Within days he was released from prison and traveled to America, where new-found friends reached out to him. When he was given a book with a picture of Jesus on the cover, his eyes lit up. "I know him," he said. "He came to me in a dream."[135]

The Jesus Film team was returning late one night from a show-ing. They saw a fire up in the mountains where shepherds were caring for their sheep. Several of the team members went up the mountain with the Jesus Film DVD and copies of the book *More Than a Carpenter.*

After a brief introduction, they offered each shepherd a DVD and book. One shepherd got all excited and proclaimed, "Last night I saw this book in a dream and I was told to read it." Need-less to say, each shepherd enthusiastically received the book![136]

A brother I personally know was telling me about seventeen people in a group of former Muslims. Every one of them had seen visions or dreams of Jesus. One of the men asked this brother if he had seen Jesus in a vision. He replied, "No." The man put his arm around my friend and said, "How blessed are you! You have not seen

Him, yet you love Him, and you serve Him." Then he added, "We have no excuse; we have seen Him face to face!"

Our God cares about the believer and those still searching for truth. He does not give up on His creation, as Nabeel's own story proves. His journey was filled with questions, frustrations, and disappointments, yet his friends continued to pray for him for four years until God's love broke through.

"Let us not become weary in doing good, for at the proper time we will reap a harvest if we do not give up" (Gal. 6:9).

Whether through dreams or visions, reading scripture, personal testimony from friends, or any of the other ways God reaches His people—I can unequivocally say that "He is a God who is jealous about his relationship with you" (Exod. 34:14 NLT).

APPENDIX 2:
ARE AHMADIS MUSLIMS?

Responding to Concerns about
My Former Sect of Islam

IN CHAPTER 7, I addressed the matter of diversity in Islam, informing readers that I belonged to the sect of Islam called Ahmadiyyat and that many Muslims consider it outside the fold of Islam. Through an account from my life, I explained why their reasoning is problematic and that Ahmadis truly are Muslims. Since that chapter was in the context of my story, I will present the reasoning more clearly here.

My position is simple: Ahmadis are Muslims because they believe and proclaim the shahada, "There is no god but Allah, and Muhammad is His messenger." That was the necessary and sufficient requirement as delineated by the traditions of Muhammad and that Muslims continue to follow today. Muhammad went so far as to say that anyone who says the shahada cannot be excommunicated no matter what, according to Sunan Abu Daud, hadith number 2526. But in addition to meeting the necessary and sufficient requirement, Ahmadis also practice the five pillars of Islam and believe the six articles of faith, putting them very close to Sunni orthodoxy, closer by far than some other Muslims such as Sufis.

Unfortunately, there are many who have been told that Ahmadis are not Muslims, and so they are concerned about this book's relevance to Islam. Others expressed concern that I said nothing to rebut Ahmadiyyat itself. Here is my response to such concerns:

1. *Seeking Allah, Finding Jesus* speaks to the common Muslim experience, and the arguments it presents apply to virtually all Muslims. The various views about Ahmadiyyat do nothing to negate the arguments presented here about Islam.
2. The criticism that Ahmadis aren't Muslim is a partisan and fundamentalist view, much like Sunnis who call Shia non-Muslim, or Catholics who call Protestants non-Christian.

3. The simplistic view that Ahmadis aren't Muslim is an unsophisticated understanding of individuals. My life is an example of a more multitextured reality than such a monochromatic view allows.

4. Although I believe that Ahmadis are a subgroup of Muslims, and by rejecting Islam I also rejected Ahmadiyyat, I had additional concerns about that particular sect that I ultimately never did investigate.

1. THIS BOOK SPEAKS TO THE COMMON MUSLIM EXPERIENCE

As you noticed in the book, my upbringing included teachings specific to our sect of Islam, but they were very much on the periphery of my perspective. What informed my worldview was the core of Islam: that there is no god but Allah, and Muhammad is His messenger. As an Ahmadi, Muhammad was my ultimate human authority and Allah was my divine authority.

That is why, when David and I discussed my beliefs, our focus was on the life of Muhammad and on the Quran, not on any sect-specific doctrine. I never suggested to David that he become an Ahmadi, but I encouraged him to accept Islam dozens of times. That is what we always talked about: the core of Islam. As a result, this book is focused on the same things: issues common to all Muslims.

At least one prominent Sunni Muslim scholar, Dr. Shabir Ally, noticed this and agrees that this book is directed toward Islam in general, not Ahmadiyyat specifically. While reviewing *Seeking Allah, Finding Jesus*, Ally was asked, "Do you think Nabeel is comparing Ahmadiyya Islam with Christianity?" Dr. Ally's response is telling: "In his book he doesn't do that.... He just compares Islam, which is known more generally, with Christianity." In his review, Dr. Ally was surprised that I do not focus on Ahmadiyyat, but there is a simple reason: I was never concerned with sect-specific teachings as a Muslim; rather I was concerned with Islam as a whole.

For that reason, even if it were true that Ahmadis aren't Muslims, that would do nothing to negate the arguments against Islam presented in this book. I contend that there is no good reason to think the Quran is inspired and that we cannot conclude using careful reasoning that Muhammad was a prophet. This is a critique of all branches of Islam, not just Ahmadiyyat.

2. PARTISAN POLEMICS

Intrareligious rhetoric can be fierce. Within Christianity, for example, polemics between Catholics and Protestants have raged since the time of the Reformation. The situation is similar within Islam, and evidence indicates that Muslims around the world are prone to accuse one another of being non-Muslim.

The Pew Research Center published the results of a survey in August 2012 titled "The World's Muslims: Unity and Diversity," which demonstrated that Muslims differ drastically on whom they consider to be Muslim, and that their opinions appear to be subjective, dependent on region and proximity. For example, Muslims disagree on whether Sufis ought to be considered part of the fold: only 24 percent of Muslims in Southeast Asia believed Sufis are Muslims, contrasted with 77 percent of respondents in South Asia.

Of course, the most well-known example of intra-Islamic discord is among Sunni and Shia Muslims. The same survey demonstrated that out of the five Muslim countries surveyed in the Middle East and North Africa with Sunni majorities, all five of them are very divided as to whether Shia are Muslim. In Egypt, Jordan, Morocco, Palestinian Territories, and Tunisia, 40 percent of Sunnis or more think Shia are non-Muslim.

However, where Sunnis live among many Shia, their views differ. According to the survey results, "Only in Lebanon and Iraq—nations where sizable populations of Sunnis and Shias live side by side—do large majorities of Sunnis recognize Shias as fellow Muslims."

I noticed a similar phenomenon in our lives as Ahmadi Muslims: When we moved to new areas and met Muslims who did not personally know Ahmadis, they started by treating us as outsiders. But as they got to know us, their view of Ahmadis usually changed. We lived like them, believed like them, and contributed to the community with them. Despite denominational differences, they invariably started to accept us as Muslims when they got to know us.

Since the reasons for including or rejecting sects are often subjective, we ought to acknowledge that the matter of religious inclusion is multifaceted, especially in Islam today. It often has little to do with what people actually believe and how they live, and instead is dependent on familiarity and proximity. We must be careful not to get embroiled in partisan polemics.

An example of such polemics that I have often heard argued against Ahmadis is a parallel between Mormonism and Ahmadiyyat: "Mormons call themselves Christian, but they are not really Christian. Similarly, Ahmadis call themselves Muslim, but they are not really Muslim." This is a false parallel. Mormonism is generally excluded from Christianity because it is a polytheistic faith, teaching that Jesus is one of many gods. It contravenes a central tenet of Christianity: monotheism. Ahmadiyyat does not deny any central tenets of Islam.

As I explained in chapter 7, Ahmadiyyat is often accused of heresy because its founder, Mirza Ghulam Ahmad, claimed to be a prophet. Since the Quran says Muhammad is the "seal of the prophets," orthodox Muslims consider Ahmadis to be heretics and non-Muslims. However, as Ahmadis, we were taught that Ahmad was a subordinate prophet, not nearly of the caliber of Muhammad himself. Ahmadis believe Muhammad was the seal of the prophets, since he was the last prophet sent with a law; the only degree to which Ahmad had prophetic authority was insofar as he pointed his followers back to Muhammad.

In response to this, I have heard Muslims say that Ahmad himself taught otherwise. But even if that were true, we were never taught anything else. We believed that Muhammad was our ultimate human authority, and Ahmad was simply directing us back to him. Thus, I saw the whole issue of Ahmad's prophethood as a semantic one. Regardless, these matters are peripheral issues, as disagreement over the precise interpretation of one verse does not constitute transgression of central Muslim tenets. Ahmadis unquestionably follow and believe the core practices and teachings of Islam.

I recently learned that a high court in India concluded decades ago that Ahmadis are Muslims for almost exactly the same reasons as mine. In the 1970 case *Shihabuddin Imbichi Koya Thangal vs. K. P.*

Ahmed Koya, the judge concluded, "The bond of union, if I may say so, consists in the identity of its doctrines, creeds, formularies and tests which are its very core and constitute its distinctive existence. Looking at the issue devoid of sentiment and passion and in the cold light of the law I have no hesitation to hold that the Ahmadiyya sect is of Islam and not alien."

It is noteworthy that this conclusion was drawn by a court in Kerala, India. Kerala is a highly Catholic region of the country, and India itself is overwhelmingly Hindu. This court appeared to have no vested interest in either party and concluded that Ahmadis are Muslim with "no hesitation."

This conclusion was based in part on precedent, with another judge in India, J. Oldfield, concluding similarly regarding Ahmadis. Oldfield's reasoning was based on yet another case, in which the prevailing Muslim denomination had charged Wahhabis of not being Muslim, an example of an intrareligious debate within Islam that Muslims have since moved past.

The fact is that Muslims around the world have called each other non-Muslim for centuries. Perhaps this is because Muslims have a very narrow view of variety allowed in Islam. The same Pew survey found that "[i]n 32 of the 39 countries surveyed, half or more Muslims say there is only one correct way to understand the teachings of Islam." The corollary is obvious: such Muslims see any divergence in Islam as non-Muslim.

Currently, Ahmadis are facing scrutiny in many regions, but other regions have already come around. In Bangladesh, for example, the Pew Forum found that 40 percent of Sunnis believed Ahmadis to be Muslim. Whatever their reasoning, their conclusion is correct, because Ahmadis fulfill the criteria of inclusion given by Muhammad and observed throughout history.

3. THE COMPLEX TEXTURES OF LIFE

I am often asked questions that attempt to put people into neat boxes, but that is not how life works. For example, many Protestants have asked me whether I think Catholics are Christian. My response is, "Some are and some are not. The same is true of Baptists, Methodists,

Anglicans, Seventh Day Adventists, etc." Denominational affiliation often tells us very little about individuals, and painting everyone with a broad brush is dangerous.

In my case, although I was an Ahmadi Muslim, I spent the majority of my Muslim life attending a Sunni mosque in Norfolk, Virginia. However, I hesitate to say that it was a Sunni mosque, because there were many denominations there. I took religious education courses through that mosque, and my Quran teacher was a Zaidi Shia. So as an Ahmadi I was learning the Quran under a Shia teacher employed by a Sunni mosque. That is what Islam looks like in the United States, much more inclusive and diverse than elsewhere in the world. We did not focus on denominational differences.

From the age of ten until my conversion at twenty-two, I often fasted with Sunnis and Shias at that mosque, celebrated Eid festivals, gathered at their homes, and otherwise was a part of the community. Perhaps the greatest indication that I was integrated into the Muslim community was that I prayed salaat with them, usually being led by them but at times even leading prayers at people's homes as the imam myself. Many Ahmadis do not pray behind non-Ahmadis, but when I reached adulthood and discovered their reasoning, I found it to be very problematic. I did not have anything against praying with other Muslims, seeing myself as one of them, and so I often did.

4. MY ASSESSMENT OF AHMADIYYAT WHILE MUSLIM

When I was investigating Islam and Christianity with my friend David, my position was rather simple: since Ahmadiyyat is a subgroup of Islam, I would investigate its evidence after investigating the evidence for Islam. If there were good reason to believe in Islam, then I would investigate its various denominations. However, if Islam proved to be historically problematic, then there would be no need to consider any of its denominations. As it turned out, the latter was my conclusion. On account of the evidence, I rejected the shahada, and in so doing I rejected Ahmadiyyat.

That said, I had come across troubling matters regarding Ahmadiyyat before rejecting Islam. While David and I were researching

Islam and Christianity, a close childhood friend of mine rejected Ahmadiyyat for Sunni Islam. Intrigued, I asked him his reasons, and he shared many arguments that I thought, if true, would pose significant problems for Ahmadiyyat.

For example, he argued that Mirza Ghulam Ahmad had issued many false prophecies. An example he gave was that Ahmad had prophesied he would live until the age of eighty, but he died about a decade before that. Another of his failed prophecies was that a certain woman would marry him; when she ultimately refused, Ahmad issued threats and tried to justify the failed prediction. My friend also suggested that Ahmad had defrauded hundreds of people; he pledged to write fifty books for them and took payment for all fifty upfront, but ultimately wrote only five. He justified this by saying, essentially, "The difference between fifty and five is a zero, and since zero is nothing, I have delivered what I promised."

These were just three of the dozens of reasons my friend left Ahmadiyyat for Sunni Islam. I knew of a handful of other people who left Ahmadiyyat for other reasons, including the accusation that Ahmadiyyat functioned as a cult, with strong central control and a tendency to excommunicate people even for minor transgressions, such as playing music at weddings. But because I had decided to visit these matters more carefully only if I determined Islam was true, I never investigated them further.

CONCLUSION

In the end, it is important to recognize the grey areas that make it difficult to draw boundaries of religious inclusion and identity. If inclusion in a religion were based on majority opinion, then Ahmadis would not be Muslim, but Sufis would not be either, nor would Shias be Muslim in some places, and Sunnis would be excluded in others. Such a measure ultimately becomes absurd.

That is why I suggest religious identity be determined by those beliefs and practices that distinguished a community from its surroundings during its inception. At the inception of Islam, what made someone a Muslim was whether he assented to the authoritative prophethood of Muhammad and exclusively worshiped the one god Allah. I think that all who do so today are Muslim, including Ahmadis.

But whether or not someone agrees with me, the fact remains that *Seeking Allah, Finding Jesus* investigates Islam and speaks to the common Muslim experience. It is my prayer that readers of this book will not be deterred by partisan polemics.

NOTES

---

1. This symbol represents the Arabic phrase *sall Alaahu 'alay-hi wa-sallam*, which means "peace and blessings of Allah be upon him," a standard Muslim formula after mentioning the name of Muhammad.
2. This formula, *subhanahu wa'tala*, is often repeated after the name of Allah, meaning "glorified and exalted."
3. A common Muslim formula meaning "I seek refuge in Allah," this phrase is verbalized after something dishonorable, blasphemous, or otherwise negative is stated or suggested.
4. In mainstream Islam, it is commonly understood that Allah has ninety-nine names. These are two, translated as "the forgiver" and "the merciful" respectively.
5. A very common formula meaning "glory be to Allah," this phrase is often exclaimed whenever good news is heard or something positive is stated.
6. An Arabic term meaning "community," referring to all Muslims.
7. Sahih Bukhari 6.61.508: "the Divine Inspiration descended upon him ... The Prophet's face was red and he kept on breathing heavily for a while and then he was relieved." See also Sahih Muslim 30.5763: "Allah's Apostle sweated in cold weather when revelation descended upon him."
8. A common formula of repentance meaning "I seek forgiveness from Allah."
9. Sahih Muslim 1.311.
10. Muslim apologists often interpret Deuteronomy 33:2 as a prophecy of Muhammad's triumphant return to Mecca.
11. The only exception being the choice of the Quranic passage.
12. Sunan Abu Daud 14.2526.
13. Sahih Bukhari 9.87.116.
14. This account is a reconstruction based on multiple conversations, some of which I overheard, and some of which I participated in.
15. This may be because of the authoritative nature of early Islam, or possibly it is on account of relatively high illiteracy rates in modern Muslim societies that require oral didactics grounded in authority structures.
16. Romans 10:9.

17. 5:72.
18. Galatians 1:6–9.
19. 4:157; 5:116.
20. Mirza Ghulam Ahmad, *Jesus in India* (Surrey: Islam International Publications, 2003). Originally published in India. This is an updated publication.
21. 4:157.
22. 4:158.
23. The Ahmadi jamaat teaches that 4:158 intends a spiritual ascension, not a physical one.
24. 3:49; 3.45.
25. This is actually a false representation of Mark 10:18 and Luke 18:19 commonly found in Islamic polemics. In neither instance does Jesus deny he is good.
26. 5:69.
27. 3:85.
28. 5:73.
29. Sahih Bukhari 1.1.1.
30. Sunnis sometimes disagree on the last three, substituting *Muwatta Imam Malik*.
31. Even the first major battle in Islamic history, the Battle of Badr, was the result of Muhammad's offensive effort against a Meccan caravan, the Nakhla raid. See Sahih Bukhari 5.59.287; A. Guillaume, trans., *The Life of Muhammad: A Translation of Ibn Ishaq's Sirat Rasul Allah* (New York: Oxford University Press, 2002), 289.
32. Sahih Bukhari 1.2.24: "Allah's Apostle said: 'I have been ordered to fight against the people until they testify that none has the right to be worshipped but Allah and that Muhammad is Allah's Apostle, and offer the prayers perfectly and give the obligatory charity, so if they perform that, then they save their lives and property from me except for Islamic laws and then their reckoning will be done by Allah.'" Cf. Sahih Muslim 19.4366: "It has been narrated by Umar that he heard the Messenger of Allah say: I will expel the Jews and Christians from the Arabian Peninsula and will not leave any but Muslim." See also Ibn Kathir's book *The Battles of the Prophet*, and the Quran, 9:5, 9:29, and 9:111.
33. Simply reading through the section on jihad in Sahih Bukhari clarifies this point: vol. 4, book 52.
34. "In reading Muslim literature—both contemporary and classical—one can see that the evidence for the primacy of spiritual jihad is negligible. Today it is certain that no Muslim, writing in a non-Western language (such as Arabic, Persian, Urdu), would ever make claims that jihad is primarily nonviolent or has been superseded by the spiritual jihad. Such claims are made solely by Western scholars, primarily those who study

Sufism and/or work in interfaith dialogue, and by Muslim apologists who are trying to present Islam in the most innocuous manner possible" (David Cook, *Understanding Jihad* [London: University of California Press, 2005], 165–66).

35. Mark 16:9–20; John 7:53–8:11.

36. Codex Sinaiticus and Codex Vaticanus.

37. The King James Version is an example of a Bible that is not a modern translation. It uses as the basis for its translation the Textus Receptus, a Greek text of the New Testament that predates important manuscript discoveries. Regardless, modern translations and those based on the Textus Receptus are not very disparate, and they certainly contain no doctrinal differences.

38. This is another common misconception held among Muslims. See chapter 42, "Hadith and the History of the Quran."

39. 5:46–47; 5:66–68.

40. Those of Arrian and Plutarch.

41. Eusebius, *Ecclesiastical History*, 3.39.15–16.

42. Ibid., 3.39.4.

43. One man, a friend of Josephus, is known to have been taken down from the cross and survived, but this was before the crucifixion process was complete. No deathblow was administered, and every attempt was made by the authorities to remove him alive. He was taken down with two others, and the three were given medical treatment. Still, the other two died. *Life of Flavius Josephus* (trans. Mason), §420–21.

44. For more, read Martin Hengel, *Crucifixion* (Philadelphia: Fortress, 1977).

45. Mark 8:31.

46. Matthew 27:19.

47. Matthew 16:21; 17:23; 20:18; Mark 8:31; 10:34; Luke 9:22; 18:33; John 12:33; 18:32.

48. David Strauss, *A New Life of Jesus* (London: Williams and Norgate: 1879), 1:408–12.

49. Gary R. Habermas and Michael R. Licona, *The Case for the Resurrection of Jesus* (Grand Rapids, MI: Kregel, 2004).

50. For a detailed discussion of the historical method in the context of Jesus' resurrection, see Michael R. Licona, *The Resurrection of Jesus: A New Historiographical Approach* (Downers Grove, IL: InterVarsity, 2010).

51. William Wand, *Christianity: A Historical Religion?* (Valley Forge, PA: Judson, 1972), 93–94.

52. 112:3.

53. Josh McDowell, *More Than a Carpenter* (Carol Stream, IL: Tyndale, 1977).

54. Luke 3:38; 1 Chronicles 28:6; Genesis 6:2; Job 1:6.

55. Romans 8:14; Galatians 3:26; Psalm 82:6.
56. Matthew 8:26–27; Luke 4:38–41; 7:14–15; 8:24–25.
57. 3:49.
58. John 10:32 and 5:19, respectively.
59. John 5:23.
60. John 20:28.
61. John 1:1–3.
62. More accurately, "a word from God," though Muslims generally do not dispute either title; 3:45.
63. The feeding of the five thousand.
64 For more on these arguments, see Bart Ehrman, *The New Testament: A Historical Introduction to the Early Christian Writings*, 5th ed. (New York: Oxford University Press, 2011).
65. Mark 14:62.
66. "For Jesus to say, 'Yes, I'm the Messiah,' is not a blasphemy; there's nothing blasphemous about calling yourself the Messiah, anymore than it's blasphemous to say, 'Yes, I'm the president of the United States,' or, 'I'm the president of the Southern Baptist Convention.' I mean I may not be, but it's not a blasphemy to say I am, there's nothing illegal about it. There were Jews that we know about who called themselves Messiah and there were Jews that we know about that the leading religious leaders of the Jews called the Messiah. 'Messiah' simply means a future ruler of the people; it's not blasphemous to say so" (Bart Ehrman, *Historical Jesus*, The Great Courses, course 643, lesson 21, 24:42–29:06, http://www.thegreatcourses.com/tgc/courses/course_detail.aspx?cid=643).
67. Craig Blomberg, *Jesus and the Gospels* (Nashville: B&H Academic, 1997), 342–43.
68. Assumed in this summation is the fact that there is only one God in the Jewish worldview. By claiming to be God, Jesus is claiming to be a part of the very identity of Yahweh. For more, read Richard Bauckham, *God Crucified: Monotheism and Christology in the New Testament* (Grand Rapids, MI: Eerdmans, 1999).
69. Psalm 110:1 is the most commonly referenced passage from the Old Testament in the New Testament at over twenty times. This indicates that it was deeply embedded in the earliest Christian notions of Jesus.
70. Philippians 2:6–7.
71. 1 Corinthians 8:6 and Deuteronomy 6:4; for more, see Bauckham, *God Crucified*.
72. Matthew 5:17.
73. A contextually inappropriate use of Jesus' words in John 20:17.
74. A commonly used attempt to argue that Galatians 1:8 indicates Paul brought his own gospel.
75. 2 Corinthians 11:23–27.

76. 5:73, 116; although 5:116 appears to construe the Trinity to be Allah, Son, and Mother Mary.

77. 2:256.

78. 9:5.

79. Found in Ibn Hisham's notes; Guillaume, *Life of Muhammad*, 691.

80. This is unlike selectively quoting from the Bible. Christians generally consider the entire Bible accurate, whereas most Muslims would concede the vast majority of hadith are inaccurate. Thus, selectively drawing from the Bible still requires the consistent interpreter to reconcile contradictory passages once they are elucidated, whereas this is not the case with hadith literature. Plus, the sheer amount of hadith material is staggering, with single collections filling nine volumes or more. Therefore, selectively drawing from the massive pool of hadith affords exponentially greater opportunities for eisegesis than does selectively drawing from the Bible.

81. Guillaume, *Life of Muhammad*, 676. See also Ibn Sa'd, *Kitab al Tabaqat*.

82. Guillaume, *Life of Muhammad*, 464.

83. 33:50.

84. Sahih Bukhari 7.62.64; 7.62.65; 7.62.88; Sahih Muslim 8.3310; 8.3311.

85. See Nujood Ali, *I Am Nujood, Age 10 and Divorced* (New York: Three Rivers Press, 2010).

86. Sahih Bukhari 3.47.786.

87. Sahih Bukhari 5.59.713.

88. Sahih Bukhari 4.54.490.

89. Guillaume, *Life of Muhammad*, 165–66.

90. Ibid., 515.

91. Sahih Bukhari 1.11.584.

92. Quran 33:37; Sahih Muslim 8.3330; Tabari, vol. 8, pp. 2–3.

93. Sahih Bukhari 8.82.794; Sahih Muslim 16.4130.

94. This is why this book does not build a case for Christianity using the Bible, and why it may appear to some that more critical attention is given to the Quran than to the Bible. However, this is not a double standard, because the comparison should be drawn between the Quran and Jesus' deity/resurrection. The latter was equally critically examined, if not more so.

95. 2:23; 10:38; 11:13; 17:88; 52:34.

96. Another name for the Quran is "*Al-Furqan.*" By titling the book written in response *The True Furqan*, the title itself is a challenge to the Quran's claim of supremacy.

97. Notification No. 78, September 7, 2005, from Anupam Prakash, Under Secretary to the Government of India, accessed July 1, 2013, *http://www.cbec.gov.in/customs/cs-act/notifications/notfns-2k5/csnt78-2k5.htm*.

98. Maurice Bucaille, *The Bible, The Quran, and Science: The Holy Scriptures*

Examined in the Light of Modern Knowledge, 7th rev. exp. ed. (Elmhurst, NY: Tahrike Tarsile Quran, 2003), 218.

99. Ibid., 214.

100. Ibid., 215.

101. "Belief in Divine Books," WhyIslam.org, accessed July 1, 2013, *http://www.whyislam.org/submission/articles-of-faith/belief-in-divine-books.*

102. The uncited information in the following paragraphs is all found in this book of Sahih Bukhari.

103. Sahih Bukhari 9.84.59.

104. Sahih Muslim 5.2286.

105. Sunan ibn Majah 1944.

106. Suyuti, *Al Itqan fi Ulum al-Quran*; Ibn Abi Daud, Kitab al-Masahif.

107. Ibn Abi Daud, *Kitab al masahif*, found by Arthur Jeffery and catalogued in his work *Materials for the History of the Text of the Quran*.

108. Sahih Muslim 8.3432.

109. Sunan Abu Daud 11.2150.

110. Tafsir ibn Kathir.

111. Sahih Bukhari 5.59.459.

112. Sahih Muslim 8.3371.

113. 5:33; "mischief makers" is a commonly used term for the Arabic *fsada*, though "corrupt" and "disorderly" also feature in translations.

114. See, e.g., Sahih Bukhari 9.84.57–58, 64, 72.

115. A prayer that means, "O Allah, by Your name I die and I live."

116. Sahih Muslim 35.6475.

117. Luke 13:22–25, 28–29, emphasis added.

118. Edyth Draper, *Draper's Book of Quotations for the Christian World* (Wheaton, IL: Tyndale, 1992), 1533.

119. C. S. Lewis, *Mere Christianity* (San Francisco: Harper San Francisco, 2001), 133.

120. Mark Mittelberg, *Confident Faith: Building a Firm Foundation for Your Beliefs* (Carol Stream, IL: Tyndale, 2013), esp. chaps. 5 and 8.

121. Ibid., esp. chaps. 10–12, where I present twenty arguments for the truth of Christianity.

122. Interested readers may view a number of my debates at *http://www.vimeo.com/licona*. A slightly revised version of my doctoral dissertation is available as a book: Michael R. Licona, *The Resurrection of Jesus: A New Historiographical Approach* (Downers Grove, IL: InterVarsity, 2010).

123. Ps. 37:7–8; 42:5–6, 11; 55:4–8, 16–17, 22; 56:3–4; 143:4–7; Matt. 6:19–34; Phil. 3:18–21; Col. 3:1–17; 1 Thess. 5:14–18; 1 Peter 5:7.

124. Prov. 4:23–27; 12:18, 25; 15:13–15; 17:22; 18:21; Lam. 3:19–24; Eph. 5:15–20.

125. William Backus and Marie Chapian, *Telling Yourself the Truth*, 20th ed. (Minneapolis: Bethany House, 2000).

126. Two of my three books on religious doubt can be found on my website, *http://www.garyhabermas.com*, without charge, under the "books" tab. Of the three, *The Thomas Factor: Using Your Doubts to Grow Closer to God* is concerned primarily with emotional doubt.

127. Christine Darg, "The Jesus Visions — Signs and Wonders in the Muslim World Introduction," accessed January 7, 2013, *http://www.jesusvisions.org/intro.shtml#top*.

128. "Accounts Multiply of Muslims Who Have Encountered *YAHUSHUA* (Jesus Christ) in Unusual Dreams," AMightyWind.com, accessed January 7, 2013, *http://www.amightywind.com/fastfood/dreams/040723muslimdreams.htm*.

129. From an email to Josh McDowell dated January 7, 2013.

130. Ibid.

131. "Dreams and Visions Move Muslims to Christ (an excerpt from National and International Religion Report," Eternal Perspective Ministries — Resource Library, accessed January 7, 2013, *http://www.epm.org/resources/1996/Sep/12/dreams-visions-move-muslims-christ/*.

132. Ibid.

133. Ibid.

134. Audrey Lee, "Why Revival Is Exploding among Muslims," *Charisma Magazine*, accessed December 7, 2012, *http://www.charismamag.com/spirit/evangelism-missions/14442-when-muslims-see-jesus*.

135. Ibid.

136. Story told personally to Josh McDowell.

GLOSSARY

Adhan: The Muslim call to prayer

Alhamdolillah: A Muslim formula meaning, "All praise be to Allah"; it is the Islamic analogue of *hallelujah*

Aqeedah: Deeply held Islamic beliefs

Asbab-an-nuzul: A body of Islamic literature purporting to detail the circumstances of specific Quranic revelations

Assalaamo alaikum wa rahmutallah wa barakaathu: An extended Muslim greeting meaning, "The peace of Allah and His mercy and blessings be upon you"

Being: The quality or essence that makes something what it is

Bucailleism: The technique of referring to the Quran for miraculously advanced scientific truths in order to defend its divine origin

Christology: An interpretation of Jesus' nature, identity, or role; for example, the Quran has a lower Christology than John, since He is just human in the former yet divine in the latter.

Criterion of early testimony: A principle of the historical method that posits that early accounts of an event are more likely to be accurate than later accounts, all else being equal

Criterion of multiple attestation: A principle of the historical method that posits that a recorded event is more likely to be historically accurate if it is recorded in multiple independent sources

Dawah: The practice of inviting people to Islam

Doctrine of abrogation: The belief that teachings and verses of the Quran have been repealed, usually by later Quranic revelations

Doctrine of the Trinity: The belief that God is one in being and three in person

Du'aa: Muslim prayers recited at specific occasions, as opposed to the ritual prayer called *salaat*; these may be memorized or improvised

Eid al-Fitr: One of two major Muslim holidays; it marks the end of Ramadhan

Fatwa: A decision or ruling by a Muslim authority

Fiqh: Islamic jurisprudence

Five Pillars of Islam: The fundamental practices required of all Muslims

371

Hadith: Muhammad's words or actions recorded in tradition

Hafiz: A man who has memorized the entire Quran

Hajj: The annual pilgrimage to Mecca

Hazrat: An honorific title meaning "respected"

Historical Jesus: Jesus as He can be known through historical records

Historical method: Criteria and techniques used by historians to systematically investigate the past

Iftar: The meal Muslims eat after fasting, often in large gatherings

Imam: A leader of Muslims, usually referring to one who leads prayer at a mosque

Injil: The book that Muslims believe Allah sent to Jesus, often considered to be the Gospels of the New Testament

Inshallah: A very common Muslim formula meaning "If Allah wills it"

Isa: The Arabic name for Jesus

Isnad: The chain of transmission for a particular hadith

Jamaat: The Arabic word for assembly, usually used to mean "group" or "denomination"

Jinn: Spiritual beings often considered analogous to demons

Jumaa: The name for the Muslim Sabbath day

Kafir: Infidel, non-Muslim

Khalifa: The position of supreme leader over Muslims; usually the title is used to refer to one of Muhammad's four successors

Khutba: A sermon, usually the Muslim Sabbath sermons on Friday

Manuscript: A physical copy of a text, whether in part or in whole

Masjid: A Muslim place of worship, often called a mosque

Mufti: A Muslim legal expert

Nafl: Optional prayers designed to invoke the help of Allah or draw the worshiper closer to Him

Person: The quality or essence that makes someone who he is

Rakaat: Units of repetition in salaat, composed of standing, bowing, prostrating, and sitting postures

Ramadhan: The Muslim holy month

Sadqa: A voluntary offering, often to prevent misfortune

Sahih Bukhari: A classical collection of hadith, often considered by Sunnis as the most trustworthy accounts of Muhammad's life

Sahih Sittah: The six books of hadith that Sunni Muslims consider most authentic

Salaat: The Muslim ritual prayers

Sehri: The meal Muslims eat before fasting

Shahada: The central proclamation of Islam: "There is no god but Allah, and Muhammad is His messenger"

Sharia: Islamic law

Sheikh: A Muslim leader, usually with graduate-level education in Islamic theology

Shia: Followers of Shi'ism, one of the two major branches of Islam

Shirk: The unforgivable sin in Islam; it is roughly equivalent to idolatry, placing something or someone in the position due to Allah

Shroud of Turin: A controversial relic, it is often believed to be the burial cloth of Jesus Himself, supernaturally bearing His image

Sirah: Biographies of Muhammad's life

Six Articles of Faith: The fundamental Muslim beliefs

Soteriology: The doctrine or study of salvation

Substitutionary atonement: The doctrine that Jesus is able to take and pay for the sins of man.

Surah: A chapter of the Quran

Synoptics: A collective term for the gospels of Matthew, Mark, and Luke

Taraweeh: Voluntary prayers offered at night during Ramadhan

Tauheed: The Islamic doctrine of Allah's absolute unity and self-reliance

Ulema: Muslim religious scholars

Urdu: The language of Pakistan

Wudhu: Ceremonial washing before salaat

Zakat: Obligatory alms

No God but One: Allah or Jesus?

A Former Muslim Investigates the Evidence for Islam and Christianity

Nabeel Qureshi

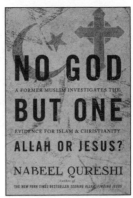

On account of the superficial points of agreement between Islam and Christianity, many don't see how tremendously deep the divides between them really are, and fewer still have considered the evidence for each faith. How is jihad different from the crusades? Can we know the life of Jesus as well as the life of Muhammad? What reason is there to believe in one faith over the other, and what difference can the gospel really make?

In *No God but One: Allah or Jesus?*, *New York Times* bestselling author Nabeel Qureshi takes readers on a global, historical, yet deeply personal journey to the heart of the world's two largest religions. He explores the claims that each faith makes upon believers' intellects and lives, critically examining the evidence in support of their distinctive beliefs.

Readers of Qureshi's first book, *Seeking Allah, Finding Jesus*, will appreciate his careful and respectful comparison of Islam and Christianity. Both religions teach that there is no God but one, but who deserves to be worshiped, Allah or Jesus?

Available in stores and online!

Answering Jihad

A Better Way Forward

Nabeel Qureshi, Author of
The New York Times *Bestseller,*
Seeking Allah, Finding Jesus

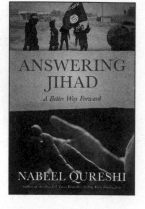

From *New York Times* bestselling author
and former Muslim Nabeel Qureshi comes
this personal, challenging, and respectful
answer to the many questions surrounding jihad, the rise of ISIS,
and Islamic terrorism.

San Bernardino was the most lethal terror attack on American
soil since 9/11, and it came on the heels of a coordinated assault on
Paris. There is no question that innocents were slaughtered in the
name of Allah and in the way of jihad, but do the terrorists' actions
actually reflect the religion of Islam? The answer to this question is
more pressing than ever, as waves of Muslim refugees arrive in the
West seeking shelter from the violent ideology of ISIS.

Setting aside speculations and competing voices, what really is
jihad? How are we to understand jihad in relation to our Muslim
neighbors and friends? Why is there such a surge of Islamist terrorism in the world today, and how are we to respond?

In *Answering Jihad*, bestselling author Nabeel Qureshi
(*Seeking Allah, Finding Jesus*) answers these questions from the
perspective of a former Muslim who is deeply concerned for
both his Muslim family and his American homeland.

Available in stores and online!

Seeking Allah, Finding Jesus Video Study

A Former Muslim Shares the Evidence that Led Him from Islam to Christianity

Nabeel Qureshi

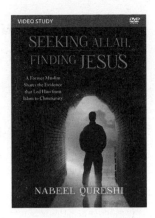

Building on the powerful story and arguments he shared in *Seeking Allah, Finding Jesus*, author Nabeel Qureshi takes viewers deeper into apologetics and evangelism among Muslims with this complete video lecture course. In eight sessions of about 30 minutes each he explores Muslim culture, the most common Muslim objections to Christianity, and the core doctrines upon which Islam stands or falls. Compassionate and clear, Nabeel's lectures will be a useful training tool for pastors, outreach leaders, and any believers wanting to winsomely engage Muslims in spiritual conversations.

Seeking Allah, Finding Jesus Video Study develops in further detail the objections to Islam and case for Christianity that Qureshi introduced in *Seeking Allah, Finding Jesus*. When used with the accompanying *Seeking Allah, Finding Jesus Study Guide*, this accessible course is perfect for adult classes, small groups, segments in college or seminary courses, and motivated independent learners alike.

Available in stores and online!

Seeking Allah, Finding Jesus Study Guide

A Former Muslim Shares the Evidence that Led Him from Islam to Christianity

Nabeel Qureshi with Kevin and Sherry Harney

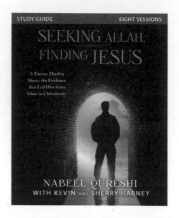

Building on the powerful story and arguments he shared in *Seeking Allah, Finding Jesus*, Nabeel Qureshi and co-authors Kevin and Sherry Harney take viewers deeper into apologetics and evangelism among Muslims with this complete study course. In eight lessons coordinated to be used alongside the *Seeking Allah, Finding Jesus Video Study*, Qureshi and the Harneys explore Muslim culture, the most common Muslim objections to Christianity, and the core doctrines upon which Islam stands or falls. Compassionate and clear, the *Seeking Allah Finding Jesus Study Guide* will be a useful training tool for pastors, outreach leaders, and any believers wanting to winsomely engage Muslims in spiritual conversations.

The *Seeking Allah, Finding Jesus Study Guide* develops in further detail the objections to Islam and case for Christianity that Qureshi introduced in *Seeking Allah, Finding Jesus*. When studied with the accompanying *Seeking Allah, Finding Jesus Video Study*, this accessible course is perfect for adult classes, small groups, segments in college or seminary courses, and motivated independent learners alike.

Available in stores and online!